Positive residential practice

Learning the lessons of the 1990s

Edited by
David Crimmens and John Pitts

blishing

First published in 2000 by
Russell House Publishing Ltd.
4 St. George's House
Uplyme Road
Lyme Regis
Dorset DT7 3LS

Tel. 01297 443948
Fax. 01297 442722
e-mail: help@russellhouse.co.uk

British Library cataloguing-in-publication data:
A catalogue record for this book is available from the British Library.

ISBN: 1–898924–51–1

Typeset by Saxon Graphics Ltd, Derby
Printed by Cromwell Press, Trowbridge

Contents

About the Authors

Brian Corby is Reader in Applied Social Studies at the University of Liverpool. His main research focuses on child protection policy and practice and he has written several books and articles on this subject. His most recent publication is *Managing Child Sexual Abuse Cases*, Jessica Kingsley, (1998).

David Crimmens currently lectures in social work at the University of Lincolnshire and Humberside. Practice experience, spanning 20 years working with children and young people, includes working on adventure playgrounds, detached youth work, juvenile justice and residential care.

Nick Frost is a Senior Lecturer in Continuing Education at the University of Leeds. His research interests include professional education, family support and looked after children. He is author of a number of publications including *Understanding Residential Care*, Ashgate, (1999) with Mike Stein and Sue Mills.

Geoff Gurney practised as a generic social worker before moving into the field of juvenile justice. He has extensive management experience with NCH Action for Children and the British Agencies for Adoption and Fostering and most recently as Refuge Service Manager for NSPCC and Centrepoint.

Chris Hume is Executive Director, Social Care and Health, for Lewisham Council. He has been a Director of Social Services for over five years and has had a varied career in Social Services including a period as a residential social worker.

David Lane started his career with eight years in residential childcare. He then moved to CCETSW as a Social Work Education Adviser. He spent ten years as Assistant Director of Residential and Day Services in Hillingdon and eight years as Director of Social Services in Wakefield. Since 1993 he has been an independent consultant. He has written extensively and held office as a member of several professional bodies, including the Residential Forum and the international childcare organisation, FICE, of which he is a Vice President.

Frank Lowe is Group Manager for Family and Mental Health Services for Lewisham Council. He has completed psychoanalytic psychotherapy training and has a particular interest in developing therapeutic services for vulnerable adults and children with Social Services Departments.

Roger Morgan is currently Chief Inspector with Oxfordshire Social Services Department. He spent three years seconded to the Department of Health advising on the regulation of boarding schools and children's homes. He remains an active inspector of homes and schools and is involved in lecturing, writing and development work on inspection of residential services for children. He is the author of the current draft national standards for welfare in boarding schools.

John Pitts is Vauxhall Professor of Socio-Legal Studies at the University of Luton. He has worked as a 'special needs' teacher, a street and club-based youth worker, a residential care worker in remand and assessment centres, a youth justice development officer in a London borough and a group worker in a Young Offender Institution. His recent publications include: *Planning Safer Communities,* Russell House Publishing, (1998), and *Discipline or Solidarity: The New Politics of Youth Crime,* Macmillan, (2000).

Georgina Rose is manager of a residential support centre for Lewisham Council. She is a social worker with several years experience of managing residential child care services.

Stephen Shaw worked for NACRO and the Home Office before becoming the director of the Prison Reform Trust at the time of its launch in 1981. In October 1999 he succeeded Sir Peter Woodhead as Prisons Ombudsman.

Sandy de Silva has been a staff training and development officer for Liverpool Social Services since 1991. She previously worked as a qualified social worker for eleven years in the childcare field. She has been involved in the Home Office project developing the NVQ Level IV Community Justice award and with the National Foster Care Association developing the NVQ Foster Care award.

Clare Sparks worked for NCH Action for Children before becoming the Policy Officer at the Prison Reform Trust.

Lorraine Wallis works for the Children's Society as a Research and Development Officer. She is also a research fellow at the University of Leeds. For the last six years her research interests have been in the field of child welfare, including family support, child protection and looked after children. Her publications include *Negotiated Friendship: Home-start and the Delivery of Family Support,* Home-Start, (1996.) with Mike Stein, Nick Frost and Liz Johnson.

Ann Wheal has a broad experience of obtaining the views of young people, parents, carers and members of the black community, and in involving them in the decision making processes that affect their lives. She has published widely in the child care field.

Carolyne Willow was a children's rights officer in Leicestershire before running the Children's Participation Programme at the National Youth Bureau. In 1998 she became an adult support worker for the Article 12 young people's organisation. She is currently chairperson of Children's Rights Officers and Advocates (CROA).

Introduction

David Crimmens and John Pitts

This book began life as a conversation between the editors about the likely impact of the Waterhouse inquiry into the abuse of children in residential care in North Wales. After all, we had already had *Pindown* (1991), *People Like Us* (Utting 1997), its more exciting Scottish companion *The Children's Safeguards Review* (Kent 1997), the various publications by the Support Force on Residential Care and Barbara Kahan's *Growing Up in Groups* (1994). If we didn't understand the problems by now, we opined, we never would. Our conversation was fairly downbeat. What, we wondered, were we likely to learn from yet more official reports, public inquiries or research reviews of the problems of residential child care, that we did not already know. What was needed, surely, was a set of policies which would underpin the development of good, safe practice, enabling the people who spent their lives working with children and young people in residential establishments to begin reconstructing the sector in accordance with the lessons of the 1990s.

Then, on 16th September 1998, the new Labour government launched *Partnership in Action* which, as Department of Health minister Alan Milburn observed, aimed to 'end wasteful duplication, make more effective use of public funds and give people the benefit of an integrated system of care'. Less than a week later came *Someone Else's Children* (DoH 98/387), a report by the SSI which bemoaned the failure of some local authority social services departments 'to provide proper care and protection for vulnerable children'. On the same day, Frank Dobson, Secretary of State at the DoH, pledged to 'transform children's services' and launched, the government's *Quality Protects* initiative, (DoH 98/388), arguably the most significant development in the sector since the implementation of the Children Act (1989) in October 1991. The initiative offered:

- An extension of the local authority's duty of care in relation to young people leaving care.
- New funding to provide a national 'voice' for children in care.
- New initiatives to improve the educational attainment of 'looked after' children.
- More effective regulation of all children's homes.
- £375 million to be spent over three years.

This was the first indication that the government was applying its much vaunted 'joined up thinking' to the plight of children and young people looked after in residential institutions. Commending *Quality Protects* to the assembled chief executives, directors of social services and heads of health and education services, Frank

Dobson stated that 'this is where bad practice ends'. Junior minister Paul Boateng underlined this message when he warned local authorities that failure to carry out the new policies to the required standard could result in them losing responsibility for local personal social services. In November 1998 Dobson was even more explicit, emphasising that 'There can be no more excuses' for not ending 'the legacy of abuse'. Moreover, in November 1998 junior health minister John Hutton, launching *Caring for Children Away from Home: Messages from the Research* announced an additional £20 million for social services training to support *Quality Protects* and as a 'lever for modernising services and raising quality'. (DoH 1998/0532). The final piece of the policy jigsaw was announced on the last day of November 1998. The White Paper *Modernising Social Services*, another step in the government's reform of the welfare state, was described as the 'most radical overhaul of the social services system in thirty years' (DoH, 1998/0557). The Secretary of State in committing the government to spending an additional £3 billion over the following three years on the personal social services said that 'things must be done properly in future' and that it was 'time to make a difference.'

Thus, by early 1999, in the residential child care sector in England & Wales, the political will and the policy framework were present. Some new money to support the *Quality Protects* initiative was on the table and existing expenditure had been effectively 'ringfenced'.

Alongside these radical reforms of, and the injection of cash into, residential child care, the government also announced its intention to spend an additional £51 million on reforms of the prison system in order to 'ensure that young offenders were effectively separated from adult prisoners'. Commendable though this objective might be, it was, in large part, the hard-line youth justice policies of the New Labour government and its Conservative predecessor which had rendered such expenditure necessary. In marked contrast with its thoughtful attempts to offer greater care and protection to youngsters looked after by local authorities, its stance on young offenders was largely politically driven.

It is probably a minority, albeit a significant minority, of the children and young people caught up in the youth justice system, who have been seriously abused or neglected. However, the remainder are by no means typical of the child and youth population as a whole. They tend to come from the poorest families, live in high-crime, high-victimisation neighbourhoods, experience poorer health, do far worse at school and have a significantly higher mortality rate (Graham and Bowling 1995). Yet, since 1991, England and Wales has been the only country in Europe which deals which a child's criminality and their care and protection in separate courts (King and Piper 1990, Hetherington et al. 1997).

New Labour has perpetuated and underscored the distinction between children and young people who are the victims of abuse and neglect, and are therefore deemed to be innocent victims and appropriate objects of our pity and concern, and young offenders who, as culpable perpetrators, are presented as the rightful objects of our disapprobation and punishment. That these children may be, and very often are, the same people is a compelling but inconvenient fact which recent governments have, for reasons of political pragmatism, sought to obscure. It is for this reason that we bring together concerns about the treatment of these two groups of children and young people in the present volume.

While governments can set standards, identify 'targets' to be achieved, and issue guidance about how these targets might be met, it is not possible to legislate for 'successful' outcomes with children and young people who have had damaging early experiences. Thus, in this book the contributors are attempting to think through the implications of the policies triggered by the crises of the 1990s for professional practice with children and young people in care and in custody. As David Lane suggests in Chapter 2, we know a great deal about the nature of institutional abuse, the circumstances which foster it and how to recognise the signs that it is occurring. The task now is to develop structures and professional strategies, which work against any future occurrence.

That these scandals were, at one level, a result of the 'residualisation' of residential child care and youth custody in the 1980s is now a matter of record. With central government exerting increasing control over local government expenditure, local authorities turned their attention to their hugely expensive children's homes and residential schools. The timely emergence of a political and theoretical critique, 'progressive minimalism', which rejected residential institutions, both custodial and 'caring', as psychologically harmful and criminogenic (Thorpe et al. 1980), governmental intervention to minimise custodial sentencing in the juvenile courts, and the fall-out from successive institutional abuse scandals, offered a scientific, political, fiscal and humanitarian rationale for radical change.

In consequence, from the early 1980s, many local authorities simply closed, or otherwise disposed of, their residential children's institutions. However, the attempt to decant the erstwhile residents into foster families or their own homes was not always successful. Cliffe, writing about Warwickshire, a local authority which closed the last of its children's homes in 1986, observes:

> *Most children were offered only one choice of foster placement and obviously, no residential placement – in other words, no choice at all. Secondly, although Warwickshire has shown that more difficult children can be fostered than was previously thought, there is still a small group – mostly adolescent boys – who need residential placements.*

(1991)

The majority of young people decanted from care were placed 'at home on trial' with their own families, but this strategy yielded its own problems. For example, a study of 39 care leavers, undertaken by the homelessness charity Centrepoint found that over half had been homeless immediately after leaving care, that nearly all of them had 'slept rough', and that 30 per cent had become homeless when social work help was withdrawn. The initial vulnerability of these young people was compounded in 1988 by the *Social Security Act*, which withdrew state benefits from under-18s, living away from the parental home. This confronted many of them with a choice between returning to the hazards of an abusive or neglectful parental home or moving onto the streets. This episode in the saga of UK residential child care points very clearly to the need for decent residential provision for children and young people who cannot live at home. This book aims to contribute to the debate about the form that this provision should take.

This residualisation of local authority children's homes and Community Homes (with Education) (CHEs) tended to erode both the quality of professional supervision and managerial surveillance. Moreover, local authorities became much less willing to spend money on a service they perceived to be withering on the branch. Meanwhile, some of the large voluntary organisations like the Children's Society and Barnardos progressively withdrew from residential care in search of new, less expensive, areas of operation.

However, there were a number of factors which meant that, even as the residential child care sector contracted and the practices within it became more opaque, it would soon be dragged back to the centre of the political stage. As Brian Corby notes in Chapter 1, if residential care was the Cinderella of the social work profession, child protection held centre stage. In the 1980s adults who were professionally involved in child care were sensitised to the possibility of abuse. As a result, they were far more likely to recognise youngsters who had been, or were being, abused, while children and young people were encouraged to reveal their abuse and far more likely to be believed if they did so. The 1980s also witnessed the problematisation of 'bullying', the legitimation of the victims of bullying and a heightened sensitivity to its consequences amongst adult professionals. Moreover, the 1980s was the decade in which the related ideas that the child in care had rights, that these rights should be claimed, with the assistance of adult advocacy, and that the child should be 'empowered' to operate in a partnership with their carers entered the vocabularies of the caring professions. These ideas were eventually to find expression in the *Children Act* 1989 and the *United Nations Convention on the Rights of the Child*, which the United Kingdom signed in 1991. It was, perhaps, inevitable that in such a political environment the routine abuses, which characterised some residential child care institutions, should come to light.

Lewisham is an authority which has run the gamut of the experiences outlined above. As Chris Hume, Frank Lowe and Georgina Rose note in Chapter 3, following a scandal in one of its homes, Lewisham's social services directorate embraced the Warwickshire model, closing their remaining residential establishments and opting instead for a foster care strategy. However, by the mid 1990s it was evident that fostering was not an effective placement for some children in care, particularly older youngsters with negative experiences of family life. It was on this basis that the local authority set out to create a new structure for residential care in the borough. The structure was built upon both the negative lessons of the 1990s and the positive potential of partnership with parents and advocacy for, and the empowerment of, children and young people in decision-making. Moreover, it attempted to establish these practices within a framework of 'rights'.

Arguably, the 'safe house' is as much a product of the 1980s as the scandals in residential child care. In his study of 1,158 first admissions to a London 'safe house', Matthew Pitts (1992) noted that 36 per cent of first admissions had run from local authority care. The safe house has served as an expansion tank for a residential sector under pressure and a safety net for many of its children and young people. In Chapter 4 Geoff Gurney explains how the safe house as a voluntary sector agency continues to:

- Serve as a test-bed for, and exemplar of safe residential practice.
- Serve as site for advocacy for the child in residential care in terms of placement decisions and the formulation of care plans.
- Exert political pressure for positive change in the sector.
- Serve as a source of surveillance of the residential sector.

In Chapter 5 Roger Morgan details 'best practice' in the regulation and inspection of children's homes. Drawing on his extensive experience in managing children's services and in establishing standards for residential child care he gives a cautious but optimistic welcome to the idea of a Commission for Care Standards.

Chapters 6 and 7 examine what we might realistically expect from a better qualified residential child care workforce. Questioning the assumptions underlying previous training initiatives, which appear to have seen education and training as a panacea for all the difficulties afflicting the sector, David Crimmens examines the potential contribution of recent initiatives in training. While acknowledging that National Vocational Qualifications may not be the ideal answer, he argues that they can provide a solid foundation for workers in residential child care. He presents a case study of a number of local authorities, which have developed successful NVQ programmes. In the following chapter, Sandy de Silva describes her own experiences in working to develop appropriate training with teams of residential child care workers in one local authority. She provides a model of unit-based training, which could easily be adapted to the training needs of staff working in other organisations.

In Chapter 8 Ann Wheal draws upon her fieldwork as a researcher with youngsters in care and her experience as an independent visitor at a secure unit, to offer first hand accounts of the residential experience. The youngsters who speak in this chapter are looking for an experience, which is as near 'normal' as it can be. They have clear, realistic, and rather modest expectations of both the setting and of their carers. Yet, the stability, consistency and fairness they are asking for has proved extremely difficult to achieve to date.

Nick Frost and Lorraine Wallis examine one way in which young people may make their voices heard. In Chapter 9 they report on research, which they undertook on behalf of a national children's charity, into the operation of the representation and complaints system available under Section 26 of the *Children Act* 1989. Like Ann Wheal, they are concerned to 'hear the voices' and garner the views and opinions of young people who are being looked after in foster placements and children's homes. Within this, they evaluate the contribution of independent persons to this process. Their findings, while creating some cause for optimism, suggest that there remains much to be done to make the system into a conduit for the authentic 'voice of the child'.

The discussion of advocacy brings us squarely into the realm of rights. And so we move from questions about whether, and in what ways, a child or young person should be represented to what it is that is being represented or, in certain circumstances, demanded. In Chapter 10 Carolyne Willows first outlines the rights of children and young people in residential care, and then spells out how such rights might be operationalised in practice. This is a crucially important discussion since, all too often, policy-makers and professionals, while paying lip-service to children's rights, pay scant attention to the circumstances in which such rights will be translated into reality.

In Chapter 11, John Pitts offers a brief history of residential and custodial disposals in the youth justice system. He notes that successive governments, in their attempts to seize the political initiative on 'law and order', have plumped for a strategy of institutional confinement for juveniles. While the evidence that custody rehabilitates young offenders is scant, the evidence that tough talking on youth crime helps to rehabilitate the flagging fortunes of political parties is stronger, and it is this evidence which tends to influence policy. Unfortunately, this often leads governments to set up youth justice systems which inadvertently draw far too many children and young people into residential and custodial establishments, thus precipitating periodic crises in the penal system.

In Chapter 12 Stephen Shaw and Clare Sparks offer a critical evaluation of the current state of youth custody. The sector is, they argue, beset by a number of major problems. These include a failure to control bullying and inmate-on-inmate violence, a failure to control suicide, para-suicide and self-mutilation amongst inmates, a shortage of resources and strict limitations upon prison managers to use existing resources in the ways they believe would be most beneficial to inmates, and staffing problems, in that staff are simply drafted in from adult jails with no necessary aptitude, or training, for work with younger offenders. This is doubly ironic when we recognise that half of the young people in these institutions have a history of residential care and, as a succession of government reports have argued, require highly skilled help. The authors argue for greater openness, effective and appropriate training, modelled on the kinds of developments we are seeing in training for residential care (see Chapters 6 and 7) and the clarification of the legal status of inmates in young offender institutions.

SECTION 1

The Lessons of the 1990s

CHAPTER 1

The Impact of Public Inquiries on Perceptions of Residential Child Care

Brian Corby

Introduction

In September 1996, the North Wales Tribunal of Inquiry held its first hearing into the abuse of children in residential care in Clwyd and Gwynedd. Under its terms of reference, the inquiry was required to examine all allegations of abuse said to have taken place in residential homes in these two counties between 1974 and 1996. Six hundred and fifty complaints were made by over 80 individuals. Allegations of abuse were received from ex-residents of 38 of the 84 homes which were in operation during the period of time under the remit of the inquiry. Approximately 70 per cent of the complaints made were about physical assaults and the remainder about sexual abuse.

This Tribunal of Inquiry which, at the time of writing, has yet to publish its findings, comes at the end of a long list of inquiries into child abuse – 70 since 1945 (Corby, Doig and Roberts 1998). Most of these inquiries have been concerned with the deaths of physically abused children while living with their parents or carers in the community. However, in the nineties concerns about the abuse of children in residential care have gained increasing prominence. The trend is clear. Only 4 of the 52 inquiries held between 1945 and 1990 were concerned with the abuse of children in residential care. By contrast, since 1990 residential child care has been scrutinised by public inquiries in roughly equal measure to field social work.

In addition to the inquiries themselves, there have been extensive joint police and social work investigations into allegations of residential abuse in other parts of the country, (Webster, 1998). Furthermore, in response to these inquiries and investigations, there have been a series of government-sponsored fact-finding and policy development reports, (Utting, 1991 and 1997, Warner, 1992, Howe, 1992) and, most recently, highly-publicised government initiatives, backed by a considerable body of research, (DoH, 1998a), to improve the quality of residential care and ensure better monitoring and accountability, (DoH, 1998b).

Residential child care is, therefore, very much in the public gaze. The establishment of the North Wales Tribunal of Inquiry is a clear reflection of the degree of concern felt about the abuse of children in residential care. Significantly, it is the first time that this form of inquiry has been used to investigate any form of child abuse. Tribunals of Inquiry are the most formidable instruments of government available for investigating allegations of negligence or wrongdoing. They can compel witnesses, use contempt of court powers for non-compliance and have unlimited access to relevant documentation. This type of inquiry is normally reserved for matters of pressing national concern and one of its key functions has been described as the restoration of public confidence, (Wraith and Lamb, 1971). Since the passing of the Tribunal of Inquiry (Evidence) Act in 1921 there have been only 21 such inquiries. It is also notable that Tribunals are expensive – the North Wales Tribunal is estimated to be costing somewhere between 10 and 20 million pounds.

There can be little doubt, therefore, given this degree of public exposure, that grave doubts are being cast on the future viability of residential care in its present form. As the then Labour Welsh affairs spokesman, Rhodri Morgan, put it before the commencement of the North Wales Tribunal hearings, 'The residential care system of this country is now on trial.' (Webster, 1998, p11).

The aim of this chapter is to provide a detached assessment of the causes for concern about residential care for children. It is important that responses to the findings of recent inquiry reports and extensive police investigations are considered ones. While it is without question that any abuse of a child in residential care is unacceptable, it is important to ensure that the whole enterprise of residential care is not 'rubbished' in the process of rooting out such abuse and preventing its recurrence. There are dangers that this may happen, and that the findings of the North Wales Tribunal of Inquiry will provide further evidence to support such a trend. With this in mind, the following issues will be considered:

1. The nature and range of concerns raised about abuse in residential child care in recent inquiry reports.
2. The reasons for the focus on abuse in residential child care at this point in its history.
3. The impact of the focus on abuse in residential care on public perceptions and public policy development.

Material derived from the transcripts and personal observations of the North Wales Tribunal of Inquiry will be used extensively to illustrate and exemplify the issues raised.

The Nature and Range of Concerns

In general terms, there have been two patterns of abusive behaviour identified in the various inquiries into residential care, (Wardhaugh and Wilding, 1995).

Abusive Regimes
The first is related to methods of controlling children's behaviour and invariably involves some form of physical and/or emotional abuse. The best publicised example of this type of abuse is that of the Pindown regime which was found to be in operation in a small number of homes in Staffordshire between 1983 and 1989, (Levy and Kahan, 1991). Here, children who were absconding, truanting or deemed to be particularly aggressive and challenging towards residential staff were subjected to solitary confinement and a punitive behavioural regime that was later judged by experts at the inquiry to be ill-considered and emotionally abusive. Perhaps the most surprising aspect of this regime was that there was no attempt at concealment by those who promoted and enacted it. Indeed, it was thought to be within the bounds of the Community Homes Regulations then in operation.

Abuse linked to control and restraint was also found at St. Charles Youth Treatment Centre, (DoH, 1991), Ty Mawr, (Gwent, 1992), Scotforth House, (Lancashire, 1992), Leicestershire, (Kirkwood, 1993) and Meadowdale, (Kilgallon, 1995). Abuse in these establishments was of a physical nature and widespread, except in the case of St. Charles Youth Treatment centre, where the focus of concern was on the use of sedatives without consent to control the behaviour of one adolescent girl.

Sexual Abuse
The second form of residential abuse identified by Wardhaugh and Wilding, (1995), is sexual abuse perpetrated by individual staff on residents. It has been pointed out that the first type of abuse may well be associated with particular regimes and linked to the task of control. However, the type of sexual abuse which has been the subject of public inquiries could not by any stretch of the imagination be understood in this way. It is notable, however, that sexual abuse has in some cases been linked with (or concealed by) a therapeutic approach or regime. Frank Beck, for instance, who was convicted of sexual offences against male residents of a children's home in Leicestershire, claimed to be developing expertise in regression therapy, (Kirkwood, 1993). In fact, he used crude infantilising techniques to further disempower already emotionally troubled children and render them vulnerable to his abuse of them.

Sexual abuse was also the subject of concern in the Castle Hill, (Brannan, Jones and Murch, 1993), Meadowdale, (Kilgallon, 1995) and Islington inquiries, (White and Hart, 1995). Castle Hill was a residential school for boys with emotional and behavioural problems – over a period of years, several of its residents were subject to abuse by the headmaster there. Meadowdale was a home for children with learning difficulties – six children alleged they had been sexually abused. In Islington, the concerns focused mainly on the exposure of children to sexual risk outside the home and the failure to identify staff with criminal convictions for sexual abuse.

It should be noted that despite the useful distinctions made between the two types of abuse discussed above, both existed together in some of the establishments subject to inquiries in the 1990s.

Physical and Sexual Abuse in North Wales Children's Homes

The forms of abuse considered by the North Wales inquiry encompassed both physical and sexual abuse. As pointed out in the Introduction, nearly three-quarters of the complaints raised were about physical assaults. Many of these were of a relatively minor nature and, although clearly in breach of existing regulations, and were part of the culture obtaining between residents and staff. The abusive incidents included objects such as board dusters and bunches of keys being thrown at children, and mock fights developing into something more serious. Some complaints resulted from situations where greater degrees of violence were used to assert control over children. A small number of residential staff were alleged to have persistently used physical force to bully children into compliance.

Just over a quarter of the complaints were about sexual abuse. Between 1975 and 1992 there were approximately 10 successful prosecutions of residential staff for serious sexual offences. Three of these offenders were convicted of offences against large numbers of children who had been in their care. All were heads, or de facto heads, of the homes where the abuse took place, a feature of other inquiries involving multiple sexual abuse, (see Kirkwood, 1993, Brannan, Jones and Murch, 1993). All used their positions of power, and two, as was noted with Frank Beck, arguably used bogus forms of therapy to establish their hold over children and provide some cover for their activities. For instance, Peter Howarth, who was the deputy headmaster at Bryn Estyn community home in Wrexham, operated a system whereby boys could come to his flat and receive special privileges (e.g. stay up late, watch television, get extra food and drink, etc.) This system, known as the flat-list, was presented as a means of reducing the impact of living in a large institution and of providing a more family-like atmosphere. It was said to have contained an element of group counselling. With hindsight it was clear that it came to be used by Howarth as a mechanism for becoming more intimate with boys in his care and ultimately as a means to sexually abuse them. In terms of forms of abuse, therefore, the picture in North Wales is similar to that found in children's homes inquired into in other parts of the country.

Broader Concerns of Inquiries

The terms of reference of inquiries into abuse of children in residential care usually require them to consider the circumstances surrounding, and possibly contributing to, the abuse, leading to a wide-ranging examination of policies and procedures, including the allocation of resources, staffing arrangements, management issues, and complaints procedures.

Resources
Several of the residential abuse inquiries have paid particular attention to the way in which poor resourcing of homes and schools can help create the conditions in which abusive activities can flourish. The best example of this is provided by the Pindown inquiry. Here a massive reorganisation of residential care services took place in the early 1980s. Combined residential and family centres replaced larger children's homes with a view to working with children at risk of coming into care within or nearer to their own communities. These changes had a very progressive ring to them, but were carried out too suddenly and too drastically (the number of residential places available to children was reduced by over a half at a stroke) and on the cheap (Staffordshire had the second lowest child care expenditure in England and Wales). The report paints a picture of poorly qualified staff in poorly furnished and resourced homes failing to cope with children with very challenging behaviours. In these circumstances Tony Latham, a residential services manager in one area of Staffordshire, established his punitive and abusive regime described earlier. Thus an apparently progressive reorganisation of residential services, largely because of cost-cutting agendas, created the conditions for an abusive regime to spring up, (Levy and Kahan, 1991).

The Meadowdale inquiry pointed to how the shift from being a general children's home to one specialising in the care of disabled children took place with inadequate resources and, therefore, placed its residents at increased risk of abuse, (Kilgallon, 1995).

Staffing
The quality of residential staff, and particularly methods of recruitment, have also been seen as important issues by inquiries. This is most notable in the Islington report, (White and Hart, 1995), and has been the subject of two separate government-sponsored reports, (Howe, 1992, Warner, 1992). Low levels of qualification and remuneration of residential child care staff compared with those of

field social workers have been persistently emphasised over the past twenty years, but little progress has been made.

Management
Management of residential care has also been a key concern of inquiries into abuse in residential care, much more so than in the case of child abuse in the community, where it has been the work and judgement of front-line workers that have born the brunt of criticism. Clearly a key difference here is that with abuse of children in care, the staff themselves are the abusers or alleged abusers. This, together with the low level of qualification among residential workers, places the onus on managers to monitor and retain close involvement with the running of homes. In nearly all the cases inquired into, this clearly did not take place and management involvement was conspicuous by its absence or ineffectiveness. The Pindown and Leicestershire inquiries, (Levy and Kahan, 1991, Kirkwood, 1993), in particular, show how higher management can become over-reliant on heads of children's homes and, therefore, less than rigorous in monitoring their work and responding to complaints made about them.

Complaints
Other aspects which have been commented on in various inquiries are the inadequacy of complaints systems, (Levy and Kahan, 1991), the difficulties staff have in passing on concerns about colleagues' treatment of children, (Kilgallon, 1995) and the poor quality of oversight and inspection, whether by councillors' visits, or by internal or external review mechanisms, (Levy and Kahan, 1991, Kirkwood, 1993).

Resource and Management Issues in the North Wales Inquiry

All these factors have also come under the scrutiny of the North Wales Tribunal of Inquiry. It is clear that for much of the period examined, residential care provision for children was poorly funded in both Clwyd and Gwynedd, and that organisational restructuring was constantly taking place. From the late 1970s onwards, residential care provision was shrinking in line with the national trend. This shrinkage was effected in an ad hoc way. Staff were inappropriately relocated in settings with which they were ill-equipped to cope and there was little evidence of retraining. It was apparent, especially in Gwynedd, that residential child care provision was a low priority.

Monitoring and Complaints Issues in the North Wales Inquiry
Internal monitoring and supervision of residential establishments in Clwyd and Gwynedd was of a low standard. As in Staffordshire and Leicestershire, (Levy and Kahan, 1991, Kirkwood, 1993), those most heavily implicated in abuse allegations were for the most part unquestioningly supported by homes advisers and

higher management. Voluntary homes were inspected and monitored by the Welsh Office Social Services Inspectorate, but the number of inspections greatly decreased in the 1980s as a result of central government decisions to reduce involvement in this area.

There was no formal system for making complaints in Clwyd and Gwynedd for most of the period inquired into. Such procedures were not required prior to the implementation of the 1989 Children Act in 1991. With regard to physical abuse, the North Wales Tribunal found evidence of many children making verbal complaints to members of staff, which were not subsequently passed on. More formal complaints were rare – usually they were dealt with by the heads of the homes concerned and went no further. Some were referred on to and dealt with by external managers – these were usually cases where there had been a violent (often public) confrontation between a member of staff and a child resulting in some form of injury. Most often the results of such complaints were warnings to the members of staff involved. Some serious physical assaults were handled without reference to external managers and resulted in children being summarily moved to other homes, often out of the county, thus isolating them further from family and friends. Generally, however, there seemed to be an acceptance of violent confrontations, particularly on the part of older male children in care during this period. This, coupled with the absence of a formal complaints system led, as noted above, to far fewer complaints being made than might be expected.

With regard to sexual abuse, some complaints were formally made which, as we have seen, resulted in prosecutions and dismissals of staff over the years. However, some persistent abusers (all high status staff members who had a powerful hold on the children in their care and on their colleagues) managed to avoid being complained against and detected for many years. The Tribunal was particularly concerned to find out why complainants did not, at the time of their abuse 'disclose' to other staff members, social workers, the police or their parents. A variety of reasons were put forward: – staff members were seen as likely to back up their own colleagues; the police were not trusted, particularly by those with backgrounds of offending behaviour; social workers were seen as either remote or likely to refer matters back to the alleged abusers and, finally, most complainants felt too ashamed to reveal such matters to their parents and friends. This combination of fear, mistrust, shame and not expecting to be believed led to two main short-term responses : acceptance or absconding.

Whistle-blowing
Another key issue for the North Wales inquiry was why there were not more complaints made by staff members about their colleagues. The paucity of such complaints is often attributed to the fact that so-called 'whistle-blowers' can suffer

adverse consequences from their actions. Indeed, this seemed to have happened in relation to Alison Taylor, the female member of staff whose concerns led to the start of the campaign for a public inquiry. She first became concerned about the physical ill-treatment of young people in the children's home in Gwynedd where she was second in charge in 1986. She made her complaint to a local councillor and the result was a police investigation. This yielded no evidence and in 1987 she was dismissed from her post. Alison did not give in and she became a focal point for complaints made by young people in residential care in both Gwynedd and Clwyd where she had also worked. However, there was little evidence of other residential staff members making serious criticisms. This might be explained by a conspiracy of silence, acceptance of a degree of physical maltreatment of children as the norm, and the ability of those who sexually abused to maintain secrecy.

The Upsurge in Concern about Residential Child Care

So much for the details of the concerns of the inquiries into residential child care establishments. In what follows, I will consider why there has been such emphasis on abuse in residential care in the last decade or so, using the case of the North Wales Tribunal of Inquiry as a key example.

Several factors have influenced the growth of concerns about residential care in the 1990s – the media, for instance, have played some part in the process, (Aldridge, 1994), as has an upsurge in fear and loathing of the paedophile, (Jenkins, 1992 and Howitt, 1995). However, two broader but closely linked developments lie at the heart of current concerns about abuse of children in care – these are what I will term the 'prizing of childhood' and 'risk elimination'.

The Prizing of Childhood and Risk Elimination
The view that childhood is a social construction has been developed primarily by Philippe Aries (1962). While his ideas have been disputed in the detail, (Pollock, 1983), they at least help us to understand why children have been seen, and therefore treated, differently at different times in history.

In modern, relatively affluent societies like our own, childhood has come to be valued by adults as a particularly precious time during which children should be carefully protected and allowed to develop largely unworried by the responsibilities and demands likely to be placed on them when they grow up. One possible explanation for this development is the fact that, for economic reasons and with the aid of advances in birth-control technology, families have fewer children than before. In addition, major advances in medical knowledge and practice have led people to believe that it is the norm now for virtually all children to survive to adulthood. Hence, the gamble on having small numbers of children is considered to be one of short odds. Society has changed dramatically in this respect over the past few decades. Individuals have become increasingly preoccupied with notions of risk and its elimination in a whole range of areas of life, of which childhood is one, (Parton, 1996 and Parton et al., 1997)). We are increasingly concerned to protect ourselves and our small number of children from dangerous diseases, dangerous situations and contact with dangerous people. For evidence of this trend, one only has to consider the national panic created recently by meningitis, which is seen as a disease which strikes suddenly and arbitrarily among children and young people in defiance of modern medicine.

The Problem of Child Abuse and its Consequences
The prizing of childhood and preoccupation with risk, therefore, have created the conditions for modern concerns about child abuse. Starting with Kempe's work on babies battered by their parents, (Kempe et al., 1962), the net of concern has spread, first to intra-familial abuse and neglect (physical, emotional and sexual) of children of all ages, and second to the abuse of children by individuals largely outside their own families, as in the case of organised and ritual abuse, bullying at school, and abuse in residential and day-care settings. One of the key factors in the spread of these concerns, which links back to the notion of the preciousness of childhood and the risk society, is the development of understanding of the consequences of abuse. It is now broadly accepted that, even though our knowledge about process, causal links and consistency of outcome is still limited, being abused as a child in any of the forms referred to above is likely to have deleterious effects, (Beitchman et al., 1991, 1992 and Calam and Franchi 1987). It can have an adverse influence on self-esteem, the capacity to make close relationships and to parent effectively, on mental health, the likelihood of self-harm and harm to others, (Boswell, 1995).

Children's Rights
Another consequence of the prizing of childhood is the assertion of children's rights and acceptance of the importance of listening and giving credence to what children say. The growth of concern about sexual abuse of children has been a key catalyst in this. The fact that often the only available evidence of such abuse is the testimony of the children themselves, has resulted in a major rethinking of the weight to be given to the words of children. The response has been cautious and, in the views of proponents of children's rights, limited, (Franklin, 1995). Nevertheless, there have been changes in law, (Cobley, 1995) and procedures, (the Home Office, 1992) in order to make it easier for children to give evidence at the trials of their alleged abusers.

Intrusion into Families
The developments discussed in the preceding paragraphs have not been without problems. For some, the consequence of the prizing of childhood has been a greater incursion into family life sometimes seen as undermining the roles and responsibilities of parents (c.f. the media reaction to the sexual abuse scandal at

Cleveland, Nava, 1988). Ritual abuse investigations such as those on the Orkneys, Rochdale and Nottingham have excited even more condemnation, (LaFontaine, 1998).

The Outrage at Abuse of Children in Residential Care
By contrast, the discovery of abuse on a wide scale in residential care in the 1990s has aroused almost unqualified public outrage and, as yet, there have been only a small number of commentators questioning the validity of the claims being made by children alleging abuse, (Webster, 1998).

Dealing with child abuse in residential care is in many ways less problematic than dealing with it in families. First, the concerns being raised are about extra-familial abuse, and certainly in the case of sexual abuse this is viewed as a less complex and more legitimate reason for intervention than intra-familial abuse. Second, in this era of the prizing of childhood, the notion of residential care has become a less and less acceptable option. It is a stark reminder of the failure of family life. We do not like to think of children living in care without parents. Residential care is equated with institutional life and the sorts of dangers and excesses depicted by Erving Goffman in his seminal work 'Asylums', (Goffman, 1968). The strongly preferred current solution to the failure of family life is to place children in other families – in foster care or in adoptive placements. Ironically, this type of thinking may well increase the likelihood of children in residential care being abused in that it can lead to lack of value placed on resi-dential services, and poorer monitoring of standards and practices.

Whatever the rights and wrongs of the situation, the fact is that for the reasons outlined above, allegations of child abuse in residential care has become in popular perception a more legitimate cause for concern than some forms of intra-familial abuse. It is therefore now generally accepted that such residential abuse needs to be brought into the open, that ex-residents of children's homes should be encouraged to speak of their experiences and that their evidence should be care-fully examined in order to identify and punish alleged abusers.

Applying this Analysis to North Wales
These developments underpin the string of public inquiries and investigations outlined in the first section of this chapter culminating in the establishment of the North Wales Tribunal of Inquiry. With regard to the latter, there were concerns about abuse of children in residential care throughout the seventies and eighties in Clwyd and Gwynedd. Between 1975 and 1987 there were 12 individuals officially investi-gated, 11 for sexual abuse and one for physical abuse, eight of whom were charged and prosecuted. There were several internal inquiries following these cases coming to light, but they had little impact on the administration of children's establishments. To some extent this may have been due to a 'culture of concealment', a term used by the Counsel to the Tribunal. More probably, however, the muted response reflected a

lack of awareness of the possible extent of abuse in children's homes at the time and the low priority attached to residential child care services more generally.

By the late eighties, however, with the increased awareness of both intra-familial and extra-familial abuse in the wider society, there was a shift in thinking. As a result, when Alison Taylor raised her concerns about the ill-treatment of children, despite being dismissed from her post, she found people, initially in local politics and the media, who were prepared to listen and pursue questions about the quality of care provided both in Gwynedd and the neighbouring authority of Clwyd. By 1991, the then Director of Clwyd Social Services, relatively new to his post at the time, was convinced of the need for a fuller investigation and North Wales police agreed to carry it out. In all, they heard complaints from more than 500 ex-residents. However, as an outcome of this investigation, only eight prosecutions were brought resulting in six convictions. This was seen as unsatisfactory by Alison Taylor and the more vociferous of the ex-residents of the homes. They suspected that since there were allegations that serving and former policemen had been involved in some of the sexual abuse activities, North Wales police had not been impartial in their investigations. In particular it was felt that there was insufficient effort being made to root out alleged paedophile rings.

By this time, concerns about abuse in residential care nationally were spreading fast – the Pindown inquiry, (Levy and Kahan, 1991) in particular raised issues not just about abuse but about the whole culture of residential care for children and the practices therein. Clwyd county council responded to the criticisms of the police investigation by setting up the Jillings Inquiry, which reported in 1996. However, the findings of their report were not made public as because of intervention by the council's insurers and subsequent legal advice. This increased suspicions of a cover-up. Soon after this, the Welsh Office set up two further inquiries, the second of which focused on current provision of residential services under the new unitary authorities that by this time had replaced Clwyd and Gwynedd, (Jones, 1996). However, dissatisfaction with the various attempts to tackle the issues of abuse persisted and the then Minister for Wales, William Hague, conceded the need for a Tribunal of Inquiry.

With hindsight, the establishment of the North Wales Tribunal of Inquiry seems to have had an air of inevitability about it given changes in popular and media perceptions, shifts in awareness and evidence of abuse being more widespread than had been previously imagined.

The Impact of the Inquiries into Residential Care

Key Outcomes of the Inquiry

As stressed at the outset, the findings of the North Wales Inquiry have yet to be published. However, they are most likely to confirm that the standard of care in large numbers of homes in Clwyd and Gwynedd was poor, resulting in environments where physical abuse was tolerated and sexual abuse could go largely undetected. It is likely that the bulk of the responsibility for this will be laid at the door of social services managers and the Welsh Office Inspectorate, and that they will be severely criticised for lack of clear policies, inadequate management of staff, poor recruitment procedures, poor monitoring and inspection practices and failure to respond properly to complaints made by children. Various recommendations for improvement, particularly with regard to the inspection and monitoring of the progress of children in care were put forward during the Tribunal's hearings. Counsel for complainants favoured the retention of guardian ad litems after care proceedings so that independent, child-focused professionals could be available for looked after children throughout their time in care. Counsel for the Tribunal proposed placing oversight authority for reviews, inspections and complaints with district judges, thus divesting local authorities of all responsibility for self-monitoring. It will be interesting to see what the final recommendations will be – it is notable that in the Government White Paper there is a proposal to establish independent regional inspection bodies to take over registration and inspection duties from local authorities, (DoH, 1998b).

The findings of the Tribunal are likely, therefore, to add to the negative image that other inquiries have already created of regard to residential care. It is very difficult to counter this. By the very nature of their function, that of uncovering abuse and satisfying the public that the truth has been established, inquiries are bound to focus on what has gone wrong, and positive aspects of practice tend to be overlooked. For instance, it is worth bearing in mind the following point raised in his opening address by the leading counsel to the Tribunal:

> *it is opportune to remark at this stage, and entirely proper that it should be said in fairness to the host of good and dedicated residential care workers who helped run the system, that of the 84 or so homes which operated within the two Counties through the 22 years we have been considering, almost exactly 50 per cent have generated no complaints of abuse of any kind of which we are aware and a further 10 per cent are homes from which one complaint only has been registered.*

(para.1.16)

How far such realities will be emphasised in the final report and the media accounts of the inquiry remain to be seen. It is also worth noting that by no means all of the complaints will have been substantiated during the course of the inquiry. Hopefully the inquiry report will make some judgement about each of the complaints so that a considered view of the number of abuse incidents and of untrustworthy allegations will be made available to the public.

Residential Care Today

Another factor to take into account is that many of the complaints considered by the North Wales Tribunal stemmed from a time when residential care was quite different from today in terms of size, aims and functions. In 1971 there were 41,000 children in children's homes in England and Wales, (DoH, 1998a p8). Many of these children were placed in large establishments by today's standards – for instance, Bryn Estyn, a community home with education in Wrexham, Clwyd, which generated the highest number of abuse allegations, catered for around 60 children when operating at full capacity. By contrast, in 1996 there were 7,000 children being looked after in local authority and voluntary homes and the number of children per home is now greatly reduced. Sinclair and Gibbs, (1998) found that four-fifths of the 48 homes they studied had less than nine residents. Department of Health sponsored research has extensively analysed the modern scene and provides a more balanced picture of the positive and negative aspects of residential care. Key findings are that homes with clearly stated objectives where heads are well-supported by external managers do best and can provide positive caring environments. On the debit side, it is notable that about two-fifths of children from a large sample of homes in one of the studies were described as miserable and unhappy, (Sinclair and Gibbs, 1998). Many of these children had considerable behavioural problems resulting from previous negative experiences, in particular, sexual abuse, (Farmer and Pollock, 1998). These behaviours pose particular challenges for residential care workers and issues about appropriate responses to such behaviour remain unresolved. It was notable also that a key concern for many children in residential care was that of being bullied by fellow residents, an area which has not been highlighted in previous inquiry reports, and was not prominent in the North Wales Tribunal. This is a finding, however, which features in official inquiries into the treatment of children in prison.(see Chapter 12 by Stephen Shaw and Clare Sparks.)

Concluding Comments

It is important that those working in and around residential child care respond positively to the concerns being currently raised. It is clear that, despite those who would wish to see all looked-after children in substitute families, residential care is still seen by large numbers of older looked-after children as having advantages over foster care. The recently published *Safeguards Review*, (Utting, 1997) has confirmed the need for sufficient residential facilities to provide choice and flexibility in placement. Thus, residential care needs to build on its strengths and eliminate its weaknesses. The recent research has provided some insights on how to do this, albeit at a rather general level.

With regard to inquiry findings, it is important that the recurring messages – the need for better recruitment practices and training, improved management oversight, better inspection procedures and methods of handling complaints, are taken on board. There can be little doubt that there is room for improvement in all these areas – for instance, the qualification rate of residential workers is still as low as

15 per cent, (Little, 1999), and current complaints procedures seem to be rarely used, (Lyon, 1997). What is important above all, however, is that these messages be taken up in a positive and constructive way. Residential work could learn much from the experiences of field social work in this respect. By the late eighties and early nineties a great deal of child abuse work had become heavily bureaucratised and proceduralised in order to ensure avoidance of the kinds of mistakes made in the past, (Howe, 1992). By the mid-nineties, however, government-sponsored research was highlighting some key dysfunctions of this approach – the lack of focus on broader family needs being the most obvious one, (DoH, 1995). It would be a great pity if residential work were to make similar mistakes. Thus, for instance, it is important that:

- Recruitment of staff to residential posts is not entirely taken over by procedures designed to weed out potential sex abusers.
- Training is broad-based and focused on the needs of children rather than on non-abusive means of controlling them.
- Complaints be managed in a way that ensures non-defensive and speedy reactions rather than becoming long drawn out and heavily proceduralised affairs.
- Managers of residential care be involved in problem-solving alongside staff rather than seeing their tasks purely and simply as measuring outcomes and dealing with complaints.

While inquiries do serve an important function in society – that of allaying public concern – they tend to emphasise negative aspects of practice and can result in defensive practice and dysfunctional policies, (Hill, 1990). Much depends on the good sense and discrimination of policy-makers and practitioners. The fact that the report of the North Wales Tribunal of Inquiry has been preceded by recently published government-sponsored research and initiatives which provide a broader and, therefore, in all likelihood, less negative picture, is a good start. It is important that this good start is built on in a positive and non-defensive way in the future.

CHAPTER 2

Often Ignored: Obvious Messages for a Safe Workforce

David Lane

The messages contained in this chapter may seem patently obvious when laid out in print, but they have often been ignored. The people who have paid the price for this failure have been primarily the children and young people in the residential services, but also residential workers and, as the ripples have spread outwards, the providing agencies and the wider public.

The main message is that safe services of good quality will only be provided if the workforce is of high quality. Residential care is essentially a human service. There are other resources which are important, such as adequate budgets and suitable buildings, but good care has been provided in some appalling buildings and on limited budgets. By contrast, if safe care has ever been offered by bad staff, it can only be attributed to luck. The quality of the workforce is the cornerstone on which everything else is built.

There is no senior manager, councillor, trustee or proprietor who would not say that the quality of their staff is of crucial importance to the safety of the children and young people in their care. Yet there are many who have failed to ensure that their staff are able to deliver high quality services by denying them the range of support systems and quality controls required to ensure high standards.

This chapter lays out the ten features required to ensure a safe workforce. Some of them are dealt with elsewhere in this book in greater detail and so are touched on here briefly. However, they are included because, unless a comprehensive approach is taken, there will be weaknesses in the system. In some cases the weakness may be trivial, but in others, failure in one feature may undermine all the other measures

The ten features have all figured in recent reports, such as Wagner, (1988), Howe, (1992), Levy and Kahan, (1991), Warner, (1992), the two Utting Reports, (1991, 1997) and Kent, (1997). If agencies, managers and practitioners were to implement all their recommendations there would be very few problems, as they contain a lot of sense about good practice.

However, the standards they describe are not achieved once and for all. It is a continual battle to maintain high standards of good practice and management, and regrettably in some aspects, standards have fallen over recent years, despite improvements in others. In human services, lapsing from standards is to be antici-pated, and in consequence it is necessary to have mechanisms to monitor quality and trigger questions about standards, though no system is a substitute for vigilance.

1. Attracting the Best People

Residential child care has had an unhappy image for some decades now. There has always been some good practice, but the public image has been moulded by scandals and the social services view has generally been to see residential care as a damaging last resort to be avoided if at all possible. In social work training, for example, many lecturers and tutors have seen residential care as being damaging, and the standard text on many courses has been Goffman's *Asylums*, (1968), which relates essentially to large institutions rather than the texts on good residential practice. People arguing to the contrary have felt themselves to be defensive, limiting the damage of the attacks, rather than confidently selling a positive image. The need to counter this perception was reflected in the title of the Wagner Report, *A Positive Choice* and its companion volume *Positive Answers*, (1988).

This point was made strongly in the Howe Report, (1992), and Lady Howe herself put pressure on the Government to produce material to attract workers into residential child care. Creating a positive image is an uphill battle, especially in view of the lack of qualifying training opportunities and the critical view taken of residential child care on many social work programmes.

The Advancement of Residential Child Care (ARCC) was set up in 1993 to promote a positive view of residential child care, but it was wound up in 1997, and this role has now been taken over by the Residential Forum.

The children and young people in residential establishments suffer, and present, the most intractable problems, thus they need, and deserve, the best staff. The residential setting provides unparalleled opportunities to address their needs. There is much to be positive about. Residential care is successfully coping with acute problems, and provides the best hope for many children and young people. A campaign is therefore needed at every level, whether nationally, at agency level and concerning each home, centre and school, to establish positive images of residential care.

Unless residential care recruits good candidates who are motivated to attempt to meet the most acute needs of children and young people, it will fail in its task, and among the symptoms of its failure will be unnecessary risk and damage to its residents.

2. Selecting the Best People

The Warner Report, (1992) made explicit the importance of good methods of staff selection, and the dangers to children and young people if the process were not carried out thoroughly. The Support Force for the Residential Care of Children followed up the Warner recommendations by encouraging higher standards of selection in a large number of local authorities, and many have implemented the Warner proposals.

The Support Force, (1995), backed up their developmental work with the publication of comprehensive guidance on staff selection. The main message to emerge from this document is that the best protection for children and young people is the thorough application of normal standard procedures, applied perceptively. There is no magic test to identify possible abusers. There are guidelines devised by psychologists to assist in screening, and there are signs to look out for, but there is no foolproof means to eliminate abusers. The selection process remains the most critical point to exclude undesirable workers. It provides an opportunity for employers not only to select staff but also to let applicants size them up and, even more importantly, to put over powerful messages about the values of the agency and the expectations which managers will have of staff. These messages can be powerful and long-lasting as they are delivered at a time of stress for the applicants, and they may both establish high standards of conduct and deter bad practice.

3. Managing the Workers

The best ongoing protection for children and young people is sound management. There are, of course, times when it comes as a complete shock to colleagues when they find that a member of staff has been involved in abusing children or young people in their care. Often, though, there are signs of poor or unsatisfactory practice which, if addressed, help the worker realise that this type of employment is not for them or which set standards by which the worker is then judged. Again, there are checklists which can be used to prompt further questions about unacceptable practice, though none provides direct evidence on its own.

It should be noted that unacceptable practice on the part of staff includes not only the obvious examples such as sexual abuse, physical abuse or theft, but also incompetence, which is sometimes more difficult to specify and justify in disciplinary proceedings, as it may become apparent by degrees and may present itself as one aspect of a wider complex of problems.

Indeed, when there is failure on the part of assistant staff, the senior staff are often implicated if only because of their failure to train or support their staff or to take action at an earlier stage. Although training opportunities for managers are increasing, line management has not received sufficient attention.

Too often, those managing heads of homes have been people who could not be found more attractive slots in departmental reorganisations, and they have had to learn about residential care from their subordinates, which is most unsatisfactory and would not be tolerated in other fields. The fact that such appointments are made is another indicator of the failure on the part of those in positions of responsibility to appreciate the complexities of the work and the need for specialist knowledge if staff and residents are not to suffer from managerial incompetence.

The relationship between head of home and immediate line manager is crucial to the effectiveness of an establishment, as the Social Care Association Management

Guide, (1999a), demonstrates. The head is of critical importance in setting the internal tone but the line manager also plays a major part in supporting the head, monitoring the quality of the head's work and holding the external boundaries. Their working relationship can be a sound bedrock for the work of the home or can create major difficulties, but its importance is insufficiently recognised.

4. Supervision

Line managers need to offer regular supervision to heads of homes, partly to offer support and partly to monitor practice. They are the people in positions of authority over the head of home who have the most regular contact, and it falls to them to be sufficiently involved to be able to note whether anything is going adrift. They need to be available to staff and residents, and to be sufficiently well known for both workers and residents to have confidence in them if there are matters of concern to report.

The supervision of heads of home by line managers sets the pattern for the heads' supervision of their staff. It needs to be regular, at least monthly, of sufficient duration to bottom out serious problems, and uninterrupted. Otherwise, it becomes irregular, of lower priority and fails to offer the opportunity to develop shared ways of resolving the major problems often met in the work.

Because the line management relationship may have to be used for policy or disciplinary purposes, there has to be an element of distance in it. Heads of homes may therefore feel the need to analyse problems and discuss their worries and failures with someone outside line management. Indeed, because of the stress involved in residential child care, it can be argued that all heads, or their staff teams as a whole, should have access to independent people whose role is only to offer support. These people may be appointed externally or may be drawn from other parts of the agency, such as training officers or advisers.

5. Blowing the Whistle

It is sometimes forgotten that the safety of children and young people in residential settings is not just a matter of senior staff checking on new recruits but may also involve assistant staff in questioning and reporting the conduct of their seniors. In some cases their managers may be burnt out and unable to function effectively, having lost the reserves needed to respond to children and young people creatively. In other cases, it may be the new recruit who becomes aware of a web of abuse, perhaps established by senior staff but involving other staff who may have been intimidated or compromised. It takes nerve to blow the whistle in such circumstances, but it is vital that such cases should be reported.

Agencies therefore need to create an atmosphere of openness, which encourages both staff and children and young people to talk and avoid secrecy, so that the possibility of abuse is reduced from the start, and so that people feel empowered to report their concerns when they believe that there are grounds.

Agencies need to have whistle-blowing policies, including arrangements with outside agencies, such as Public Concern at Work, who can help potential complainants to frame their concerns and handle the process constructively, and clauses to protect bona fide whistle-blowers from recriminations. Concern in this area has grown over recent years. Many agencies now have whistle-blowing policies, and there is a growing literature, (c.f. Hunt, 1998).

6. The Supportive Agency

Good management does not end with the head of the home. The senior managers to whom the head is answerable have key roles both to be supportive and to monitor practice. In nearly every report on scandals in residential services, there have been failures on the part of senior managers, who have turned a blind eye to malpractice or failed to involve themselves sufficiently to identify abuse.

Again, the best protection for children and young people is provided by sound standard management practices, such as :

- regular visiting by senior managers
- monitoring visits by councillors, proprietor or trustees
- planned professional supervision at all levels
- the maintenance and checking of records
- regular explanations to residents about complaints systems
- reviewing systems which involve the children and young people fully
- regular visits by field social workers
- the availability of independent persons to speak to, and on behalf of, the children and young people.

By corollary, the children and young people who are vulnerable to abuse are those who have no-one to turn to outside the home or who have no opportunity to speak confidentially to outsiders.

While all these points may seem obvious, the fact is that agencies often fail to deliver good practice as described above. For example, local councillors may have rotas to visit council children's homes, but the frequency and value of visits are often very patchy. In part, this may result from the lack of guidance on the purpose of the visits and on what to look for, so that the councillors feel unsure of themselves and of what they should be doing. A Management Guide prepared by the Social Care Association, (1999b), offers guidance to agencies wishing to organise such systems.

Again, large agencies, whether they are local authorities or voluntary bodies, are multifunctional and they have other agendas besides the provision of residential childcare. At times, these functions clash and other priorities may over-ride the interests of children and young people in residential care. Councillors, for instance, are accountable to their electorates, who may be supporters of 'nimbyism', regardless of the needs of the children, and decisions may be taken about the opening, closure or siting of homes that reflect political priorities rather than children's interests.

In the management of local authorities, systems may be introduced where the purchasing of household goods and equipment, the upkeep of the grounds or the maintenance of buildings are not under the control of the residential staff. If, however, the aim is to bring up children and young people as independent, responsible, confident adults, they need adults who themselves offer such a model. If the staff are seen as pawns in the game, pushed around by other forces, the primary purpose of the service may be unwittingly undermined.

If residential care is to fulfil its function properly, the agency needs to be geared to support the residential task rather than fit the home to the agency's requirements. The Secretary of State has made it quite clear in directives and in *Quality Protects*, (DoH, 1998), that councillors have a major responsibility for the quality of the care offered to children and young people by the local authority. Responsibility for the services has to permeate the whole organisation.

Although the examples given above all relate to local authorities, there are similar constraints on other types of service provider. A large voluntary body will have multiple functions, for example, into which it may require its homes to fit, and private proprietors face the constant tension between the need for a degree of profitability and expenditure on providing a quality service.

7. Pay and Conditions

If a good workforce is to be attracted and retained, it needs to be reasonably rewarded. This point has been made at intervals from the Residential Care Association's *Dalmeny Papers*, (1974), through to the Howe Report in 1992.

Where pay and conditions are bad, there is liable to be high staff turnover, which is damaging to children and young people. What is worse, the only people liable to stay and provide any degree of consistency may be those who are less competent, or who cannot obtain other jobs, or who obtain other types of pay-off by seeking power over children or at worst indulging in abuse, unchecked by the flow of temporary colleagues. In themselves, high pay and good working conditions do not make children and young people safe, but poor pay and conditions can contribute to their vulnerability.

The residential child care service is highly vulnerable to the impact of hidden consequences, and there have been a number of examples over the last twenty years. In order to implement the introduction of the fixed working week in 1971, employers upped staffing numbers. Later in the 1970s, they imposed realistic rents, which in effect drove resident staff out. Both were justifiable measures, as workers had previously been exploited, as they lived on the spot where they worked and their working hours were frequently over a hundred hours a week. However, the combined effect of these two measures was to make children's homes places which adults visited to do their shifts, and they became homes only for children and young people, changing their nature and effectiveness. However, the changes did not result from professional thinking about the best ways of meeting children's needs, but were a sort of backwash from developments in conditions of services.

Other conditions of service affect the quality of childcare and the safety of the children. Research has demonstrated time and again the need for children to enjoy continuity of care, and yet agencies make frequent use of agency staff and of peripatetic teams, so that children and young people often do not know the people who are caring for them. Frequent changes of carer inevitably make relationships more shallow at a stage when children and young people need greater stability if they are to confront and cope with the intense personal problems they often bring with them into residential care.

The examples above are historical, but what will be the effects of the European Directive on Working Times? Like the historical changes mentioned above, the Directive has not arisen from a considered view of meeting children's needs, but is having a direct impact on practice. No doubt the unintended consequences will emerge over time.

Ideally, when devising rotas, arranging conditions of service or negotiating pay, the primary consideration should be the best way of meeting the needs of the children and young people. Unfortunately, history teaches us that the employers' and employees' needs come first.

8. Setting the Standards

The discussion of professional ethics is not high on most practitioners' or managers' agendas, as it sounds too theoretical and unrelated to practice to be a priority in the current professional culture in the United Kingdom. Awareness of sound ethical practice is of critical importance, however.

A code of ethics can establish good practice. It can reassure the public that the profession has explicit standards by which it is prepared to stand and by which it may be judged. It offers guidance to individual workers in difficult situations. It can act as a template against which to test conduct when it is transgressed, and transgressors cannot plead ignorance once standards have been made clear. It also offers a target for reformers to use in clarifying modifications which need to be made.

The British Association of Social Workers has a Code of Ethics. The Social Care Association, (1999), published a Code of Practice for social care workers in 1982, preferring this title to emphasise its relevance to the task, and this has been adopted by a number of employers. A modified form of the SCA Code was adapted by Caring for Children for use by child care workers in 1992. The Fédération Internationale des Communautes Éducatives, (FICE, 1998) published an International Code in five languages, appending explanations of the importance of codes and how to prepare them.

In the production of the International Code, it became apparent that different countries approached questions of professional ethics from very different standpoints. In some,

- The professionals were keen to make them consistent with legislation and to work closely with their government.
- Professionals wanted to establish a code in order to demonstrate that they were self-governing and independent, not dictated to by their government.
- A code was seen as a creed to strengthen their resolve to fight for children's rights against corrupt governments or police.

Clearly, codes of professional ethics need to be related to the settings where they are to be used. They are not just for professional associations. It is helpful if employers make clear the standards of conduct expected of their staff and volunteers. Otherwise there may be variable practice and there could be inadequate grounds for criticising or disciplining staff in the event of alleged misconduct if standards have not been made explicit. Indeed, some trades unions have opposed the adoption of codes of ethics because their members might then be vulnerable if they were to fail to comply.

More important than the actual code is its preparation. The process can involve staff, set them thinking, help them to be precise in devising the wording of the Code and encourage them to identify with the agreed standards. Involvement in the process of thinking about best practice is more valuable than unthinking acceptance of edicts set in stone. Residential child care is a creative task that continually needs new answers to human problems, and no rule book is sufficient to resolve all issues. All it can do is to help indicate current accepted practice and the underlying principles, which need to be borne in mind in deciding what to do.

When the General Social Care Council (GSCC) is established, among its first tasks will be the preparation of Codes of Conduct for both staff and employers. These will supersede any other Codes and will be applied nationally.

However, the national authorisation of the Codes by the GSCC will not mean that debate on ethical issues should be closed. Such discussion should be ongoing, whether in addressing new issues or in revising thinking on current policy. Residential care is forever changing and developing, and new answers need to be found. It is more important, therefore, that workers should question and attempt to solve problems creatively than that they should work by a rule book. The purpose of codes of ethics is to assist in establishing good practice, not to stultify it.

9. Checking for Quality

At present, the only systems to regulate workers in the field of child care are the statutory registration and inspection of child minders by local authorities and the availability of checks on police records for a wide range of people who work with children and young people. Under the GSCC, a statutory system of registration will be introduced. In due course this will probably cover a number of professional and para-professional groups of workers, some of whom will be working with children and young people.

The two groups identified as priorities are field social workers and residential child care workers. The process will be to identify the training relevant to the group of workers, to ensure that it is available in sufficient volume to meet the needs of the workforce, and to check that a critical mass of the workforce has the necessary qualifications before setting up a register. In the case of field social workers, this is likely to present few problems as virtually the whole workforce now holds recognised qualifications in social work validated by the Central Council for Education and Training in Social Work.

However, the number of qualified workers in residential childcare is much lower, and the Government proposes in *Quality Protects* to establish the register within its guidelines by accepting training undertaken at National Vocational Level 3 as an adequate qualification . This approach fails to recognise the complexity of the task and the level of skills and knowledge required, and is only acceptable if it is acknowledged as a staging post en route to higher standards to be adopted in due course.

The Institute of Childcare and Social Education, has been unhappy at waiting until the GSCC is established, and has prepared its own proposals to commence the voluntary registration of all people working with children and young people. Their checks would involve the identity of applicants, their work records, their academic records and their police records, so that any potential employer would have as a full and reliable picture, checked and confirmed wherever possible.

Of course, such a system cannot be fool-proof, and it is always possible that undesirable workers will slip through. In particular, potential abusers may be latent, awaiting their time, and there may be no untoward signals or symptoms by which to identify them at the point of registration. Nonetheless, when unacceptable conduct has been identified, it will be possible to exclude perpetrators more easily, and the very existence of a register may dissuade some possible abusers from seeking employment.

The price to pay for providing protection in this way is that the careers of some workers could be put in jeopardy, for example if they are subject to false allegations. On balance, however, it is necessary at this point to swing the balance in the favour of protecting children. If, on the balance of probabilities, it seems that a worker has been involved in abuse, it is more important to protect the children and young people than the careers of the workers.

10. Training and Developing the Workforce

The last element in the protective armoury is the provision of training. In terms of the safety of children and young people in residential care, it has been pointed out that some of the worst abusers, such as Frank Beck, have been qualified. Obviously, training is not a guarantee of probity. However, the power wielded by Beck and other abusers was in part enhanced because of the dearth of other qualified staff with the authority to challenge them.

Training is not only the provision of knowledge and skills but it also carries messages about the values implicit in the work. This is as true of professional qualifying training as of staff development exercises put on by employers. In both cases, it is important to emphasise the need for high standards and the refusal by the profession or agency to tolerate abuse.

Training needs to start from induction, for which the National Children's Bureau, (Gabbidon et al., 1999) has recently published an excellent pack, carry on through ongoing staff development, and include team training and individual personal development, up to qualifying and post-qualifying levels. The Government has just published proposals for post-qualifying training for child care workers, including those working in the residential setting, which is welcome, as there have been few opportunities for residential child care workers since specialist advanced courses were abandoned by CCETSW.

The Residential Forum, concerned at the continuing inadequacy of current training, recently published *A Golden Opportunity*. In much of Europe all residential staff are qualified, following three-year training courses. In this country, the volume, content and quality of training are all inadequate to meet the needs of the workforce. The report argues for training specific to direct work with children and young people, criticises the existing Diploma in Social Work model, and proposes a new professional identity for workers under the heading social education, with its own leadership group. Several universities and agencies are now experimenting or planning courses for residential child care workers outside the CCETSW format. While these developments may lead to short-term confusion, they indicate the wish to set up courses which provide the skills and knowledge needed in this specific setting, and the dissatisfaction with what is currently on offer. (Issues of training for residential care are dealt with in greater detail in Chapters 6 and 7 by David Crimmens and Sandy de Silva.)

Certainly, many staff could do with a boost to morale and self-confidence, so that residential childcare is seen as a credible professional activity, and not just a stepping-stone to field social work.

A Comprehensive Approach

This chapter has dealt with a lot of themes briefly in order to emphasise the initial point that we need to take a comprehensive view of the scene if we are to succeed. If we attract the wrong staff, we will fail. If we attract some good staff, but appoint the wrong ones, we will fail. If we train staff inadequately, however good they are, they may well lack competence. If we manage them badly however well we train them, our practice is likely to be poor. If we reward staff badly so that they leave, we may well harm the children and young people in residential care. In short, if any of these things happen, we can fail even if we are doing a lot that is right. Investment in a lot of good practice may be undermined by failure in one field, and result in poor unsafe practice.

At present, of the ten planks in the platform described in this chapter, some are in good shape, some are rather creaky, some are in places rotten, and some are missing. Residential child care workers and the children and young people whom they serve deserve a more solid basis for their work.

Why Have We Failed?

The failure to develop an effective, reliable and safe service for children and young people over the last twenty-five years is perhaps the most serious short-coming of the social services since they were set up. If the mistakes are not to be repeated, the cause needs to be sought. Perhaps the residential child care task is seen as being easy, the sort of activity which any parent can undertake and not needing the types of support described above. Perhaps residential care is the victim of decades of criticism within the social work profession. Perhaps the best staff who are needed to provide leadership have been put off from joining the service, seeing other fields as being go-ahead and innovative. Perhaps the criticisms have become self-fulfilling in driving standards down.

Whatever the reasons, the service needs to be turned round. The current attention paid to this service is most encouraging, an opportunity which must not be lost. In particular, the Government interest is most welcome, and the services must respond by helping them to ensure that there is a safe workforce, which will keep the children and young people resident in the homes, centres and schools safe.

Safety Versus Quality? A Caveat!

Finally, in emphasising safety, professionals face a serious dilemma. Of course we wish the children and young people in residential services to be safe, and we want the staff and volunteers who work with them to be safe as well. However, safety is not the main aim of providing residential services. The purpose of residential care is a blend of resolving the problems which children and young people bring with them, providing a sound normal upbringing and creating opportunities for their futures. We may wish to achieve these aims safely, but safety is in itself a desirable quality rather than a primary objective.

Indeed, it can be argued that an over-emphasis on safety risks detracting from quality of care. A child or young person needs to experiment and to take risks if it is to learn to walk, to find out what is dangerous or to move towards independence. With proper preparation and supervision, the danger associated with calculated risks is minimised, but it would not help children and young people if they were brought up wrapped in cotton wool.

The same is true of staff. If they are always placed under pressure to act safely, there is a real risk that they will fail to respond to situations creatively and will work according to the book, in order to avoid criticism and liability. Staff who are aware of the risk of allegations, for example, may decline to be left alone with a child, even though the child may be going through a phase when personal individual attention could be critical to resolving their problems. Again, staff who are reluctant to cuddle or touch children in order to avoid being subject to complaints and allegations may leave children feeling uncared for.

There are no easy answers to this dilemma. There are aspects of good child care practice which help to make it manageable, such as full discussion with colleagues, talking the risks through with the children and young people, and recording events carefully so that the staff involved can be accountable and explain their actions subsequently if necessary.

Ultimately, however, each worker has at times to make judgements, balancing up the risks, and sometimes best practice may not be the line of action which is superficially the safest. The ultimate test is which line of action is in the best interests of the child or young person.

It is important in a book such as this, or in a report such as Sir William Utting's, *People Like Us*, (1997), that lessons should be learnt from the past and that proper attention should be paid to the safety of children and young people in residential settings. It is also important, however, that we do not fall into the British trap of creating policy solely by reacting against previous bad practice. Good child care is much more than the absence of bad practice but that is the subject for another book.

SECTION 2

Re-structuring Residential Child Care

CHAPTER 3

Building in the Lessons: A New Start for Residential Care in Lewisham

Chris Hume, Frank Lowe and Georgina Rose

Introduction

In 1985, the officer in charge at Leeways Children's Home in South London, was convicted of indecency against children in his care, (Lewisham Council Report, 1995). Within a few years Lewisham had closed all its children's homes and was pursuing a policy of relying on foster placements for children in care. This dramatic change in policy was in part a response to the abuse inquiry, but more a response to the national trend of moving away from residential care and instead placing an emphasis on fostering. The Warwickshire experience was seen in Lewisham as setting the tone. The view was that foster care provided a better form of placement for children in care and that sufficient supply could be generated to meet all needs. At the time, Lewisham had a successful fostering service and was investing in a capacity to recruit, support and retain foster carers for all types of young people taken into care. The policy took effect at the beginning of the 1990s. However, the reality of this decade has been somewhat different from the policy.

Firstly, it was not long before residential placements were being made. In the absence of local authority provision in the borough, placements were made in private and voluntary homes often some distance from the place of origin of the children concerned. The decade saw a creeping use of private and voluntary residential care. In 1990, 40 children were placed in private and voluntary residential homes. By the end of 1998 this had risen to 70 children. At the same time there were year on year budget reductions. All budget areas were allocated efficiency savings, and this included the fostering service but fostering was also targeted for additional savings. In 1991/92 the fostering and adoption budget was £574,000 and there were 12 fostering social workers producing a ratio of one social worker for every ten carers. By 1996/97 the budget had risen to only £603,000 (despite inflation and increased demands on the service) and there were only seven social workers in the fostering team with a ratio of one social worker to 21 carers. Alongside this was a growing realisation that fostering was not always an appropriate placement for children. As with other inner city areas the demand on children's placements was growing through a combination of a rising child population and an increasingly challenging group of young people with higher needs.

By the middle of the decade it was clear that the policy was out of line with reality. And a re-think began. Initially this was budget-driven with a recognition that not only were residential placements necessary but the Council was paying over the odds in the private and voluntary sector. As part of the annual budget process for 1995/96 a decision was taken to develop a residential home in the borough in partnership with Barnados. However this was *not* part of an overall policy review or part of a strategic approach to children's placements.

At the same time the Department experienced pressure for change from two other directions. Firstly, Lewisham was the subject of a pilot joint review by the SSI and the Audit Commission, and secondly, in preparation for a new senior management team, the Council commissioned a review by consultants of the Department's structure and overall strategic approach. These events set the scene for an overhaul of the department's strategic approach to children's services.

A Strategic Approach

Both the pilot joint review, and the review by consultants, concluded that there was an absence of strategy across the department, and highlighted the approach to children's placements as a particular example. The new Departmental Management Team and elected members took this as an opportunity to fundamentally review the department's strategies. This was to be done by the production of a series of strategic plans for each of the five main user groups. This approach began with elderly services in late 1995/early 1996. And was followed immediately by a strategic planning exercise on children's services.

The approach to strategic planning included the following stages:

1. A review of levels of need and demand for services.
2. An examination of resourcing levels to meet those needs then and over the five years of the plan.

3. An examination of the strengths and weaknesses of current services.
4. An examination of best practice in service provision.
5. Establishment of access and eligibility criteria in order to match resources available with levels of need and demand for services over the lifetime of the strategy.
6. A blueprint of change in the provision and mix of services in order to best meet need and demand – in line with best practice identified.

The process adopted in producing the children and families strategy was an inclusive one. A project group chaired by the Director of Social Services was established in early 1996 containing a mixture of operational and strategic managers. The focus of the project group was initially on estimating need for services and reviewing research and literature on best practice- such as *Messages from Research* and reports of the Support Force for Residential Care. This group reported to a steering group of councillors who considered the information analysed by the officer group and reviewed drafts of the strategy. At an early stage a draft of the strategy was discussed at a staff conference. Practitioners, supervisors and managers were given the opportunity to comment on, and shape, the strategy. A draft was then approved by elected members and consulted on widely, involving service users, carers, interest groups and key partner agencies. A re-draft of the strategy following consultation was approved by the Social Services Committee in February 1997.

There is nothing remarkable about Lewisham's strategy. It reflects many of the key policy themes of the day. Essentially it has two aims:

1. To shift the emphasis of child protection work more towards family support.
2. To develop an improved range of local placements for children looked after to better meet their needs.

The second aim was the key to the re-introduction of residential care in Lewisham. The analysis in the strategic plan showed that many private and voluntary residential placements were not effective in delivering care plans and long term outcomes for children. Many of the placements were at a considerable distance from the borough and this did not assist achievement of care plans or best outcomes for children. 46 per cent of children looked after in Lewisham are black but many private and voluntary homes in the home counties are ill equipped to provide a relevant environment for these young people. The analysis of cases indicated that the majority of children looked after returned home, but none of the available residential placement options supported this objective. The strategy set out the need for a range of placements to meet the different needs of children looked after. This range envisaged:

- Two new residential units, one for shorter term placements and one for longer term placements.
- A residential respite unit for children with a disability.

- Investment in foster care to enable foster carers to more effectively accommodate children with high needs, challenging behaviour and mental health difficulties.
- Development of family support services to prevent children being looked after in the first place.
- Development of non residential adolescent services to prevent adolescents entering care and assist the aim of rehabilitating children looked after.
- A review of youth justice services to improve the effectiveness of work with young people who were offending to prevent them becoming looked after.

The strategy identified that the delivery of these aims needed to be underpinned by improved planning and review of cases by social workers to ensure that the new resources were used most effectively.

The development of the strategy coincided conveniently with the production of the 1997/98 budget. The Council operates a policy of exceeding the level of budget reductions required in order to create a fund to redirect to new projects. Social Services secured new funding for the key projects in the strategy:

- £500,000 to develop a new local short term residential unit.
- £250,000 to introduce improved support to foster carers including specialist assistance for children with challenging behaviour and therapeutic needs.
- £650,000 to develop a range of family support services in conjunction with Education, Early Years and the Community Health Trust.

Resources had already been secured for the longer term residential unit.

It can be seen, therefore, that the re-introduction of residential care was not an isolated development but part of a broader strategic plan and as part of a range of placement and other services for children to offer a greater choice to social workers and families.

The next task was to take the broad prescription for the local residential units and develop the new service. This was seen as a key project with a high profile within the Council. Again the Director chaired a project team to develop the new residential service. The Director also chaired, at the same time, a group overseeing the implementation of the whole children and families strategy. This ensured that the co-ordinated approach envisaged in the strategy would be delivered. This has proved essential in overcoming the difficult issues of implementing an effective residential unit. The project team developing the residential unit contained a finance officer, a personnel officer, social workers, placement officer, social work supervisors, strategic managers, an adviser from Barnados and a representative of children looked after.

The first task was to clarify the purpose and target group for the unit. The strategy had identified that the majority of children looked after return home. It was decided therefore that the focus of the unit would be to work with young people for whom the care plan was rehabilitation. Analysis of children looked after statistics in the department showed that the majority of people in residential care were aged 12–16, so it was therefore decided that this would be the target age group of the unit. Further analysis of cases was undertaken which confirmed that a large proportion of children placed in residential care, especially those accommodated, had a care plan for return home. This analysis of commissioning need was accompanied by an examination of best practice. This was achieved by visits to existing units and a look at the material produced by the Residential Care Task Force (particularly the strategic planning material) and other literature. This work indicated that the style of working should be therapeutic, and involve families as well as children. As a result of the commissioning process and the review of best practice we developed the concept of a residential family support unit.

Developing the Statement of Purpose

Child care legislation and policy, as well as social work jargon, often dilute the core business of child care work. The vast majority of children in public care have suffered and are suffering emotional pain. They have experienced loss, sexual and or physical abuse, abandonment, rejection and other trauma. These experiences have lifetime effects. Social care staff have a crucial role to play in determining the severity of impact of these events. We believed it was important that the Unit was able to understand and work with the pain and suffering of the young people. Where possible there needs to be a shared understanding with the young person and his/her family, in order to help them find more effective and satisfying ways of coping with their difficulties.

Although we were clear that the unit was going to provide a short term residential service to adolescents, there were still many unanswered questions. For example, what should be the unit's referrals and admissions procedures? How will cooking and cleaning be organised? It was important that we could translate theory into practice. A small sub-group of the project team, which included the placements manager and the unit's manager, spent some time addressing more detailed operational issues. We noted that there were a significant number of young people placed in the past year who had been accommodated under Section 20 as a result of various family crises. These children spent varying time in care, had numerous placement breakdowns, and would often return to their families for short spells, but generally were spending longer periods in the Authority's care. We therefore felt it was essential that the unit had a clear purpose and was designed to address such issues as crisis management, family work, and boundary maintenance and containment. The sub-group drafted a statement of purpose, eligibility criteria and a referral and admissions procedure.

A young person would not be accommodated by the unit unless there was a reasonable chance of the young person's returning to his/her family. The social worker making the referral was expected to assess the potential for rehabilitation and would have to outline how they thought the unit could make a positive intervention to help the young person, and their family, resolve their difficulties. We also agreed that the maximum length of stay at the unit was six months, but in line with messages from research we set a target of a return home within six weeks.

The Statement of Purpose

It was intended that the unit would seek to provide young people with a positive experience in a safe and homely environment. The main emphasis, however, would be on providing an environment where parents and children can feel understood and helped to better deal with the difficulties they face. Where a return home is not possible, the unit will work with the young person, their parents or carers, their social worker and other professionals to achieve a permanent placement consistent with their long term needs.

The key elements of the statement of purpose were therefore as follows:

- To be a Residential Family Support Centre (not a traditional children's home).
- To seek to return children to their families as soon as it is safe and possible.
- To work with families in a flexible way including providing shared care and aftercare.
- To provide a safe and empowering environment for residents.
- To develop a theoretical and practice model which promoted effective work with families.

Core Values

We are committed to helping young people experience family life, preferably within their own family or with carers within their own community. Too often young people in difficulty are seen as the problem and are treated by professionals in isolation from their families. Even when the family is regarded as the primary source of the difficulty, it is still common for professionals to work largely or solely with the young person. At the Residential Family Support Centre, because we believe young people are best looked after by their own families, we are committed to helping parents or carers find a way of overcoming difficulties to enable them to meet the needs of their adolescents.

We regard parents and carers as essential to the process of reuniting young people with their families. We will at all times seek to work in partnership with young people and their parents/carers. Young people often need the support of their families to make changes. Sometimes it may be the adults who have to make changes first. We will work with families and young people to develop a programme of support that will meet their particular needs. We will negotiate with the young person and their family the targets for change and agree a programme of activity that will help achieve the targets set.

The unit expects the young people to be involved in all plans and decisions affecting their future. We hope to empower young people within a context of mutual respect and positive communal living. The centre will value and respect the race, gender, sexuality, culture and unique individuality of each young person. It will strive to provide an environment which does not disadvantage a young person or their family because of their gender, race, culture, sexuality, disability, health, religion and linguistic background.

Placements which are assessed not to be in line with the unit's statement of purpose or as detrimental to the needs and safety of those already accommodated will not be offered. The centre's manager was given full authority to make such decisions.

Why Work with the Whole Family?

We thought that if we were to achieve our aim of reuniting children with their families, it was essential that the unit was able to work with the young people in context – the context of their family, carers and community. To meet children's primary need for love, acceptance and security, it is clear that this can only best be done through working positively with their families.

> *The dynamics of any family have a real influence on the progress any child can make in life*

(Department of Health, Nov 1998)

Because children are the ones in our care, or involved in anti-social behaviour, it is often easier to target our effort on them. However, when one member of a family is experiencing difficulties, other family members are affected. They may have ideas about the origins of the difficulties, how they are sustained and how best to resolve them. It may be that one or more member of a family needs to make changes in order to make a difference. Young people in particular need to know that their parents or carers are thinking of ways to help them and are primed to notice and praise any changes the young person makes. Children and young people need the support of their families to make changes. Work with families can run alongside work with young people on their own; they are not mutually exclusive.

When working with a young person, it is important to have an understanding of their family context, including their social and economic situation. It is therefore necessary to have an understanding of the family's cultural and ethnic origin and how this may be reflected in the family organisation and how racism may impact upon their lives and self-esteem. Class and economic status will also have an effect on how the family live and also how they see themselves. Any work with families has to pay attention to their context, otherwise work with them may not fit with their experience or expectations.

The Value of Theory in Residential Child Care

To paraphrase the literature:

> *Theory without practice is barren, practice without theory is blind.*

Residential child care, particularly in the statutory sector, has generally not invested in theory. Homes at best may describe themselves as eclectic, or at worst may be led by charismatic heads, like Frank Beck, the serial abuser who impose their own homespun theoretical models without open challenge or critique.

Residential care staff need to have a good understanding of children's needs and their development. This is becoming more necessary because of the growing number of very disturbed children entering residential care. In developing the unit we therefore embraced Roger Bullock's (1991) view that:

> *Homes must have a guiding philosophy, not one that is exclusively limiting but one that is sufficiently coherent to shape staff perspectives on children's problems, to relate to cause and to justify practice.*

We looked for a theoretical approach that would practically help staff with their tasks as residential child care workers. We thought this approach should offer an understanding of:

- children's needs and their development
- children's behaviour
- families and their functioning
- group living and its management
- staff relations in institutional settings

as well as:

- staff with skills to achieve care plan goals in a non-abusive way
- staff with skills to work creatively with families
- managers to provide effective support and supervision
- managers to create and maintain a genuine enabling environment for children
- managers with skills to exercise empowering leadership

There appear to be two basic theoretical approaches which have guided practice in children's homes: behavioural modification and psychodynamic interventions. We thought a psychodynamic approach would be more suitable for a short-term residential unit aimed at reuniting children with their families. Psychodynamic theories, offered us a rich understanding of the difficulties which arise from parental failure to meet children's needs, as well as offering useful methods of working with the child and the family to achieve desired goals.

Psychodynamic Theory:

- Is rooted in the study of child development and pays particular attention to emotional development.
- Offers both an understanding of families and their functioning and techniques to engage and work with families.
- Offers understanding of unconscious forces (unhealed wounds and conflicts) in children, staff, parents and institutions.
- Offers a practical and coherent perspective for the management of group living.
- Contains an understanding of crisis intervention/management.

We believe that if we provide staff with a good grasp of psychodynamic theory we would help them develop ways of meeting children's primary needs, helping them to grow and develop emotionally. This approach would also support staff to develop and maintain empathy in the face of attack, manipulation, seduction, and other alienating and hostile behaviours by children or families they are attempting to help.

Psychodynamic theory offers a thorough understanding of the importance of appropriate boundary management, and will enable staff to cope with the frequent testing of boundaries that characterises work with adolescents. Rule/boundary breaking can be understood as more than just adolescent anti-social behaviour, but as testing behaviour arising from fear and the expression of a need for containment and reassurance. Staff have been introduced to the concept of transference, and trained and supervised to deal with feelings transferred from other people and situations onto them in the unit.

Designing the Building
The design was overseen by the project team which represented a wide range of interests. We involved a group of young people (a mixture of care leavers and children currently in care) in the plans for the building. The overriding aim was to create a welcoming, non-institutional, non-stigmatising environment for young people and their families. The unit was decorated with sturdy but fashionable Ikea furniture and walls were painted in a range of modern colours. Each room had individuality and staff offices were located centrally but unobtrusively. A separate entrance was created for professionals and trades people to minimise traffic through the unit.

The greatest care was taken with the kitchen and dining room. It was a challenge to meet health and safety requirements as well as to create a warm, homely and inviting communal environment. Food, its availability, accessibility, cooking and eating, is a major part of our lives, providing both physical and symbolic nourishment. It was imperative that we got the kitchen and dining room details right. After careful consideration we created a kitchen-diner, so that cooking and eating could take place next to each other. The space was also large enough to accommodate everyone who lived and worked there. We provided one large dining table to symbolise one community, and to encourage closeness and communication.

Other important features of the design were maintaining a similar appearance to the other buildings on the street. This involved retaining a front garden and tree instead of developing extra car parking space. A large comfortable conservatory was added to complement a large back garden.

Building the Staff Team

A high quality staff team comprising three managers and twelve residential social workers (two social workers to each child) was sought. The utmost care was taken in selecting the staff team. All the lessons of the Warner report were drawn upon, (DoH 1992). This was not only to select out potential abusers, but on a positive note, to ensure that the most competent staff were recruited. A selection process was set up which included the following elements:

- personality testing
- occupational testing (chosen to be relevant to day to day work)
- group exercises
- interviews by young people in care
- interviews with managers

Great care was taken over references and police checks. Major insights were provided by two elements: personality testing and involvement of young people. Without these processes key issues about many individuals would not have been unearthed.

The staff selection process was linked to the management of the overall project. This meant that the manager was appointed nine months before opening the unit to contribute to the development phase. The staff team were in post a month before opening to enable training and team building to take place. However, it is important not to remain complacent after such a thorough recruitment process. We have built in careful monitoring of the staff group.

Training

The initial staff team comprised people with previous residential care experience, some with a CQSW and all with previous in-service training. Before the unit was opened all staff went through a planned induction and team building programme. They also commenced a one year accredited 'Certificate in Therapeutic Childcare' with the Caldecott College. The course covered such topics as child development, psychodynamic concepts, boundary management, creating a therapeutic environment, group dynamics, play and symbolic communication and working with families. Most staff have found the course intellectually demanding. Many have shown its helpfulness in thinking about practice in the unit, especially around boundary management, attachment, and communication issues. It is expected that 75 per cent will gain the certificate at the end of the programme.

Monitoring
We have in place the standard arrangements to monitor the unit: Registration and Inspection visits, Regulation 22 visits and line management relationships. In addition, we have created a management committee which includes three councillors. The councillors have volunteered, been trained and police checked. Their task is to befriend the unit and visit regularly. This arrangement goes beyond the usual 'visiting member' system.

Opening the Unit and Providing the Service

Having planned a service with all the lessons in mind, covering purpose, building, staffing, selection and training, we did not anticipate that establishing the service was going to be as difficult as it turned out. There were six main issues we encountered:

1. *Attracting staff of sufficient calibre at Assistant Manager level.*
Despite offering an above average salary, plus an attractive training and support package, the unit had difficulty attracting appointable candidates to these posts. Most of the qualified candidates did not have sufficient residential care experience, and the experienced candidates did not have the knowledge required to provide the quality of practice leadership needed - especially as regards working effectively with families. This resulted in the unit opening without its full management complement, and consequently not being as well equipped to deal with the challenges of establishing a practice culture.

2. *Managing the field social work pressure for placements.*
Having planned the unit with the involvement of all stakeholders, it was surprising to encounter the demand for emergency and other unsuitable placements, and the vexation it produced when they were turned down. The enormous pressure on the unit by social workers to accept referrals, not in line with its statement of purpose, was essentially a product of the unavailability of suitable local placements. Budget pressures and a culture of social work practice that is predominantly reactive and finance-led as opposed to planned, timely and goal-oriented.

3. *Securing enough developmental space.*

Events after opening the unit demonstrated that the planning team had underestimated the size of the task. Reinstating a children's residential service within Lewisham was a bigger challenge than we had realised. At the strategic level there was clarity of purpose and a commitment to excellence. However, a well functioning residential service requires similar understanding, co-operation and support from front line practitioners and managers in both education and social services. Unfortunately, this understanding and co-operation cannot be assumed, it has to be built, and this takes time, especially if there has not been a residential unit in existence within the authority for the past 10 years.

Getting the building and staff right is only the beginning, not the end. A new unit in a borough without residential units is in many ways highly vulnerable. Vulnerable from a real lack of knowledge of residential care within the organisation and therefore of an appreciation of all the factors which are needed to make it work. In such a context the unit is more likely to have to cope with unrealistic expectations and isolation. Therefore, it was necessary to build a new infrastructure across the whole department, including practice and procedures.

As an in-house resource the authority's social workers did to some extent understandably expect the unit to be more accessible, flexible and responsive to their needs than it was. The unit was also vulnerable from its own staff who again were understandably wanting to demonstrate their value and credibility quickly. But just as children need space and time to develop, services, especially ones as complex as residential care, need space to create and establish an effective culture with values, rules, boundaries, expectations, responsibilities, routines, which is not only carried by staff but by its residents as well.

If the unit comes under too much pressure to make admissions without adequate care and consideration being given to such issues as the mix of residents, level of disturbance in the group, level of violence, acting out and boundary testing, then the task of establishing a containing environment will become harder if not impossible. Our experience has taught us that the first three to six months of a unit is a delicate and critical stage of development and must be handled with the greatest care. We would suggest that it would be wise to err on the side of caution and be fairly selective in the choice of the unit's first resident group, because taking on too much too soon can result in unmanageable boundary breaking, loss of staff confidence and the need for robust containment in the unit.

A new unit, like its staff, should be allowed to be new and be given space and time to acclimitise itself to the task before it is expected to perform fully.

4. *Building-in external support from day one.*

The need to succeed felt by all staff and managers involved in the project made it imperative for the unit to have external consultancy early, to help us deal with our limitations without getting overwhelmed. Criticisms received by staff in a high profile, well-resourced unit were painful. One of the issues staff needed support with was addressing the overwhelming sense of failure many experienced during the unit's first 3–6 months of opening. Particularly intense feelings of uselessness, isolation and unpopularity increased the need for support, understanding and management leadership.

5. *The historical inferiority of residential care staff vis à vis field social workers seemed to be reinforced by the current purchaser-provider division.*
One of the ironies of current social work practice is that social workers have the statutory powers, responsibilities and duties with regard to looked-after children, but spend little time working with or developing real relationships with them. When the purchasing role is added to the social workers statutory keywork duties, it seems to produce an unbalanced power relationship with care providers. One deleterious consequence of this situation is that the field social worker often comes to see provider services as being accountable to them for their practice and never the other way round. Developing a mutually respectful and joint approach to looked-after children with shared accountabilities is obviously essential, but is still not a common reality. It is an issue we in Lewisham have learnt needs persistent attention. Partnership is something which is essential but still not enough of a reality.

Conclusion

Developing a residential unit in a local authority which currently does not provide residential care is a monumental task. Issues which will need to be addressed and not underestimated include:

- Managing the expectations of field social workers.
- Getting all parts of the organisation to own the statement of purpose, in order to make it a common purpose.
- Designing all elements of the system: staff selection, the building, training, procedures, and fieldwork practice to reflect the statement of purpose.
- Developing effective working relationships at all levels.
- Ensuring the unit has adequate developmental space in the first 3–6 months.
- Ensuring staff, especially in the early months, are regularly supervised and supported, including the use of an external consultant.
- Getting the right management team within the home to provide the leadership to maintain boundaries, establish a supportive culture and develop reflective practice.
- Developing a confident and united staff team, especially when subject to regular criticisms from colleagues and challenging, dangerous and provocative behaviour from residents.

Establishing the purpose for the unit is a much easier task than making it work in practice. The main obstacle to successful operation is matching social work practice and the purpose of the unit. Understandably, social workers, faced with high bombardment rates, see making placements as a priority in itself rather than ensuring that the placement's purpose is matched with a unit's ability to deliver. As a result we decided that strong gatekeeping was essential. Any placements in the unit would have to go through the placements panel followed by assessment by staff of the unit to agree the appropriateness of the placement. The problem with this approach was that it does not match social workers timescales and their need to make placements. As a result, initial referrals and placements were low despite the evidence collected in the commissioning exercise. There is a need to market the unit and its purpose to social workers and to make accessing the unit fast and easy – without compromising the unit's purpose. We have stuck to our guns and taken the view that social work practice needs to change and not the purpose of the unit. Planning and review by social workers does not always match up to the process of making accurate placements. We have made some improvements in this area, but are delighted that *Quality Protects*, with its emphasis on improving assessment, planning and review, will provide us with the opportunity and resources to make further progress.

Many of the difficulties associated with residential care will not be resolved until the shortcomings on the other side of the equation – social work practice – are resolved. Social workers themselves are not to blame for this. The reason is lack of management direction and accountability, allied to lack of resources. However, residential units also need to be more proactive and accessible. In Lewisham we have therefore ensured that managers from the units go out and meet with social workers and are available to pick up referrals in duty rooms. A key lesson we have learned is the importance of achieving both strategic planning across the service and also bringing this down to the real world of assessment and care management within field social work teams. Grand plans such as Lewisham's will fail unless social work practice is also targeted and included in the project.

Re-introducing residential care in Lewisham has also been a great opportunity. So much has been written about children's homes, and there is plenty of guidance available. It is more difficult to graft this on to an existing service. We had the opportunity to build the lessons into a new service, without any legacies. But even with these advantages it has still been a huge task. There is no substitute for proper resourcing, proper planning and time to think through all the issues.

CHAPTER 4

As Safe as Safe-houses?

Geoff Gurney

Introduction

Young people running away from their own homes, children's homes and foster placements is a growing problem. In 1989 it was estimated that there were around 100,000 incidents of young people under 18 running away. A study of missing persons statistics in four police areas showed that running away occurred in all regions, both urban and rural, but much higher numbers came from disadvantaged areas. The vast majority stayed in their local area and were only away for a short time, but this did not necessarily diminish the risk, (Abrahams and Mungall, 1992). A subsequent survey of over 1200 young people indicated that one in seven young people under the age of 16 had run away and stayed away overnight, (Rees 1993). A questionnaire survey of 102 young people in contact with streetwork and refuge projects in 1994 revealed that most young people in the sample had run away a number of times and lacked support networks. There was a high level of detachment from their families, social services and education systems, (Stein et al.,1994). A small, but significant, number of these runaways are minors, under the age of 16.

The London Safe House, (the Refuge), aims to provide a breathing space for runaway children and young people, aged 16 and under, to help them to return to parents or local authority care, or to sort out some other solution if a return home is not appropriate. Centrepoint, NSPCC, NCH Action for Children, and Safe in the City are working together to make such a provision in a well-structured and responsible way.

The Refuge can accommodate up to ten young people, but it is fairly crowded if seven residents or more are staying. The Refuge provides for four or five boys and four or five girls, in a mixture of single and double rooms. Two thirds of the 200 or so children we deal with annually come from the greater London area while one third – about 70 young people in 1998 – come from outside London. With the help of Childline, and a variety of street agencies, runaway children and young people find their way to us, and are provided with a safe place to stay, sometimes within hours of their arrival in the city. Consequently, they are offered protection from the very real risks to unaccompanied minors in Central London, and some breathing space in which to think about and negotiate a return to their home area.

Since it opened in October 1993, Refuge workers and managers have wrestled with the task of making sure that the London Safe House is, indeed, a safe house. This chapter presents a range of professional and managerial techniques and strategies designed to make this short residential experience a safe and positive one for children and young people who run away, and a rewarding one for the adults who care for them. Our efforts are set against a backdrop of the growing concern about weaknesses in services for children which have precipitated, amongst other things, the Government's *Quality Protects* initiative which represents a commitment to delivering high quality, well-managed and effective children's services. Beyond its central role as a service for young runaways, the London Refuge provides a unique 'window' on the operation of mainstream services to children in need and in danger.

A Statement of Purpose

Section 51 of the Children Act 1989 sets out the terms and conditions for voluntary organisations to provide refuges for children and young people who run away. Refuges are there to protect young people from harm, and to provide a safe place to stay, and to return young people to their parents or carers when it is safe to do so. Refuges cannot provide placements for children and young people at the request of parents, Social Services departments or other organisations, but are expected to work together with all of these in the best interests of each young person. Young people may be helped to refer themselves to the Refuge once they have run away from home, but the agreement to provide refuge is always between staff employed at the Refuge and the young person. Refuges have a confidential address, and the maximum length of stay (the legal limit) is 14 days. Currently there are only three of these 'Children Act' refuges in England and Wales, two run by the Children's Society in Leeds and Cardiff, and the London Refuge.

Listening

It is our experience that many social workers and their managers are unwilling to listen to the young people who run away or, indeed, to us. We invariably contact the responsible local authority within hours of a young person's admission to the Refuge because we want to know if the young person or their family is known to social services. We attempt to discover the name of an allocated social worker if there is one. When the young person is not known, and we are requesting a meeting with a duty social worker, it is not uncommon for social workers and their managers to say they do not want to see the young person and that we must simply tell them to go home.

Why is this? We think that sometimes it is because they assume that we are a hostel, like Centrepoint, for the 16–25 age group, and that we have neither the legal right nor the expertise to be involved with younger children. We usually explain the statutory basis of the Refuge, offer them information about it and refer them to the relevant sections of the 'big yellow book' (DoH, 1991), Volume 4 of the Children Act Guidance and Regulations. We also emphasise that we provide this service in partnership with NSPCC and NCH Action for Children.

Yet, even where social workers and their managers do understand the nature of the Refuge and its work, they are sometimes unwilling to acknowledge that the young person's account of events has any validity, even in some cases where the youngsters are indicating that they could be in danger if they returned to the place from which they ran. Perhaps these social workers and their managers refuse to interview young runaways because they believe that they should ration their time or the additional services which might be required if the young person's account of the problem was accepted. Sometimes, they appear to believe that we are creating a storm in a tea-cup. Yet the dangers in not listening to the concerns of the young person and the Refuge workers can be very great, as Rachel's story illustrates.

Rachel, Age 15 Years

Rachel ran away from home and stayed with a friend's family for a few days. Rachel telephoned Social Services and told them that she had run away because she had been sexually abused by a male cousin when she was only 10 years old. Rachel's mother died when she was 11 and she now lived with her father and two younger brothers. Rachel absolutely refused to go home, but the social worker she spoke to said that she must go home. Her friend's mother said that she couldn't stay with her because she would get into trouble, and Rachel spent two nights sleeping on a park bench near Covent Garden, in central London. Cold and hungry, Rachel phoned Childline and talked to a counsellor about her situation. She was given the telephone number of the Refuge. Rachel talked about being raped by a male cousin who still sometimes visits the family. She also told her keyworker about two suicide attempts soon after the death of her mother. She said she hated her father but wouldn't say why. Rachel admitted to being sexually active since soon after her 14th birthday. She sometimes stayed away from school, and there were lots of rows with her father about school, and boyfriends, and what he saw as her bad behaviour. Rachel said she would never return home. She said she would kill herself if anyone tried to make her go home.

Rachel didn't want us to talk to her father. When we tried to contact the father, the telephone was either constantly engaged or off the hook, and at other times not answered. We asked the local police to speak to Rachel's father and to explain what was happening. The police did this and gave the telephone number for the Refuge. Rachel's father did not telephone the Refuge and had not reported to the police that his daughter was missing from home. With Rachel's permission, her keyworker asked for a meeting with a duty social worker, explaining that Rachel wanted to see a social worker on her own, and not with her father present. The keyworker told the duty social worker what Rachel had said to her about her situation, and faxed information about the Refuge. The duty social worker and the team manager refused to arrange a meeting. They said that Rachel was 15 and that she must go home. Rachel stayed at the Refuge for seven days while we tried to negotiate for a meeting. Rachel helped her keyworker write a report about her situation.

The duty social worker and the team manager again refused to start any work until Rachel went home, and soon after this was explained to Rachel she took an overdose of paracetamol tablets, and began to self harm (small cuts to her arms and legs). Rachel was admitted to hospital and seen by a social worker and a psychiatrist there. The psychiatrist's opinion was that Rachel had been abused by her father, but Rachel did not confirm this. On receiving the psychiatrist's report, social services agreed to a meeting with the father and Rachel together on the following Monday (Day 14). They would not see Rachel without her father, and reluctantly Rachel agreed to the meeting if her keyworker could be present. At the meeting Rachel's father said that Rachel was not telling the truth, but agreed to Rachel being accommodated for a short time. Rachel was placed in a children's home close to her home address. Rachel ran away from the children's home several times, and spent some nights sleeping on the streets, before returning. Her social worker said that if she didn't want to be at the children's home she should go home to live with her father. Rachel made many telephone calls to the Refuge, and two months later she asked to return to the Refuge because she was being bullied at the children's home. Staff saw a marked deterioration, both physically and mentally. Rachel overdosed again and self harmed again whilst at the Refuge, and moved to an adolescent psychiatric unit at the end of her second stay.

The Children Act 1989 requires social services to make assessments of children in need, and to carry out investigations when abuse or neglect is suspected. Nearly all the young people who come to the Refuge talk about ill-treatment or neglect at home or in the placement in which they are being 'looked after' by their local authority. Moreover, they often feel that they have been unable to communicate what is happening to them to their social workers. For many, running away is a drastic step, which they take when they believe that all other options have been exhausted. While social workers and their managers express a commitment to 'listening', our experience is that the children who run to the Refuge have not been listened to and that they have often encountered formidable barriers when they have tried to have their say.

The objectives of *Quality Protects*, (DoH, 1998), aim:

- To ensure that children are securely attached to carers capable of providing safe and effective care for the duration of childhood.
- To ensure that children are protected from emotional, physical, sexual abuse and neglect.
- To ensure children in need gain maximum life chance benefits from educational opportunities, health and social care.

For any of this to be achievable, social workers must first learn to listen to what young people have to say.

Towards a Protocol with Social Services Departments

In the past we have sought to establish agreements with all social services Departments to work in partnership with the London Refuge. These agreements have included the following elements:

- An acknowledgement that young people who run away, including those who run away from foster carers or children's homes, need access to a safe and confidential refuge.
- An understanding that the confidential nature of the location of refuges is an essential factor in their success with young runaways.
- A willingness to act on a telephone referral, followed by a written report, which requests an assessment for a child in need, or a child protection investigation.
- to agree to a meeting with the young person and a keyworker to continue an assessment of need.

Although the Association of Directors of Social Services has expressed its approval of and support for the work of the London Refuge, to date it has proved impossible to establish the type of 'protocol' itemised above. This is in spite of the fact that Section 51 of the Children Act,1989 requires social workers and their managers to co-operate with refuges.

The Work of the Refuge

The Refuge seeks to return the young person home, unless there is cause for concern about the young person's safety at home. Then the Refuge negotiates with Social Services to try to find an alternative place to stay while an investigation and full assessment are carried out. When the decision is to return home, the young people and their families will be offered support from the Refuge to work things out so that the young person can stay living at home. This support may mean the continued involvement of family support workers based at the Refuge, or a referral to Social Services or to a voluntary organisation, which can provide services to help keep families together.

Work with young people at the Refuge can be divided into four stages:

1. Inquiry into what is currently happening to the young person: information from the young person, their parents or family members, and from social workers and others if appropriate.
2. Consultation about what is likely to happen next, and what the different parties think the options are.

3. Assessment by the keyworker and duty manager to establish what constitutes the best interests of the young person in the circumstances.
4. Planning and preparation for a discharge from the Refuge.

The Refuge staff team acknowledges that their 'duty of care' requires them to share any information they may gain from the children about past abuse or their concerns about further abuse if they return. Any evidence of abuse, including an account of what the young person tells us, will be recorded and reported to the responsible authorities, the relevant social services department and/or the Police Child Protection Teams. The fact that this will happen, and that confidences about abuse cannot be offered or kept at the Refuge, is explained to the young people at the time they are admitted.

Often, the keyworker is able to act as an advocate for the young people, helping them to say what they want to say to parents and/or social workers, or sometimes speaking on their behalf. Occasionally, we take the view that the young person needs a service which they do not wish to receive or, despite our negotiations with the relevant service provider, is not available. In these circumstances their keyworker will advise the young person to contact an advocate from Voice for the Child in Care, or a solicitor to act on their behalf.

The young person will usually be accompanied to a discharge meeting by their keyworker. If this is a meeting at their own home, or on neutral ground, with parents and family, and without the involvement of social services, the keyworker will offer continuing support from the Refuge staff team.

Managing the Refuge to Maximise Safety

In an agency established specifically to deal with crises, the supervision and management of front-line staff can be difficult. In pursuit of greater efficiency, worker satisfaction and a more child-centred approach, we have moved away from problem solving by 'consensus', where everyone gets to say what they think should happen to every young person, to a 'need to know' practice which allows decisions and plans to be made between the keyworker, the young person and the duty manager.

Trying to deal as effectively with the residential task as we do with problem solving, has led us to experiment with project workers preparing food with the young people and with project workers and volunteers leading small groups of young people in recreational and educational activities during their stay at the Refuge. Keyworking has replaced a more ad hoc allocation of tasks.

Day training events, team meetings and individual supervision sessions have often been stormy, because these changes have meant giving up old ways of working and seem to some workers to be 'change for change sake'. Some of these changes have meant putting children's needs before staff needs. Managers have known that staff expect to be – and should be – consulted and involved with planned changes to policies and procedures, and that change will always be more painful for some more than for others. Managers at the Refuge also know that managers have to lead change, and hold staff accountable for implementing prescribed as well as agreed procedures.

Quality Protects has emphasised the need to ensure compliance with administrative and child care procedures in order to provide a safe environment for children. Compliance is more likely to be obtained by shared and accepted aims and attitudes to the work, rather than by verbal or written instructions and disciplinary action for non-compliance. However, in a small unit, often working under a great deal of pressure, this is more easily said than done, and we have not been able to avoid the conflicts between managers and workers, nor conflicts between the 'stakeholders' – Centrepoint, NSPCC, NCH Action for Children, and the Department of Health.

Nonetheless, we are all, stakeholders, managers and workers, agreed about the essential functions of the Refuge, the tasks to be accomplished and the fact that the motor of the project are the demands made upon it by the children and young people in crisis who seek its services.

There are bound to be individual differences amongst such a large staff group, and the personalities and problems of individual young people will inevitably impact on the keyworkers who listen to them and spend time with them. So policies and procedures are continually challenged. For example, the criteria for admission to the Refuge are set out clearly. If the young person is under 16 and they have run away then they should come to the Refuge. If they are over 16, it is necessary to ask more questions before deciding if this is an appropriate admission. But it's never as simple as that, and we have to make time in team meetings to discuss individual young people and whether our criteria are being used correctly or incorrectly. We have to keep coming back to this and to other procedures that are affected by the differences in staff opinion, and the differences in young people.

Managers are expected to be more distanced and objective, but not so far away that they can't understand these pushes and pulls, and support their staff as they deal with these situations and their feelings about them. To date we have resisted introducing forms of non-managerial supervision or external consultancy, believing that the management team has sufficient experience and expertise, but there is an argument for using these techniques. The closest we get to this model is a discussion in team meetings which is led by project workers. However, the 'us and them' element in the relationship between project workers and managers is never far away, particularly at times when we have reached the implementation stage of changed procedures and ways of working. Managing such a situation is not such an impossible task, but it is a never-ending one and the manager must be constantly alert to the emotional climate within the Refuge and how, at any given moment, it is constituted.

Quality Assurance

Centrepoint, one of our key stakeholders, aims to link the Quality Assurance Standard ISO 9002 – the internationally recognised service standard – to all of the organisation's housing and social support services for the young homeless by November 1999. Work has been completed to provide a set of service promises, and a system for controlling procedures documents, improving documentation, monitoring and audit, is already in place. The service promises have been developed through consultation with young people, staff teams and service users/purchasers. There is a core set of procedures, which cover all areas of project work. Each project or service manager has developed local procedures to 'sit behind' the core documents. Together they form the *Housing and Social Support Quality Manual.*

Many of Centrepoint's core procedures, drawn up with hostels for the16 to 25 age group in mind, do not easily fit short-term work with the mainly under-16s at the Refuge. The Refuge procedures are complex. The Refuge is subject to regular inspection by the Social Services Inspectorate (SSI). Refuge workers struggle to adhere to the principles and standards for Children's services developed by NSPCC and NCH Action for Children, as well as Volume 4, Guidance and Regulations, of the Children Act 1989. It has been necessary to develop summaries and interpretations of procedures for both the induction of new staff and the use of existing staff, struggling to do the right thing in an increasingly complex legal and administrative environment.

Below, we reproduce, by way of illustration, some of the local procedures of the London Refuge. These procedures highlight the practice principles the organisation is committed to in its work with young runaways.

The Admissions Procedure
This aims to:

- Ensure young people are made welcome and helped to manage any anxiety or uncertainty.
- Ensure that the young people are given the necessary information about the Refuge, its values and the way it functions in order to help the young person feel at home.
- Begin the work with the young people, aimed at rehabilitation home or back to where they were last living when it is safe to do so and whenever possible, or a move to an alternative safe place with family, friends or to social services care when it isn't possible.
- Gain the necessary information to start off the Refuge programme of Inquiry, Consultation, Assessment, Planning.

Child Protection Procedures
These cover the responsibilities and actions to be taken to ensure the safety and protection of children and young people resident at the Refuge. The purpose of the procedure is to:

- Ensure that staff members will provide empathy and support when a young person begins to disclose their own past or current abuse.
- Ensure that staff members inform the young person about the limits to confidentiality before any detailed disclosure.
- Set out the procedure for when a young person alleges abuse by a member of staff at the Refuge.
- Set out the procedure for when a young person alleges abuse by another young person resident at the Refuge.
- Provide guidelines for male and female members of staff working with children and young people at the Refuge.
- State the meaning of Regulation 20 concerning the notification of significant events at the Refuge.
- Ensure that staff have read and understood the Child Protection principles and policies supported by Centrepoint, NSPCC, and NCH Action for Children.

Care Planning, Review and Recording
These procedures symbolise the commitment to ensuring that young people are fully involved in making decisions about their future and working in partnership with parents, local authorities and other adults concerned with the welfare of each young person to ensure that:

- All young people are involved very soon after admission in developing their care plan, which is periodically updated.
- Parents/carers, social services, and significant others are involved in developing the young person's care plan.
- The care plan includes a Refuge assessment of the situation and the options therefore available for discharge from the Refuge.
- To ensure risk assessment is part of the care planning process, and of the Refuge assessment.
- Appropriate recording practice.

The Assessment and Management of Risk
There are two kinds of risk to be assessed at the Refuge, the risk that a young person is to themselves and/or to other residents and staff, and the risk to the young person if they leave the Refuge without permission and against the advice of staff. The London Refuge offers a breathing space to children as young as 11 or

12 who have run away from home perhaps because of abuse or neglect, or because of bullying at school. Many are vulnerable because of their age and because they are easily influenced by adults or their peers. This same Refuge provides a service to 15 and 16 year olds who walk out of care placements because of abuse by staff or bullying by other young people, or because they are not happy with their social worker or with their care plan. Some have been moved more than 20 times and have spent time in secure units and therapeutic communities. Young and old, many of these young people are using drugs and alcohol, are out of mainstream education, are seeing or have seen educational psychologists or psychiatrists or counsellors for help with difficult behaviours at school and at home. Some are offenders. Some are victims of serious sexual abuse. Some continue to self harm.

Participation

The London Refuge is committed to ensuring that young people have a voice at the Refuge, and contribute to the way the Refuge is run for young runaways. Residents meetings are called to discuss anything of importance to the whole group – a visitor to the Refuge, some earlier behaviour by one or more young people which necessitates a repetition of the rules and expectations, perhaps some information about a planned activity.

Centrepoint supports the commitment to a service user perspective through the 'Complaints and Suggestions' procedures, as well as the Refuge user feedback forms. Every young person is told about mechanisms for consultation during their initial interview, and this is reinforced in written documents: *Information for Young People coming to the London Refuge*, and *The Placement Agreement*.

Actually, there are not many formal complaints at the Refuge. Young people are encouraged to say what they think about us, and staff and managers deal with these things immediately – some trivial and some more serious. If there isn't enough fresh fruit or orange juice, then we can do something about it quickly. If a young person says that they have been treated differently because they are white or because they are male, then there are two things that have to happen; an immediate enquiry and discussion with the staff involved and the young people in order to give a satisfactory response to the young person who has complained.

Keyworking at the London Refuge

The keyworker is responsible for making sure that the young person has the correct information about the Refuge and what can happen or may happen. In particular, the confidential address, the way we work, including our position on confidentiality about child protection concerns, staying safe at the Refuge, and respect for other young people and staff. This may have been done by someone else at a 'welcome meeting' or by staff on duty at the time of the admission, but the keyworker still needs to check this out. It's always a good idea to go over these things again, and is a good way to start a series of keywork sessions. Sometimes the 24-hour, six week rolling rota for project workers makes keyworking difficult, but the intention is that the same project worker will help the young person through their admission, our attempts at problem solving with them and for them, and their discharge from the Refuge. The keyworker is also responsible for any follow-up contact that has been agreed with the young person. Perhaps a single phone call a few days later to see how things are, perhaps an introduction to a Family Support worker who will continue to work with the young person and the family. Throughout the young person's stay, the keyworker is responsible for the young person's file record, including the daily shift hand-over sheets and daily comment in the file record by the young person.

Care and Control

Most of the time, the London Refuge is like a warm, comfortable, quiet, children's home. User feedback forms and what young people say to us confirm that they feel well looked after during their short stays, and thankful to staff who seem to understand and are ready to listen, and can help with their problems. Staff and children eat together, watch videos and TV, play Monopoly and talk about sports and fashion so that the Refuge often feels cosy.

But some of the time the Refuge is anything but cosy. Younger and more vulnerable residents are threatened and intimidated by older, sometimes 'institutionalised', young people. Sometimes the group of residents – three, four or five young people who have met for the first time at the Refuge – gel in such a way that staff and volunteers need to spend their time patrolling and supervising, using their skills and abilities to calm individuals and the group, and to divert young people away from destructive behaviour.

So staff need to regularly discuss risk assessments for the individual young people and for the group. We have chosen not to use a precise scoring system for risk assessments. Even 'high, medium or low' assessments do not seem appropriate to the work we do. Instead, a brief discussion at each hand-over meeting (morning, afternoon and evening every day) is used to inform staff coming on shift about events and behaviour at the Refuge over the preceding hours. Significant events, behaviours and fears are recorded in the young person's file and discussed with the young person. Serious incidents may trigger a 'warning' or a decision to ask the young person to leave the Refuge or, in particularly serious cases, Child Protection procedures may be invoked.

As a Housing Association, Centrepoint must have the ability to evict young people aged 16 to 25 from accommodation that is provided for them, for non payment of rent, or for behaviour that is unacceptable or a danger to themselves or others. The London Refuge invites young people to stay for up to 14 days. The placement agreement makes it clear that unacceptable behaviour may result in them being asked to leave or made to leave. But if a young person has run away and is refusing to return to a safe environment – or if the environment is not considered safe – then "eviction" back on to the streets of London is not an option. The procedures that cover Warnings and Decisions must include a bold statement that we can only ask or demand that a young person leaves if there is another safe place for them to go to. A 12 year old who is vulnerable and at risk from older residents will sometimes be asked to go home or to a Social Services office for a discharge from the Refuge. Sometimes they are given no choice.

But a 12 year old who won't go home and for whom the Social Services assessment is that they must go home, may choose to run away from the Refuge. Our procedures say that if he/she leaves without permission and against our advice, then we will immediately notify the local police and give a description of the young person. At 12 years old the risk is that great, and we expect the police to try to pick them up.

If a 16 year old is asked to leave or told to leave, an appointment will be made at Social Services or a Housing Advice Centre or Hostel, and the offer of a worker to go with them. If this 16 year old refuses our help and walks out the door, then the police and those with parental responsibility are notified, but there is no expectation of any further action by the police. If a 16 year old refuses to leave, then we will ask the police for their help to escort the young person off the premises.

But what about 13, 14 and 15 year olds? The younger the child then the greater the risk if they have nowhere else to go, and the more effort that staff must put in to persuade the young person to improve their behaviour, take advice, or accept an undesired option. Some 15 and 16 year olds are as vulnerable because of their inability to cope with the pressures of street life. The Refuge operates a curfew, and young people will be reported missing if they fail to return at an agreed time.

The Children Act 1989, Guidance and Regulations, applies to the London Refuge as to any other voluntary children's home. The SSI guidance for the Control of Children in the Public Care: Interpretation of the Children Act 1989 (Department of Health *Dear Director* Letter, 20 February 1997) defines responsibility to provide direction and guidance for the young person, and the right to control, direct, or guide their upbringing in a manner that is consistent with their stage of development and particular circumstances.

Project workers at the Refuge are no different in many respects to any residential child care worker with troubled and troublesome young people. From time to time they experience difficulties in maintaining complete control of the young people for whom they have responsibility, given the variety of problems faced by the young people in need of refuge, and the influence that these problems have on their behaviour. The Children Act does, however require that staff do everything in their power to protect young people from harm or from harming others.

The Refuge lacks the formal legal authority of parental responsibility, which is retained by parents and sometimes shared with the responsible local authority. But this does not weaken our authority to control the young people in our care. Section 3(5) of the Children Act makes it clear that those who do not have parental responsibility, but none the less have the day-to-day care of a young person, may do what is reasonable in all the circumstances to safeguard and promote the welfare of that young person.

Parents (and sometimes local authorities) may have wishes about the control of 'their' children, which must be taken into account, but cannot constrain day-to-day carers to the extent that they are unable to control the young person properly.

Concerns have been raised that the Children Act may have gone too far in stressing the rights of children and young people at the expense of upholding the rights and responsibilities of parents and professionals in supervising them. Young people must be listened to at the Refuge, and their wishes and feelings taken into consideration. But this does not mean that staff are constrained to abide by all the wants of the young person. Their wishes and feelings can and should be over-ridden in decisions that affect them if this is necessary to safeguard and promote their welfare and protect others.

Volume 4 of the Children Act 1989 Guidance and Regulations, and the Department of Health's *Guidance on Permissible Forms of Control in Residential Care* (LAC(93)13) remain the primary source of guidance, and these have been used to provide written policies and procedures for the use of sanctions and the control of young people at the London Refuge. But it is different at a refuge which is so short term, that on the whole, young people want to be there and therefore we are working with their consent. Our procedures reflect this.

Conclusion

In the five years since its inception, the London Refuge has forged an effective partnership between three voluntary agencies and now provides a safe and effective service to young runaways. We could do better of course. A more structured programme of daily life at the refuge, improved advocacy for young people, better partnerships with parents, working more co-operatively with social services are all goals we are struggling to achieve.

Of all these imperatives, co-operation with Social Services to protect the children and young people who run away from, or feel forced to leave, their homes or their placements is most pressing. *Quality Protects* is about improving the well-being of the children for whom the local authority has responsibility; children and young people who are 'looked after' or the subjects of child protection proceedings, and other young people who, while not presenting such dramatic or clearly definable problems, require active support from local authority social services departments.

Across the country, social services departments have prepared Management Action Plans to meet new national objectives, many of which are directly relevant to the needs of young runaways. These plans are supported by additional new funding. As we have noted, the central thrust of these developments is fourfold, and it intends that:

1. Children should be placed with carers capable of providing safe and effective care for the duration of childhood.
2. Children should be protected from emotional, physical and sexual abuse, and neglect.
3. Young people leaving care, as they enter adulthood, should not be isolated and can participate socially and economically as citizens.
4. Referral and assessment processes discriminate effectively between different types and levels of need and produce a timely service response.

Refuges can help social workers and their managers to improve their services in all these areas, but Social Services have to listen to us, and to the children and young people we work with. Running away is always a significant event and always puts children and young people at risk. Running away also often highlights weaknesses in procedures and provisions which social services departments need to know about.

The new millenium may see a significant growth in the numbers of refuges in the major towns and cities of the UK. This creates an opportunity for local authorities to enter a beneficial partnership which can only serve to further the interests of children and young people who run away from home, residential homes and foster care.

CHAPTER 5

Positive Residential Practice: The Contribution of Inspection

Roger Morgan

Regulation of residential care, the combination of registration and external inspection with powers of enforcement, is generally and rightly seen as one of the major safeguards for children living in residential accommodation. It is however only one amongst others.

Registration offers two safeguards. Firstly, it offers the assurance that persons, premises and services have been checked against specified requirements important to the safeguarding and promotion of children's welfare before a 'licence to operate' is granted. Secondly, it enables action to be taken if a serious failure to safeguard and protect children occurs. Crudely and at its extreme, this would be to remove a service from the register and thus outlaw its continued operation.

Inspection offers a further four safeguards:

1. A regular monitoring appraisal of the service (home or school) by an independent external inspector against specified standards of operation.
2. An external but statutorily powerful inspectorate to investigate complaints or allegations of failure to safeguard and promote children's welfare.
3. A powerful source of specific recommendations for change or correction to restore satisfactory standards of care.
4. The ability of someone outside the home to take formal action to change its operation or to close it if necessary.

However, the processes of registration, inspection and enforcement are limited. Some inspectorates may unfortunately have stated that their aim is to 'ensure' that welfare is protected, but no regulatory process can absolutely 'ensure' anything. Registration checks on a service before it begins to operate, however precisely done, are vital protections for the children who will subsequently live in the home concerned, but at best involves conducting a limited list of selected checks. Interviews and references to assess the fitness of an applicant for registration to look after children suffer from all the limitations of any interview and reference process, and cannot guarantee that no inappropriate person will 'pass' as fit, any more than any appointment panel (even supported by sophisticated assessment procedures) can guarantee that no poor job appointment will ever be made. Furthermore, the most complete set of police and official checks against lists will always fail to predict the first offender.

Similarly, no inspector, however competent, diligent and independent, and however much time he or she spends in a home, can know all about the operation of the home. An inspector can see records, observe practice (which of course changes when an inspector is watching), gather facts and information from staff, resident children, relatives and other observers of the home, and appraise policies and premises, but if in a home for (say) three days in a year, he or she does not know for certain what is going on the other 362 days of the year. No inspector can aspire to omniscience; even if some enquiries may regard inspectors as failing if they miss something that subsequently proves to be vital. No inspection can do more than comprise what is effectively a welfare MoT test – a competent check on specified criteria using approved methods on a particular date, which gives massive assurance but no guarantee that nothing can subsequently go seriously wrong.

Registration and inspection, and the enforcement processes that may follow, are thus limited and imperfect tools – but they are nevertheless still essential tools to contribute to maximising welfare for vulnerable children. The Social Services White Paper *Modernising Social Services* summarised the government's view that:

> *no regulatory system can absolutely guarantee consistently good standards everywhere, but we must make sure that the system we put in place does everything that is possible to prevent and root out the abuse and neglect of vulnerable people.*

(DoH 1998)

The present chapter aims to identify some of the strengths of inspection, some of the means whereby the protective efficacy of registration and inspection can be maximised, and some of the limitations of regulation that need to be addressed. Inspection has certainly failed to prevent some recent tragedies and scandals – just as management of homes, personnel practices, government guidance and the monitoring of individual children's welfare by families and placing social workers have failed to prevent the same tragedies and scandals. As is the curse of prevention, we will never know how long is the past 'shadow catalogue' of potential tragedies and scandals that have not occurred because of these preventive measures. However, in line with stated government policy, we owe it to future children looked after away from home to maximise the contribution of inspection to improving the future shadow catalogue of scandals and tragedies that are prevented from occurring.

The Legal Basis of Registration and Inspection – and its Anomalies

All registration, inspection and enforcement work is based on the law, which determines what types of service must be registered in order to look after children, the minimum legal requirements that such services must meet, the extent of inspection or other monitoring of services once operating, and the actions that can be taken against unsatisfactory services. By implication, the law also defines by exclusion those types of services looking after children which do not require either registration or inspection.

Through its White Paper *Modernising Social Services*, the government has recognised that changes are needed to resolve some of the anomalies in current legislation – for example, to apply the same legislative requirements to all types of children's home, to extend welfare inspection to all types of boarding school, and to place local authority run homes under the same external regulation that currently applies to independent sector homes. These are welcome developments, and will contribute to the consistency and coverage of welfare regulation for the benefit of children looked after in various forms of establishment. It remains important however that the detail of legislative anomalies should be rectified logically in the envisaged future changes to the Children Act 1989 and its attendant Regulations.

Regulation of homes looking after children derives from one of two Acts of Parliament. Most are regulated under the Children Act 1989 and its attendant Schedules and Regulations. Section 63 and Schedule 6 of the Act, together with the Children's Homes Regulations 1991 (as amended), govern the registration and inspection of private children's homes. Sections 60 and 62 and Schedule 5 of the Act, together with the same Regulations, govern the registration and inspection of voluntary children's homes; these are homes run other than for profit, not necessarily by charities or voluntary organisations. Section 62 of the Children Act concerns the monitoring of accommodation of children by voluntary organisations, including the very important sector of non-maintained special schools. Finally, Section 87 of the Act governs the welfare monitoring of independent boarding schools. Some homes accommodating children are not regulated under the Children Act, but under the Registered Homes Act 1984 and its attendant Residential Care Homes Regulations 1984 – this Act governs homes which accommodate and provide board and personal care for persons, including children, for reasons, amongst others, of disability, 'mental disorder' or substance abuse.

The law determines five main issues in the regulation of homes or schools:

1. Whether, and by whom, the service has to be registered in order to look after children.
2. Whether the provider of the service has a specific welfare duty towards the children looked after and what that duty is.
3. Whether and how the service must be inspected.
4. Who can inspect the service.
5. What enforcement action can be taken against the service if it fails to safeguard and promote the welfare of children.

Positive Residential Practice

The table below identifies the current (1999/2000) legislative position on each of these five issues for the main categories of service looking after children. This information relates to registration, inspection and enforcement in relation to welfare rather than other functions of the establishment. The enforcement measures listed relate to changes or loss of registration rather than the possibility of prosecution through the courts.

Type of accommodation	Duty to register	Welfare duty towards children	Duty to inspect	Available enforcement
Private children's homes with under 4 places	None	None	None	None
Private children's homes with 4 or more places	With local authorities	Safeguard and promote welfare, use local services, prepare for leaving; consider child's / others' views, religious persuasion, racial origin, cultural and linguistic background in decisions	Twice a year by local authorities	Change of conditions of registration or cancellation of registration
Voluntary children's homes (any number of places)	With Secretary of State for Health	Safeguard and promote welfare, use local services, prepare for leaving; consider child's / others' views, religious persuasion, racial origin, cultural and linguistic background in decisions	Annual particulars sent to Secretary of State; inspection through Department of Health; local authority to visit and satisfy itself regarding welfare	Change of conditions of registration or cancellation of registration; local authorities may remove children placed or exercise other Children Act provisions relating to child
Non-maintained special schools	None	Safeguard and promote welfare, use local services, prepare for leaving; consider child's / others' views, religious persuasion, racial origin, cultural and linguistic background in decisions	No inspection requirement – local authorities to satisfy themselves and visit the children from time to time regarding welfare	None against school, but removal of child or exercise of other Children Act provisions in relation to a child
Independent boarding schools accommodating children under 295 days a year	None (although registered as schools by DfEE)	Safeguard and promote welfare	Every four years by local authorities; some more frequently – criteria for frequency in circular LAC(95)1	Notification of failure to Secretary of State for Education and Employment – who may cancel school registration

Independent boarding schools accommodating 4 or more children over 295 days a year	With local authorities (and as schools with DfEE)	Safeguard and promote welfare, use local services, prepare for leaving; consider child's / others' views, religious persuasion, racial origin, cultural and linguistic background in decisions	Twice a year by local authorities	Change of conditions of registration or cancellation of registration; notification of failure to Secretary of State for Education and Employment – who may cancel school registration
Residential care home (e.g. for children with disability)	With local authorities	Provision of board, accommodation and personal care	Twice a year by local authorities	Change of conditions of registration or cancellation of registration; notice requiring change to comply with specific Regulations
Unaccompanied holiday accommodation or language school run for profit	None (unless qualifying for registration otherwise)	None	None	None
Local authority run community homes	None	Maintain the child, safeguard and promote welfare, use local services, prepare for leaving; consider child's / others' views, religious persuasion, racial origin, cultural and linguistic background in decisions	Twice a year by the providing local authority itself	None

There are some major anomalies and exclusions in the current regulation of accommodation for children, which remain to be resolved by government in forthcoming legislation. Some of the main issues to be considered are identified below.

Definition of a Children's Home and Requirements to Register

There are currently historical differences in registration and inspection, although not the operating regulations to be complied with, between voluntary and private children's homes. This is to be resolved under current government proposals.

Children's homes with fewer than four places do not have to be registered or inspected if they are run for profit, but do have to be both registered and inspected if they are not run for profit. This inexplicable anomaly will be resolved by current government legislative proposals, with interim guidance on attempting to minimise the problem meanwhile by voluntary means.

A private home which accommodates children, but which mainly accommodates those over the age of eighteen does not have to be registered or inspected as a children's home. This is because Section 63 of the Children Act only requires children's home registration if the home is 'wholly or mainly' to accommodate more than three children. This means that an establishment such as a semi-independence hostel which accommodates young people from say 16 to 21 may escape any form of regulation for its care of its youngest residents if they are in a minority, even though logic suggests that they may be more vulnerable in such circumstances than if they were accommodated with younger children. Interestingly, the exclusion does not apply if the home is not run for profit. It is to be hoped that forthcoming legislative changes will provide children's home regulation for all homes accommodating children or young people under eighteen.

The definition of a children's home is based on the criterion that both accommodation and care are provided. There are two problems with this. Firstly, there is no generally accepted definition of 'care', nor any government guidance on how to determine whether accommodation involves care. It has, however, become common and sensible practice to assess the extent to which staff rather than young people themselves make day-to-day decisions. Secondly, because a home only becomes registerable and inspectable if care is provided, it is perfectly possible for a hostel which accommodates children, but does not care for them, to evade any form of regulation.

This effectively excludes from all welfare regulation independence hostels and hostels accompanying non care activities, such as sporting, educational and cultural provision. It could, however, be strongly argued that children looked after away from home in any form of hostel require the added protection of registration and inspection, regardless of whether the hostel is intended to provide care or simply to accommodate them for other purposes such as cultural, sporting or educational activities. The latter can just as easily harbour health, safety or abuse risks to children and young people. Including the care criterion in defining what residential accommodation of children requires regulation may be valid in relation to selecting provision to which detailed specific requirements for care provision should be applied, but it is not seriously justifiable in determining where children living away from home should be protected and where they should not.

It would be better to accept that all residential accommodation of children should be regulated, but to publish specific regulations covering hostels which are not intended to provide care. These could still cover all necessary child protection measures without the specific care requirements applied to children's homes through the Children's Homes Regulations. The government has already done something similar in applying lightened regulations to independent schools that also require registration as children's homes.

Enforcement and Improvement Action

Present legislation does not provide any means for the immediate closure of a children's home in an emergency – yet this is provided for in the case of a residential care home, usually caring for adults. It is to be hoped that an emergency closure provision (with proper safeguards) will be provided in future legislation.

The law does not provide for children's homes the very useful provision of issuing a notice statutorily requiring specific changes within a defined timescale that Regulation 20 of the Residential Care Homes Regulations 1984 provides for registered residential care homes. Again, it is to be hoped that this provision will be included in future legislation.

In the positive direction, the Children Act does provide for the registering authority to include any reasonable conditions within a registration, while the conditions of registration are severely limited for residential care homes. This enables local authorities to require changes to the operation of a home by use of the power to impose conditions, an option extremely limited for residential care homes. This provision should certainly be preserved in future amended legislation – providing regulating bodies (the future Commissions for Care Standards) with the option of using conditions of registration to direct vital but specific aspects of the operation of a home, while reserving the option of issuing an enforcement notice requiring specific action to rectify specified shortfalls should these occur.

The Subject of Registration

It is odd that for a residential care home, it is a person that is registered (a manager or person in control of a home), while for a children's home, it is the home itself rather than a person that is registered. The difference matters when there is a change of person in control, or proprietor, a new registration then being required for a residential care home, while the registration continues for a children's home. This lesser emphasis on the registration (or refusal or cancellation of registration) of the person in charge of a home in the case of children's homes is odd, given that the fitness of the person looking after children in a children's home is just as vital as the fitness of the person running a residential care home. It would better benefit children to focus future registration for all types of home upon the persons responsible for and in charge of the home rather than on the vaguer entity of the home itself.

Homes for Children with Disabilities

Where children are looked after in an independent sector residential home because of disability, the home fails to be regulated under the Registered Homes Act 1984, which is more geared towards the needs of adults than children. Where the home is intended to accommodate children, it would seem preferable in future for it to be regulated as a children's home, with specific additional requirements relating to the care of children with disabilities, rather than for it to be excluded from the general regulatory provisions applying to children elsewhere. This is also an issue likely to be dealt with through current government proposals.

Night Care by Nurseries

The law is currently unclear on the proper categorisation of nurseries which extend their service to add night care to their more usual day care provision. Day care for children under eight is registered and inspected under Part 10 of the Children Act 1989, but such regulation does not easily apply to night care. Indeed, the issue begs the question of whether the word 'day' is to be defined as 'waking day' or '24 hours'. Such services need clear regulation to protect very young children away from home, and it is important for future legislation to clarify the position of night care by nurseries. The most effective measure would probably be to confirm that such provision should be registered and inspected as a children's home, but incorporating and adapting as conditions of its children's home registration those requirements that would usually apply to day care of such young children. It is also necessary to remove the present legislative 'gap' here that allows such night accommodation to be provided for up to 28 days as a holiday without requiring children's home registration.

Non-maintained Special Schools

Current legislation is very weak in regulating the welfare of children in non-maintained special schools. Such schools cater for vulnerable children with severe problems of learning disability, physical disability, or emotional and behavioural difficulties, and care for those who may but for the accidents of their referral history just as easily find themselves in children's homes as special schools. Their regulation is, however, weak in that no statutory registration is required; the local authority has no enforcement powers in relation to such schools. Since no registration is involved, there can be no cancellation of registration nor conditions of registration, although the local authority may remove individual children. The government has made no regulations governing the operation of such schools in the manner of the Children's Homes Regulations for similar children in children's homes. Formal inspection is not required either – under Section 62 of the Children Act, both the local authority and the placing authority for each child must satisfy itself about welfare, and visit the children from time to time. There is no required frequency or guidance on how often 'from time to time' is intended to mean. These monitoring requirements are very differently interpreted by different authorities.

Under the present legislation, children in non-maintained special schools are protected by these measures to an unacceptably variable extent. Sir William Utting, in his report *Children Like Us*, highlighted the weakness of regulation of care of children in non-maintained special schools and recommended that all boarding schools be brought into the ambit of Section 87 of the Children Act, where schools have a duty to safeguard and promote welfare and are inspected in fulfilling this duty. It would be preferable also for the government in its future regulatory changes to add to this regulation the application of specific regulations for the care and protection of children in non-maintained special schools, as in children's homes.

Accommodation of Children by Voluntary Organisations

There is currently an anomaly in that Section 62 of the Children Act 1989 requires local authorities to satisfy themselves about the welfare of children, and to visit children from time to time, where any non profit-making organisation accommodates any child. This applies whatever the purpose of the accommodation, whether or not care is provided, whatever the age of the child under eighteen, and for however short a period the child is accommodated. It is clearly anomalous that this requirement does not exist for the accommodation of children for profit, while it does exist where their accommodation is not for profit. While in practice authorities do not implement the letter of this requirement, it is to be hoped that the legislation will be rewritten in the future to remove this poorly defined requirement.

Future Rationalisation of Anomalies

The current legislation, primarily the Children Act 1989 and its attendant Schedules and Regulations, provides very differently for the regulation of different types of home, and it is hoped that this will be rationalised in future legislation. Under Section 63 of the Act, private children's homes intended 'wholly or mainly' to accommodate four or more children must register and be inspected by their local social services department, while voluntary children's homes (not run for profit) must be registered and inspected by the Secretary of State for Health, and also visited from time to time by local social services authorities. Private homes for fewer than four children do not require registration or inspection, although the government has issued guidance about accommodation standards, checks on staff and voluntary inspection arrangements. The main welfare protection for children in these 'small private children's homes' is currently monitoring of the welfare of individual children, at the time of placement and at regular reviews subsequently, by placing local authorities, under regulations under the Children Act governing placements and reviewing children's cases. Community homes for children run by local social services authorities are not subject to registration (being run at present by the same authorities that carry out the relevant regulation – something current government plans will change), but under the Inspection Unit Directions, (DoH, 1994), must be inspected by social services inspection units. If a child is accommodated in a home because of his or her disability or substance abuse, the home is likely to be regulated through the

Registered Homes Act 1984 and its attendant regulations, rather than the Children Act, even though the Registered Homes Act relates more appropriately to adult rather than child care (although authorities may refer to relevant guidance under the Children Act).

Many children are accommodated by special schools. If run by local education authorities, these are unlikely to be subject to any form of welfare inspection – although if children are resident for over three months, social services welfare monitoring is required, and if run in the voluntary sector as non-maintained special schools, there is no provision for welfare registration or inspection of the school but social services staff are expected, under Section 62 of the Children Act 1989, to satisfy themselves about welfare and to visit the children from time to time. If children are accommodated in local authority secure units, the homes accommodating them will be subject to licensing (for restriction of liberty) by the Secretary of State for Health through the Social Services Inspectorate of the Department of Health. As such units are also classified as community homes, they will also be subject to the local social services authority's own inspections under the Children Act.

The government has described present regulatory arrangements as 'incomplete and patchy' (*Modernising Social Services*, DoH, 1998). As well as anomalies in the legislation itself, some children living vulnerably away from home are still not covered by any form of welfare regulation. Furthermore, the present regulatory system involves different local authorities adopting very different standards and methods for registration and inspection, and differently interpreting the relevant government requirements, which are generally broadly stated outside a relatively small number of specific Regulations. This latter issue is to be addressed through the creation of the new regional Commissions for Care Standards, operating to the same national standards and methods, to which will be transferred the current variable welfare regulatory duties of local social services authorities.

The Process of Inspection

Inspection is essentially the process of seeking information from and about the welfare provision of a home or school in order to report a comparison of its functioning against stated standards. Usually, specific methods are used to assess policies and practice in relation to a number of different criteria which together add up to an appraisal against each standard. Of necessity, inspection samples the available information and cannot possibly review all the information that is available about a home. As has already been said, inspection is one process amongst many, and is akin to an 'MoT test' at a given time. Like a research report where a researcher states the extent to which the evidence found supports or opposes an hypothesis, no inspection can prove that welfare is always satisfactory, but rather it provides evidence for or against the hypothesis that the home is operating in line with the required standards.

Importantly, inspection is not the only appraisal tool – nor sometimes even the most important appraisal tool – of a regulatory authority. Important information is also provided by statutorily required systems for the notification of certain events or incidents to the regulatory authority. Under the Children's Homes Regulations, a home is required to notify the local authority of the death of a child, of any conduct by a member of staff which indicates that they are not suitable to work with children, of the outbreak of notifiable disease in a home, and of any occurrence of significant harm, accident or serious illness involving a child in the home. There is also a legal requirement for the home to notify the registration authority of the absence of the person in charge of the home, or of a change in the person in charge. The regulatory authority should use information from these notifications as a means of monitoring the home, in addition to inspecting the home against set standards. Such notifications enable the authority to check for emergent problems or trends in major problem areas, to check the suitability of a new person in charge, and to satisfy itself where a significant and notifiable welfare event has occurred, that necessary precautions had been satisfactory and that the management and staff of the home responded appropriately to the incident.

In addition to receiving statutory notifications, the regulatory authority will from time to time receive and investigate complaints made to them about regulated services. Information about child protection enquiries carried out under the Children Act by social services authorities are a further vital source of information about problems, preventive child protection measures and a home's response to any occurrence, suspicion or allegation of child abuse. At best, such investigations will include risk assessment as well as investigative data. It is essential that when legislative change separates inspection and child protection enquiries into different authorities (Commissions for Care Standards and social services authorities respectively), provision is made to require regular communication between social services child protection staff and those inspecting (and carrying enforcement powers) in relation to the home or school.

Enforcement is often triggered by receipt of a complaint between inspections, rather than through routine inspection. With many residential care provisions for children, an important source of information is the placing authority for each child accommodated, since that authority has statutory duties to monitor the individual child's welfare. It is important that any regulatory system for children living away from home maximises the communication of concerns, and the cross checking of routine information, between inspectorates and placing authorities where these are involved.

Inspection evidence is rarely entirely objective. It is the nature of monitoring personal care of people of any age that judgements of the inspector must play a major part in the many assessments that constitute an inspection. It is, however, important that inspection methodologies are designed to maximise the representativeness of the inspector's sampling of information, and to maximise objectivity rather than subjectivity. There is currently little formal training or professional qualification available for inspectors, and it is to be hoped that this will be rectified in the future with a national system for training and accreditation of welfare inspectors. Both inspection methods and training of inspectors is needed to maintain inspection objectivity, for example by using methods that seek evidence from more than one source to corroborate significant findings, that seek evidence to check on the implementation of policies in day-to-day practice, to corroborate the assurances given by heads of establishment and senior staff about the operation of the home or school, and to avoid inspection information being unduly influenced by what is recent rather than what is typical.

Because an inspection is an appraisal against standards, it is unlikely that any home or school will fully satisfy every single inspection criterion and standard, or that any home or school, however it may be failing, will fail to satisfy some criteria. An inspection report is therefore essentially a profiling of the home or school against the applicable standards, and a good report will comment on both positive and negative aspects of the establishment, commending establishments for exceeding required standards or for progress in particular areas. Good inspection is a means of reinforcing progress as well as pointing out short-comings, and may often usefully do both in the same report. For the same reason, although it is certainly true that there are some 'either or' outcomes of an inspection – it will, for example, either lead to recommended changes or enforcement action, or it will not – it is important that inspection reports are seen as a source of external feedback and not solely something to 'pass' or 'fail'.

Of course, a provider will prepare for an inspection in order to present the home or school in as good a light as possible, and the imminence of an inspection will therefore often trigger a self appraisal and self-correction by the establishment. In many ways, this self checking in preparation for an inspection is as important as the inspection itself – rather as most of us check our own speed on the road before we reach the speed camera we see ahead of us. Some of the most satisfactory inspection findings are those which identify a shortfall that the staff of a home or school have just identified themselves and for which they have commenced a sound corrective action programme.

Inspection Methods

The methods used to inspect a home or school are as important as the content of the standards against which it is evaluated. Just as researchers declare their methods, use methods of recognised validity and reliability, and have their findings themselves evaluated according to the power of the research methods used, so the methods used to inspect an establishment are vital to the value and validity of the findings. Currently, inspecting authorities are free to determine their own inspection methods, and there is no statutory requirement about

precisely how inspectors should go about gaining information, beyond requirements determining frequency of inspection and whether unannounced visits are
required. Some national guidance and good practice exists, but there is currently
no equivalent inspection methodology to equal the 'gold standard' of techniques
such as the controlled trial for researchers.

The law also places differing burdens of knowledge upon inspectors for
different types of establishment – for children's homes, statutory requirements
refer specifically to inspections being carried out and used for functions such as
the review of registration of a private children's home. However, for the vital
sector of non-maintained boarding schools, there is no statutory requirement for
inspection as such, only for measures to satisfy the authority regarding welfare,
and for visits to children, while for independent boarding schools, Section 87 of
the Children Act 1989 does not specify inspection or visiting at all (although this
is specified in subsequent guidance), but imposes the very different duty upon the
monitoring authority of maintaining a constant state of being satisfied (or not
satisfied) with the school's safeguarding and promotion of welfare.

It is essential for the law to be clear on whether the future Commissions for
Care Standards should maintain close contact with, and awareness of, welfare in
homes and schools between formal visits, or whether they are instead only
required competently to carry out assessments on set occasions such as inspections or when specific notifications or complaints are received, without any expectation of monitoring or awareness of welfare between such occasions.

Current inspection methods used by local authorities with children's services
include important and sophisticated means of discovering and corroborating
information and of securing the views of children, an issue importantly emphasised in recent government announcements. The variety of available methods
provides good opportunity for corroboration of information about particular
issues by securing that information in different ways and from different sources –
for example, from children, parents, placing authorities, staff, records and by
direct observation.

Inspection methods currently used merit inclusion in any future national
standard methodology for Commissions for Care Standards, as either core
required inspection methods or as optional additional corroborative or investigative methods usable on the authority of local Commission managers.
Examples of current methods are set out below.

**Examination of day-to-day practice against the establishment's policy
documents**, through information from discussion with staff and children about
what happens in various circumstances (with recent examples) and checking
records of actions and incidents against what policies and statutory requirements
determine should happen.

Discussion to gain information about aspects of the operation of the home or
school, and the experience of day-to-day living there, with a range of children and

staff, looking for information corroborated by different children and staff, as well as issues needing to be pursued further because of their significance.

Use of survey questionnaires to children, staff, parents and/or placing authorities, to secure information which (where numbers allow) can be compared with norms from use of similar questionnaires in other inspections, and repeated on successive inspections to enable trends to be monitored. A survey can for example be used to assess how child-reported levels of bullying compare with other homes or schools, or are changing over time. This does not determine whether the reported level is acceptable, but is vital in assessing the home or school's performance in relation to what other establishments are achieving in countering this problem. Surveys also allow all children or adults in the relevant group the opportunity to provide information and views to the inspector, helping to avoid the risk of only the most voluble – or the most positive or dissatisfied – being heard. As well as a 'traditional' completion of a written form, questionnaire formats may be used as the basis for structured interview with children or adults, or for group discussion. Enabling those in a home or school to provide written information to an inspector also enables specific concerns or even allegations or 'whistle blowing' to be conveyed for investigation. Careful interpretation of survey findings is essential – there will always be a proportion of 'spoilt responses' – but inspectors can be reasonably expected to exercise professional judgement in interpretation, and to pursue significant concerns made by appropriately seeking corroborative information. My own experience is that children are remarkably thoughtful and perceptive in what they write for inspectors, and that even children who include 'silly' or pornographic comment will often write balanced and reasonable comment elsewhere in the same document. The extent of input from the children living in an establishment on which corroboration is sought and taken into account is an important measure of the quality of an inspection.

Inspection of premises and physical facilities against premises standards – an inspector can often be guided round the building by children who can provide information about how various spaces and facilities are used, and will valuably provide both positive and negative comment.

Inspection of statutorily kept and other records – as a permanent source of information on specific issues and incidents, often providing the source of information for corroboration in other ways, and enabling inspectors both to identify trends (e.g. in accidents or absconding) and to check the establishment's use of records as feedback information for its own management of the home or school. A vital element of checking of records is commonly the checking of personnel records of staff appointments, usually to ascertain, from a sample of such records, written evidence that required recruitment checks and safe recruitment procedures have been followed.

Interviews with key staff (often including new or junior staff, whose knowledge and induction to the home are important in their own right, but who are also commonly a vital source of the perceptions of 'fresh eyes' about daily life in the establishment). Such interviews can cover both life and practice in the home, and how different issues and incidents would be handled.

Discussions with children – these can include both arranged group discussions about particular standards, issues raised by children or staff, or issues identified by the inspector, as well as important informal discussions with children when in and around the home and at the meal table. One technique worth noting is that of one authority where a pair of inspectors may discuss the same issue or issues simultaneously but in different locations with two small randomly selected groups of children, enabling a rapid assessment of the degree of corroboration of child views on those issues. Many inspectors have a range of vital standard issues to be covered in discussions with children – for example, whether there are any times of day or week, or places in the building or grounds, which are danger times or places for bullying to occur.

Observation of practice – although the presence of an inspector changes practice, 'straight' observation is valuable in giving an inspector a view of what is regarded as 'standard practice' in the home or school, in corroborating some issues (e.g. whether children do have to queue for facilities such as telephones or toilets at peak morning or evening times), and in observing 'live' issues which are not planned – such as fights or arguments between children, how staff respond to challenging behaviour, and the extent and nature of communication between children and between children and staff. Although the inspector still affects these exchanges, what is observed will inevitably be within a reasonable range of what is usual in the establishment.

Requests for information from other relevant bodies involved with the home or school, such as the fire service, child protection staff of the local social services department, environmental health service, and where relevant, the Department for Education and Employment.

Lay assessors will be involved in many inspections of homes, although not of schools. Lay assessors are people from different backgrounds to the providers or inspectors of the homes visited, with no prior interest in the establishment concerned, who are involved in inspection alongside professional inspectors to contribute the lay person's view, counter any tendency of inspection to accept the long accepted, and to bring 'fresh eyes' to practice within homes . There are two main categories of lay assessor in practice, each with a very different contribution to make to the assessment process. The first is the 'genuinely lay' person recruited from the general public and intended to bring the views of the 'person in the bus queue' to inspection. The second is the user or former user of the type of service being inspected, who is in this case likely to be someone who has themselves lived in a children's home, who can bring with them to the inspection both a vital 'child's eye' view and an ability to discuss issues with children more 'from the inside' than can be achieved by many inspectors who have not themselves experienced residential care. Lay assessment brings a vital outside perspective to inspection, although since lay assessors, more than inspectors, contribute through their own personal life experiences rather than having been trained and experienced in inspection and expected standards, their contribution may be somewhat more subjective than that of other inspectors.

In evaluating an establishment against pre-set standards, inspectors must balance the routine gathering of information on criteria with the pursuit of issues particular to the home or school being visited which may have been raised by children or staff, identified from past inspection, notifications or complaints, or which arise during the inspection.

Occasionally, routine checking against sets of standards must give way to pursuit and corroboration of a particular or idiosyncratic issue important to the welfare of children in the establishment. If an inspector suspects or receives an allegation of abuse of a child, he or she must refer this to the local social services authority's child protection investigation staff for enquiries under Section 47 of the Children Act, but all inspectors of children's establishments need to be able to receive and appropriately deal with the early stages of an allegation of abuse. Immediate measures will include any immediate protection arrangements that may be necessary following a disclosure, and recording information appropriately without inappropriately guaranteeing children secrecy for the information they have disclosed, without using leading questions with a child, and without pre-empting subsequent possible statutory interviews and enquiries.

I have referred to the importance of corroboration of information that is to form the basis for significant findings, recommendations or action. Routine discussions and checks against standards criteria will normally be constructed to enable a core of required information to be gathered from more than one source. Where an important issue for children's welfare or the future of an establishment is being evaluated, the inspector should attempt to 'triangulate' the information on which findings are based, seeking corroboration from two reasonably independent sources as well as the original source in order to provide strong evidential confirmation for the consequent finding, recommendation or enforcement action.

It is, however, an uncomfortable fact that inspectors must select and prioritise the statements and information they will attempt to corroborate from a different source, such as by asking a member of staff or another group of children, neutrally and without revealing identities, about an issue of concern raised by an individual child. Resources do not usually allow more than a selection of facts to be corroborated by such means. This is where the inspector's experience and judgement is vital, and there must be an acceptance that inspection is bound to 'miss' some issues that could with hindsight have been pursued for the welfare of children.

It is a requisite of all inspectors of children's establishments that they can communicate readily with children, and be regarded as credible, trustworthy and fair by children of different ages, both genders, and from a range of very different backgrounds, in order to receive and give due weight to children's views and concerns. Children themselves are not only the direct consumers of welfare provision in homes and schools, but are the most candid and important informants about their own lives in residential settings. Communicating with children and evaluating their views and information is central to the task of any inspector of a home or school.

As in any form of inspection, inspectors of homes and schools must differentiate between the inputs of what is provided or done, and the outcomes of that provision from the children's viewpoint. For many provisions, the correlation between what is objectively provided and how children perceive it or are affected by it can be expected to differ between different groups of children, or even the same children at different times. As an example, the level of privacy of telephone, toilet or shower provision may objectively be physically the same in two buildings, but the children in each setting may have different evaluations of that privacy. This is sometimes for good reasons. For example, toilet cubicle doors which have large gaps beneath or above them may be no problem to privacy for one group of children, while in another there may be one or more children who are in the habit of looking under or over the door, thus making the same physical provision totally unsatisfactory. Both physical provision and care practice needs to reflect the social characteristics of different groups of children and the differing histories of different groups and establishments. Again, children's views are a vital touchstone in evaluating their welfare. Inspectors need to assess what the establishment is providing, and then discover from the children how that provision works in practice for them.

What Constitutes Welfare

There is no succinct universal definition of what constitutes welfare in a residential setting for children, but much has been written about the subject. The definition of welfare will always derive from a combination of four main sources – firstly from the law together with statutory regulations and guidance, secondly from the local standards and criteria documents of the regulatory authority itself, thirdly from recognised reports on aspects of welfare provision and, most importantly, fourthly from the views and wishes of the children currently resident in the establishment.

The government is a main source of guidance on standards, through statutory documents such as the Children's Homes Regulations supplemented by statutory guidance documents and circulars issued to local authorities under the Children Act and 'practice guidance' documents from sources such as the Social Services Inspectorate of the Department of Health. These must be taken into account by inspectors, although they provide a valid but not always constant yardstick – for example, the Children's Homes Regulations define many aspects of welfare in children's homes, although with some significant gaps such as the remarkable absence of any regulation concerning prevention of child abuse. Local authorities currently produce their own local detailed standards within these wider government requirements. These local standards are at present problematically variable between local authorities, but should under the future regulatory Commissions be based on clear national sets of standards and therefore inevitably and appropriately will be more definitive as effectively a 'welfare blueprint' for the type of provision concerned.

National reports provide an important source of well researched guidance on aspects of welfare. Much current guidance on use of punishments in homes derives from *The Pindown Report* by Levy and Kahan, together with the government guidance document *Permissible Forms of Control*. The recognised source of good staff recruitment practice is the report produced under the chairmanship of Norman Warner, *Choosing With Care*. For boarding schools, the Department of Health publication *School Life* gives a résumé of the views of children about what constitutes 'best buy' welfare provision and practice, and must be taken into account, providing a valid if not necessarily constant yardstick of the establishment's welfare practice.

Key issues in children's welfare will always include, in addition to child protection, major issues such as the level and countering of bullying, and the relationships between children of different ages and with different needs. The age and need mix of children is a vital factor in the welfare of all in the resident group, and there also needs to be an examination of the roles (if any) given to older or senior children. Some homes give significant roles to older or more responsible children, while many schools operate prefect systems or the equivalent. No home or school is free of bullying, and it is essential that establishments have well understood and effective countermeasures, both preventive and to respond to incidents and reports of bullying, which will not be the same in all homes, with all groups of children, or at all times. An important question for both inspectors and staff of homes and schools is to identify, primarily from the children themselves, what are the current local factors most effective in countering bullying, and to utilise that information in recommendations or strategies against bullying.

A related key issue is that of the people to whom children will go with personal problems. Usually, the most likely are friends or parents. Friends are often the recipients, before staff, of significant welfare concerns, including allegations of abuse, and this raises the importance of children themselves knowing to whom major problems may be taken and how they may be responded to. Children may well go to different adults for different types of problem, and may often choose to confide in junior or ancillary staff rather than necessarily their own keyworker, tutor, unit or house staff. This in turn emphasises the importance of sound induction training and supervision of staff at all levels, and of clearly understood and practicable policies and practices for responding to welfare issues raised by children. From the inspection point of view, inspectors can make a major contribution by assessing the pattern of adults to whom children may turn, through discussions with children and through survey work. The extent to which children state that there is a range of adults to whom they feel they may turn with personal problems is a measurable indicator of this aspect of the welfare health of an establishment.

Staff are clearly central to the welfare and protection of children in residential settings, and an essential part of every inspection should be the evaluation of staff recruitment procedures. The government has, through its response to Sir William Utting's report on children's safeguards *People Like Us*, committed itself to defining as the future gold standard the recruitment checks and processes contained in the Warner Report on staff selection for children's homes (*Choosing With Care*). This is an important and welcome definition of a national recruitment standard, which must form a core standard for checking at all future full inspections of homes and schools.

Alongside safe staff recruitment, and the attendant factors of effective staff induction, training, supervision and appraisal, must run the awareness in all children's establishments of which adults 'on site' have been checked as suitable to have substantial unsupervised access to children, and which have not. Staff who have not been so checked should not be given such access – they may well assist in activities and work with children, but should not able to spend long with children (particularly any child alone) outside the sight or hearing of others. It would perhaps be helpful for both residential staff and inspectors to reinstate the old concept of chaperoning children – so that any individual child or group of children is effectively chaperoned by one or more staff who have been subject to the necessary recruitment checks with a satisfactory outcome.

While it is not the case that staff who have been satisfactorily checked are automatically always safe with children, it is not proper protection of children if staff or other adults who have not been subject to such checks at all are given substantial unsupervised access to them. Such staff checks need to be in place for visiting, ancillary and contract staff who do have such access, but may not be directly employed to work with the children. It is axiomatic that as staff we pay great attention to fire precautions requirements in homes and schools, although the risk to children from fire is statistically less than the risk to them from abuse. It is also axiomatic that we expect to impose greater protective measures and procedures against theft of money than we necessarily do against potential abuse of children. Sound staff recruitment, proper recruitment checks of all adults with substantial unsupervised access to children, and effective chaperoning are the triple protections for children which merit as high a profile as either the protection of the establishment's money or its protection against fire.

Further issues that merit consideration in inspection of all children's establishments include the availability of telephones for children to use to make contacts outside the establishment. This availability should avoid erosion on either the grounds that children should not have telephone access for a period after arrival in a school in case this encourages homesickness, or that some children frequently vandalise the telephone. There also needs to be provision for children to make complaints with a proper expectation of investigation and response, and for staff to 'whistle blow' outside the line management within the home or school. These are all measures increasingly and properly required by government, which provide the means for significant welfare concerns to be surfaced by those within homes or schools. They certainly carry a cost in terms of potential for misuse or malicious use, but that is a reason for proper and skilled evaluation of issues raised through these routes rather than an argument that residential establishments should remain more closed.

Three final issues merit noting as special issues in children's establishments. The first is the opportunity given for children to achieve and develop educationally and in terms of personal interests and social skills, recognising that children are by definition in a developmental stage of life. Secondly is the fairness and acceptability of the disciplinary system employed within the establishment, including the extent to which there is effective prohibition on the introduction of potentially unacceptable sanctions idiosyncratic to some staff rather than contained in the inspected disciplinary policy. Thirdly is the use of any therapeutic interventions in the home or school, and where these are used, the extent of staff training and competence in the techniques, and the presence of external consultancy and monitoring of the use of the therapeutic approach. In many homes and schools, the disciplinary system will include use of restraint where necessary to prevent injury to a child or others, or major damage to property, and use of restraint will form part of any inspection.

Risk Assessment and Welfare Audit

Inspection is at best an occasional, if thorough, process. Equally important to children's welfare is the establishment's own self assessment and self correction or development processes. Two processes are of particular importance here. One is the regular self assessment of welfare provision by staff and their managers, which would appropriately involve children. A useful agenda for such self assessment is provided by the standards and criteria against which the home or school is externally inspected, supplemented by both the recommendations made by the latest external inspection, and also by those issues or development points identified by the staff themselves or their managers (for example through monthly visits on behalf of the provider organisation).

Risk assessment is a more specific process increasingly used in establishments and indeed expected through inspections, and effectively involves regularly identifying hazards to the safety and welfare of children (including risks of bullying or abuse, as well as the more obvious physical risks in a building), considering the extent to which those risks can and should reasonably be reduced, and following through an action plan for such risk reduction. If a disaster occurs, it is important to all involved that the staff of an establishment exercised reasonableness and due diligence in identifying risks and deciding reasonably which could and which could not reasonably be reduced. The greatest risk to both children and to the future of an establishment is failure to foresee the clearly foreseeable, not the 'act of God' that occurs despite reasonable practice and could only reasonably have been prevented with the luxury of previous hindsight.

In conducting an internal risk assessment, it is helpful to follow six steps. Firstly, the responsible member of staff should list apparent hazards from the locations and activities taking place in those locations – remembering that risks may arise from illicit as well as approved activities, and that what caused no problem in the past may do so in the future. It is also important to include any foreseeable significant hazards from occasional activities, journeys and periods spent 'off site'. In practice, it is helpful to tour premises and grounds, and to go through daily and weekly activity routines, with selected children as well as with key staff, and to pay particular attention to anything that may have been the subject of a 'near miss' in the past.

The second step in risk assessment is to identify the harm that might arise from the risk identified, rating (perhaps on a three point scale) its likelihood, and also identifying what might occur as the 'worst occurrence'. This can then be used to prioritise in the third step, which is to decide what action can be taken to minimise each risk. It is reasonable to take practicalities and resources into account, as well as the fact that one cannot eliminate all risks. The aim is to avoid 'unnecessariness' in foreseeable risks, and to reach reasonable decisions on what action to take and not to take. Such decisions may need to be demonstrably justifiable should the hazard turn into an accident in the future. The fourth step is to draw up an action plan for risk reduction - and to implement it. Fifthly, it is wise to clarify what action should be taken should the harm or accidents now identified actually occur – including any identified 'worst occurrences'. This forms the establishment's 'disaster plans', which may include protocols for staff to manage major crises such as an occurrence of fire or widespread infectious disease. Finally, it is important to review and repeat the exercise to ensure that the action plan is implemented, that the value of risk reduction measures is evaluated, and that any new reasonably foreseeable risks are identified.

The Future of Inspection

At the time of writing, the future of inspection of children's homes and all types of residential school is about to change following the government White Paper *Modernising Social Services*, together with the government's announcements in its *Quality Protects* initiative and its response to the children's safeguards review.

Structurally, these proposed changes are designed to achieve three important changes in the regulation of homes and schools. Firstly, they are intended to establish full independence of the regulatory bodies (the future Commissions for Care Standards) from local authorities which also provide homes. This is now an appropriate measure, given that the current enforcement regime is inevitably different in relation to independent and local authority homes. Secondly, they are intended to establish common national standards to be followed in inspection throughout the country. This is a long awaited and welcome principle, as the present differences between numerous local authorities has proved difficult to justify and unnecessarily inconsistent. However, on this initiative, the important effect will come not from the principle, but from the content and quality of the national standards themselves once brought into practice. It is essential that these are clear, detailed where they need to be, without uneasy compromises which leave too much to the individual positioning of Commissions or inspectors, acceptable to both providers and experienced inspectors as well as to government, in tune with the views and wishes of children, and containing appropriate provision for variations in specified areas where Commissions are satisfied that there is good reason for a particular provider.

The third change now designed into the proposed Commissions is that of ensuring that the profile of regulation of children's establishments remains high and separated from the risk of becoming 'swamped' by the regulation of other types of provision such as adult residential care homes. It is a welcome development that each Commission will have a Children's Rights Officer to oversee the regulation of children's services within the Commission, and that from the outset that Officer will have specific powers and duties to report on children's issues to the national Chief Inspector. Less clear however is the extent to which Commissions will eventually preserve the inspection of children's establishments as an identifiable specialism within their overall work, with individual training and accreditation of inspectors to undertake such work. It will also be important to establish how each Commission will link with complaints systems operated by children's placing authorities, and at a very practical level, to what extent children will be able to approach the staff of the regional Children's Rights Officer instead of using their local authority's complaints procedure to raise a concern about their home. It will be vital to establish how precisely the Commission will link with the individual child protection investigation systems of the numerous local social services authorities in its region.

Wide consultation will also be important to ensure that the government's declared intention that many current anomalies in legislation and the regulation of different types of establishment will be effective and avoid the creation of too many new anomalies. Many questions currently remain over the establishment of the Commissions – not least the sufficiency of their funding for the frequency of inspection and investigative work they will undertake. It is important for children that there are the resources available to respond rapidly to significant concerns raised by children or about their welfare between statutory inspections.

Conclusion

Inspection of children's homes and schools is an external check on welfare provision and its effectiveness that is one, but not by any means the only, means of endorsing good practice and identifying problems needing to be rectified. The presence and expectation of external inspection is also an encouragement for self evaluation by establishments, and it provides standards against which such self assessment can be made. The world of children's services and of their inspection is currently about to change dramatically, generally in a very positive direction but dependent on the detail and day-to-day operation of new structures and processes of regulation being appropriate and working satisfactorily.

Inspection should never decline to the level of solely generating lists of short-comings, like a poor house survey report, but should, where effective, be seen as a tough but fair source of external feedback, identifying what is going well as well as what needs rectifying – even as a form of external consultancy for the management and operation of the establishment. Perhaps the most important measure of the value of inspection for any home or school is the extent to which the children regard inspectors as known people who can make an impact on their welfare if necessary, and to which staff regard inspectors as a relevant and positive influence on their practice between inspections as well as on inspection days.

CHAPTER 6

'Things Can Only Get Better!' An Evaluation of Developments in the Training and Qualification of Residential Child Care Staff

David Crimmens

The aim of this chapter is to review developments in the training of residential child care workers since the publication of *The Pindown Report*, (Levy and Kahan, 1991). Recent research and policy will be reviewed to expose the potentially over-optimistic expectations invested in training. Questions will be raised as to why the value of training is regarded as self-evident in light of the fact that:

- The proportion of residential child care staff with any qualifications remains low.
- Traditional forms of training, particularly the continuing reliance on the Diploma in Social Work as the only professional qualification recognised by most employing local authorities, do not adequately equip staff for the contemporary residential child care task.

Recent developments in training, especially the availability of a relevant National Vocational Qualification (NVQ) will be evaluated. A cautious optimism will be adopted in assessing the potential for training to raise the professional status of residential child care workers in the current political climate. The relationship between higher levels of qualifications and training and the quality of care for the young service users will be critically appraised. The chapter will conclude by examining the potential of continental European models, which have developed a more focussed and specialised approach to training residential child care workers.

Dispelling Damaging Mythology

The Residential Forum, (1998), a group of experts working under the auspices of the National Institute of Social Work, expresses concern about the findings of recent research into training for residential child care. Concern focuses on an important but often misunderstood quotation from the Utting Report, (1997), which states that:

> *no statistical association could be found between the measures of quality of care and the level of qualifying training within the staff group.*

> (para 12.8, p125)

The Residential Forum is concerned that this could create a myth that training is ineffective in improving the quality of residential child care. Utting poses the paradox with which all those involved in residential child care continue to struggle. On the one hand, he makes the point that trained staff provide more effective services which will improve the quality of care and consequently keep young people safe, (Utting, 1997, para 12.7 p125). On the other hand, research demonstrates the continuing low level of training and qualifications and suggests that current approaches to training are not relevant to the tasks faced by residential child care workers. Utting does go on to say, however, that training:

> *can only be effective in improving the quality of care for children if trained staff are working in settings in which the whole staff group can work coherently towards explicit objectives for the children.*

> (para 12.9 p126)

In spite of all the research, and efforts invested in development, the effect of relevant training on the quality of care remains unclear. Authors such as Sinclair and Gibbs, (1996,1996a), maintain that their findings should not lead to the abandoning of training, which they regard as a potentially key mechanism for improving the quality of care. They suggest that the task is to continue to develop training until we discover what works, and that what works will be evident in improvements in the effectiveness of residential child care, (Sinclair and Gibbs 1996a, p358).

Low Levels of Training and Qualification

The problem of the low proportion of trained and appropriately qualified staff in residential child care has been a constant theme in relevant reports since the war. It is worth noting that contemporary concerns, which emerged at the beginning of the 1990s, with the publication of the *Pindown Report* (Levy and Kahan, 1991), linked the absence of trained staff with the evolution of an unhealthy and unethical method of controlling children in residential homes in one local authority area (p167). The government responded to these issues by requesting the then chief inspector of the Social Services Inspectorate (SSI) to carry out an urgent inquiry. *Children in the Public Care*, (Utting 1991), provided something of a renaissance in residential responses to looking after troubled and troublesome children in the UK. The report reiterated the fundamental importance of the residential option as:

...an indispensable service: that should be a positive, joint choice, primarily for adolescents...residential homes fulfil a specialist role as partners in a range of preventive and rehabilitative services designed to meet specific needs.

(Utting, 1991, p62)

Affirmation of the importance and value of residential child care flew in the face of the conventional professional and political consensus, which had dominated debate during the 1980s. One outcome of this debate was a significant decline in the number of children living in residential care. The trend towards family support and the use of fostering as the preferred option for looking after children, influenced by changing ideas about the scope of the welfare state and financial pressures, was common among the majority of continental European countries, (Colton et al., 1993).

Importantly, for our present purposes, Utting made a number of significant recommendations about the qualifications and training of residential child care staff. It is worth briefly reviewing his perception of the situation, before moving on to evaluate the impact of his recommendations during the 1990s.

All heads of homes and a proportion of care staff, possibly amounting to one third in all, should hold the Diploma in Social Work or a relevant professional qualification. The remainder should possess the appropriate level of the National Vocational Qualification.

(Utting, 1991, p65)

Utting found that 70 per cent of the residential child care staff surveyed had no relevant qualification. This figure represented:

- nearly one in five (19.59%) of officers in charge
- more than half (56.20%) of assistant officers in charge
- four out of five (78.90%) of other care staff

This demonstrates that at the time of the survey only one out of five residential child care staff held any relevant qualification. Utting commented that his survey:

speaks eloquently of the low esteem accorded residential child care

(1991, p17)

The publication of the Utting Report was followed by a flurry of official action including:

- The Committee of Inquiry chaired by Lady Howe, (1992), which looked at pay and conditions across the sector.
- The Warner Report, (1992), in response to a further child care scandal involving Frank Beck rapidly following on the heels of Pindown.
- An 'expert group' was established by The Central Council for Education and Training in Social Work, (CCETSW, 1992), to determine an appropriate professional response.

- the Residential Child Care Initiative, which aimed to increase rapidly the proportion of professionally qualified heads of home and their deputies. Additional funding was provided by the Department of Health through the Training Support Grant (TSG).

The Residential Child Care Initiative (RCCI)

It is worth reflecting on the experience of the RCCI because it is the official response to some of the issues raised in the Utting Report. It represents an attempt to address major problems in residential childcare via training, in this case, senior residential staff. It was set up in haste without time to consider the relevance of course content on existing Diploma in Social Work (Dip.SW) courses. It was in a sense a political act of faith seen to be responding to the issues raised by Utting. It presumed that training would resolve the problems. Issues identified above about how many staff would need to be involved in the longer term and how far the training offered would be relevant to the residential child care task, were not addressed.

The first intake of RCCI students was in September 1992. Nine universities across England were chosen to achieve an effective geographical spread in providing training to the target group identified by Utting, namely heads of homes and their deputies. The initiative was essentially short term in the absence of a longer-term strategy to ensure the maintenance of a qualified workforce, at least at this senior level.

David Lane, (1994), in his independent evaluation of the RCCI for CCETSW, suggests that this was one of the major shortcomings of the programme. He applauds the fact that around 500 residential child care staff were able to qualify with the Dip.SW. but questions what contribution this increase is likely to make in the longer term to the inadequate levels of qualified staff in the sector. He suggests that the reduction in levels of secondment for professional training by many local authorities at the time, along with the tendency towards wastage, identified by Utting and others, indicated that there was never likely to be a significant increase in qualified staff in the medium and long terms. This situation was created by a continuing reluctance of the Conservative Government to provide sufficient resources to support a training strategy capable of achieving the objectives identified by Utting.

The Tavistock Institute, funded by the DoH, also carried out an evaluation (Hills et al. 1997). The evaluation found that, at the time of the research, nearly 90 per cent of residential child care staff seconded onto the RCCI remained in residential child care and the majority of the 13.5 per cent, who were no longer directly involved, continued to work in related activities. Karban and Frost, (1998), maintain that one of the key outcomes by which to judge the relative success of the RCCI is the extent to which qualified staff remain in residential child care. They produce less optimistic findings in their research, which surveyed three cohorts from one RCCI-providing university. They found that five of the 30 RCCI graduates surveyed had already left residential child care at the time of their survey and a further ten expressed their intention to leave at some time in the future. This would suggest a loss of up to 50 per cent of newly qualified staff from residential care within two years of qualification. This loss of qualified staff raises a question about what kind of return is reasonable to expect in relation to the length of time staff remain in residential child care posts, and was particularity crucial given the short term nature of the initiative. Utting, (1997), acknowledges that the RCCI 'could only be remedial in the short to medium term'. He expresses a fear that with the initiative ending 'there is a danger that a haemorrhaging of qualified staff will reverse the gains, which have been made.' (para 12.17, p127)

Overall, the Tavistock evaluation provides some optimistic findings on training for residential care staff. Hills et al., suggest that the Dip.SW enhances career progression of residential care staff and increases promotion prospects into management posts. This raised the possibility of residential staff occupying more powerful positions in their organisations with the ability to influence policy developments and decision making, (p127).

Those who had been seconded, and their colleagues in the residential units, received exposure to a broader range of theoretical and practical approaches to social work. This suggests that there may be some 'cascade' effect where those attending training can pass on some of what they learn to colleagues in their team. There was a belief that training enhances status, particularly in relation to dealing with field social workers and other professionals. Residential workers:

> *are consequently keen to acquire this higher status and in doing so it enhances the status of residential care and improves the standards of care not just within the unit but also in the process through which a child is taken into care and assigned a case worker.*

> (Hills et al., p126)

This question of who benefits from training remains controversial. The Tavistock evaluation provides some evidence that, along with improved salaries and better supervision and support, enhanced training opportunities can lead to, for example, reductions in the loss of qualified staff. What is harder to demonstrate is the impact on residential child care staff morale and levels of job satisfaction, and crucially whether and in what ways better training and professional qualification leads to a higher standard of care for the young residents. None of the research provides conclusive evidence that better trained and qualified residential child care staff provide better quality of care in more effective children's homes. But the fact remains that any positive relationship will be impossible to measure while the level of training remains so low, and the majority of residential child care staff are untrained and unqualified.

There are also major outstanding questions about the relevance of existing training to residential childcare tasks. An overview of recent research sponsored by the Department of Health (DoH) maintains that:

> *It is questionable whether the social work training of residential workers is as useful as it used to be and whether the skills transferred are relevant to the residential context or apply to other aspects of children's services. Therefore continually tinkering with the conventional social work training in an attempt to meet the special requirements of residential care is unlikely to achieve much.*
>
> (DoH, 1998, p36)

The research concludes that clarity about the nature of the tasks must be achieved prior to designing relevant training. Consequently, the research is scathing about any attempt to discover evidence, which links training with positive outcomes in relation to the quality of care provided for young people. However arguments about developing further training cannot be sustained unless efforts are made to demonstrate that better trained staff make an appreciable difference to the quality of care.

Low Levels of Training and Qualification...Continue!

The fact is that the RCCI only involved about 500 senior residential child care staff. What improvements in training and qualification emerged for the majority of residential child care staff in the mid 1990s? The answer appears to be 'very few'. What does appear to have happened is a continuing decline in numbers of children's homes and in the numbers of young people looked after. Smaller homes, looking after up to six young people, have become the norm. Smaller homes with smaller numbers of young people suggest some changes in the nature of the residential child care task. Smaller group dynamics should reduce issues of control and raise questions about the nature of the relationships which develop between residential workers and young residents. While this is not the place to examine these changes in any detail, questions are raised about the implications for a relevant training. Size of group and staff team may not lead to major changes in professional values. The new context, quite different from the larger group experience which was historically the norm, requires the development of relevant skills and knowledge.

It is worth further labouring the point about the low level of qualifications among residential child care staff. Constant reminders about the lack of progress made in the past few years, should produce an impetus for future activity and change. It is significant that, in spite of a recommendation to collect workforce data annually, (Utting, 1991), the Department of Health does not routinely collect such information, (House of Commons, 1998, p.xliv). The latest available information provided by the Social Services Workforce Analysis Main Report 1996 indicates that:

- 30 per cent of officers in charge and deputies
- 69 per cent of other supervisory staff
- 78 per cent of child care staff

hold no relevant qualification.

This picture is reinforced by recent research, which confirms the above situation with respect to heads of homes and their deputies, but states that 'it was very rare for any other member of staff to have any qualification at all,' (Sinclair and Gibbs, 1996a, p46). All the evidence indicates a consistent picture of little improvement to date in the proportion of residential child care workers with any relevant qualification.

It is within this overall context that questions of appropriate qualifications, their level and the means of acquiring them must be debated. Arguments about why residential child care workers need any qualifications in the first place can be summarily dismissed. Abundant research evidence demonstrates that young people living in residential children's homes are among the most troubled and troublesome in the wider population. They need consistent and highly skilled help to come to terms within their current difficulties and to have any chance of developing the level of maturity required to participate in modern society.

Horwath and Morrison, (1999), identify the purposes for training social care staff, an occupational group which includes residential child care workers:

- To meet service users and carers needs.
- To contribute towards the achievement of organisational goals.
- To meet the professional development needs of individuals.

They suggest that training alone will not provide what they term a 'competent workforce'. They define competence as:

> *The ability to perform the activities within an occupation...to the standards expected in employment.*

> (DoE, 1991)

The idea of identified standards, which are universally applicable across an occupational area, underpin the emergence of National Vocational Qualifications, (NVQ). Critics of NVQ argue that activities like residential child care cannot be reduced to a set of competent behaviours. Joss, (1991), cited in Horwath and Morrison, (p57), suggests that competencies show what people must do but not how or why they do them. He maintains that all social work activities require the exercise of discretion and that working in different situations requires different responses. Horwath and Morrison examine this and other critiques of NVQ before reaching an essentially pragmatic view which focuses on the potential benefits of NVQ qualifications for the largely unqualified workforce in social care:

Competence based training ensures that training is continually linked to performance in the workplace through its firm emphasis on the need to demonstrate the application of knowledge, values and skills in the workplace.
(Horwath and Morrison, 1999, p58)

A Competent Workforce; The Potential for NVQ

The arrival of the relevant award at NVQ level 3 for residential child care work 'Caring for children and young people' should be welcomed. NVQ can provide the basis of a qualification for all residential child care workers, given the low level of existing qualified staff in residential child care and the recommendation in the Utting Report that NVQ should be the appropriate structure. The award provides a structure for rewarding competent practice, which is based on an explicit set of standards derived from an analysis of the tasks involved in residential child care practice. This suggests that the content of the award is more likely to be seen as relevant to the task by residential child care staff, and should produce the following positive outcomes:

- Relevance to task increases motivation by appealing to common sense understandings of their experience as workers.
- Increases the sense of value of the award as something which will enable them to improve the quality of the practice.

The following case study describes how one local authority is committed to raising the levels of qualifications of residential child care workers. The study highlights the positive aspects of an investment in defining occupational standards for residential child care and later linking these to NVQ awards.

Northborough: An Example of Good Practice

Northborough provides an illustration of a development in competence-based awards for residential child care staff. Northborough was a large northern metropolitan authority, since reorganised into four separate unitary authorities. In January 1993, the authority was managing 19 children's homes employing nearly 200 staff as residential child care workers. At this time, the majority (89 per cent) of this workforce were without relevant qualifications.

Standards Development Officers were appointed prior to the introduction of NVQ to improve standards specifically for residential child care. They spent a year developing relevant occupational standards by meeting regularly with staff working in each of the children's homes. Their task was to identify what residential workers were doing in their day-to-day practice. Consequently, the standards were seen as relevant to residential child care practice because they were developed with the participation of residential child care workers. The occupational standards emerged from the pragmatic realities of residential child care practices.

Using this model the Standards Development Team developed an NVQ level 3 award 'Supportive Living' which was piloted with a cohort of 80 residential child care workers without relevant qualifications. The task was to take these workers through to the award in a period of eight months before local government reorganisation led to the break up of the authority. 20 workers were selected from each of the four authorities, which would become the new unitary authorities after the reorganisation.

Each of the children's homes was allocated 20 hours per week to enable staff to be released to attend 'guided learning workshops'.

As far as possible the workshops involved members of a working team who were able to build up their knowledge together in each children's home. These workshops were not only intended to provide the necessary knowledge for the award. Each week two hours were spent on learning about legislation, policy and practice issues. Most importantly, two hours were allocated each week to enable workers to record what they were learning; this reflects the reality of working in any children's home where there is rarely any opportunity to write up and record. It also confronts the problem of enabling staff to collect all their learning together for assessment, rather than the potential for unfinished pieces of work to be left lying around in different children's homes.

NVQ has been criticised by Chris Payne, (1999), among others, for the potential lack of learning involved in a process described as the collection of evidence, which is then produced in a portfolio for formal assessment. NVQ has been criticised as a technical process by which candidates achieve awards by demonstrating competence in the specified standards. The language used smacks of the new managerialism and it is possible to collect evidence of, for example, prior learning, without learning anything new. The experience in Northborough suggests a more dynamic collective learning process, which increases the potential for residential child care workers to become more effective in working with the young people they look after.

More than 50 per cent of the original cohort achieved the award in the target period January to August 1993. A total of 45 residential workers were successful with 18 out of 20 workers achieving the award in one of the authorities. Other factors contributed to this high success rate:

- A policy of regular supervision was introduced into the authority. Workers were expected to receive individual supervision once every three weeks.
- Personal Development Profiles recommended by Warner, (1992), became the norm for every worker and were monitored through supervision.
- Each children's home had a staff meeting every two weeks. It became part of the culture of residential child care in this authority that both supervision and team meetings occurred on a regular basis.

Simultaneously all children's homes managers were given parallel training in 'Supervisory Management' with an award provided by the Open College. This ensured that managers were developing their skills and knowledge at the same time as the wider residential child care workforce. The NVQ award became a desirable factor in enabling successful candidates to apply for promotion to supervisory posts when vacancies occurred.

The New Award in One Unitary Authority, Northtown

Northtown is one of the unitary authorities which replaced Northborough after local government reorganisation. It maintains a commitment to qualifying residential child care staff using NVQ. There are currently five children's homes in Northtown. The majority of staff are involved in preparing for NVQ level 3 awards.

The model of the weekly guided learning workshop has been retained. The average time spent completing the awards is a year, though the authority remains committed to the original pilot period of eight months. Emphasis is placed on the successful achievement of an award rather than allowing individuals to complete in their own time frame in an authority committed to a fully qualified residential child care workforce. There is a clear timescale for completing work and gaining the award.

Pathfinding: A Beacon of Best Practice

Northtown is committed to the creation of a qualified competent residential child care workforce. Completion rates are high by comparison with my own experience of a similar training programme for residential child care workers, where only 20 per cent of those who started successfully completed an award. Low completion rates are unlikely to be attractive to employers or to the political members of local authorities who make the decisions about investing in training the staff they employ. High completion rates reflect the credibility and relevance of a training programme among residential child care workers. They reflect the time and energy which workers are willing to invest in further developing themselves as competent residential child care workers. They also reflect the level of resources which employers are willing to invest in developing their staff to enable them to be more effective workers.

Northtown is committed to enabling the young people they look after to achieve NVQ level 2. Significant numbers of ex-service users with a breadth and depth of experience of residential care are training to become the care workers of the future in residential child care and day care with people with learning difficulties.

There is a clear mechanism for continuing personal and professional development. For example, a number of workers are currently embarking on level 4 awards. The status and credibility of NVQ is further enhanced by the links with a local university. This provides local arrangements for level 4 NVQ to be integrated into the Diploma in Social Work. Additional traditional academic units combine with the NVQ award to make up level one of the Diploma.

Why have NVQ awards relevant to residential child care practice only recently become available? One significant factor was the essentially permissive position taken by a conservative government, post 1991, which was reflected in policy from the DoH, and the paucity of funding sufficient to create changes in investment in NVQ, and ambivalence by CCETSW arising from fears about de-professionalisation. Changes in policy have led to funding becoming available to local authorities to meet the goal of achieving a fully qualified workforce for residential child care by 2001/2. Residential child care workers possessing the child care award at level 3 will be entitled to registration by the General Social Care Council. These developments will be addressed in more detail later in the chapter.

Evidence from the case study and the work of Sandy de Silva, which follows this chapter, highlights a number of factors which are important for creating a successful learning environment in which residential child care workers can acquire relevant training and awards like NVQ. This is not to suggest that there is a blueprint which can be applied in any situation, but that there are a number of factors, taken together with local conditions, which combine to create the potential for success. It is important to emphasise the local level as the essential point of organisation, in order to reflect the particular requirements of workers to demonstrate their competence in their normal places of work, (Crimmens and Vaughan, 1992). Organisation needs to reflect local conditions but there are a number of important factors, which combine together to provide successful outcomes.

The case for advocating that training is best delivered to residential child care workers as a working group and in their normal place of work is based on recognised expertise, (Kahan, 1994), and research evidence, (Whitaker et al., 1998, Sinclair and Gibbs, 1996a). I have argued elsewhere, (Crimmens, 1997), that competent working groups of residential child care workers make effective child care units. The group care nature of residential child care needs to be recognised at all times in designing training.

Consistent and competent supervision is a key determinant in ensuring high completion rates. Successful organisations create clear policy and practice procedures for support and supervision. They invest simultaneously in the development of supervisory staff as an integral and essential element in a successful NVQ strategy.

Residential child care workers must be allowed time to learn, and reflect on their experiences. They have to gather together information on the development of their professional values, skills and knowledge. Residential child care will never be an easy task. Shift patterns and unsocial hours already create pressure and stress for workers. Additional staff may be required to ensure that care workers preparing for an award are freed up from normal rota patterns to participate in training, record their evidence, and reflect on their progress with supervisors and mentors. Residential child care workers cannot be expected to complete any NVQ award successfully if they attempt to fit their training into the already unsocial demands of shift working which includes working at weekends and sleeping in overnight.

Residential child care workers need to take some responsibility for their own personal and professional development. Two major factors hinder successful outcomes in training and development. The first is the pragmatic and anti-intellectual position taken by some workers. Experience can be taken for granted as the key to competent practice and 'knowing' the job, leading to an inherent resistance to any type of training. The other factor is the perception that training is the employer's sole responsibility. Professional development requires a personal investment by any worker wanting to achieve an award. This has to include the use of personal time to study and record. Personal investment must be part of a balance reached through negotiation and matched by investment by the employer as indicated above.

Residential child care staff need to know how they will be rewarded as workers successfully completing NVQ. Many recognise that the acquisition of new skills and the understanding of different ideas will enable them to become better practitioners. They also need the recognition, which goes with higher levels of training and accreditation to be reflected in the opportunities available for career advancement. Some employers have recognised NVQs as additional relevant qualifications leading to higher salaries and promotion. Further research is required to identify how far qualification levels and the increased status and salaries, which should follow, make residential child care a more attractive proposition and reduce loss of experienced and qualified staff to other areas like field social work.

The Government Expects...'Modernising Social Services: A New Agenda'

This illustration of NVQ development suggests that, in some local authorities, consistent efforts are being made to provide relevant training to residential child care workers.

The White Paper *Modernising Social Services*, (Department of Health, 1998b), provides a much wider context for locating developments in training. The government makes a commitment in the White Paper to raise standards across the board in social care. The key mechanisms for raising standards are:

- The General Social Care Council (GSCC).
- A national training strategy.

These mechanisms are new. The idea of a national training strategy for social care is unique in the long and troubled debate about qualifications and training. There appears to be a commitment to a competent and confident workforce, to be supported by:

- *Clear definition of social care roles by employers.*
- *Wider objectives related to service objectives.*
- *Better supervision and management.*
- *Improved education and training which is geared to the new agenda.*
- *A new status for social care which fits the work they do.*

(DoH, 1998b, para 5.5 p85)

It is possible to identify a qualitative difference from previous official commitments. The White Paper can be seen to represent the most radical shake-up in the Personal Social Services since Seebohm in 1970. For our current purposes, this is the first time that a national training strategy and institutional changes to make the strategy work consistently across the country have underpinned major policy changes in this area. The National Training Organisation, (NTO), which is strategically responsible for training and development of all staff working in the personal social services, will:

- *Identify training needs and ensure that they are met.*
- *Carry out workforce analysis.*
- *Maintain the occupational standards.*

(DoH, 1998b p94)

There is a clear and explicit commitment for the first time to provide a basic qualification for residential child care workers at level 3 NVQ. This award will be a prerequisite for registration in the professional register maintained by the GSCC, and the government expects to register residential child care staff as well as those who already hold a recognised professional qualification in social work, (para 5.22). While the professional register is only one element of the responsibilities of the GSCC, it is significant in the potential it has for enhancing the status of residential childcare workers and for sustaining a longer term commitment to their training and development. For a more detailed discussion of the role of the GSCC, readers are invited to look at the earlier chapter by David Lane.

There are indications of a radical new policy agenda, which articulates clear and specific objectives for all social care and social work activities to be achieved by systematic processes of modernisation. The question is whether current developments in training address the critical findings of government sponsored research, which was completed some years ago. The pace of recent change has been rapid, and most of the new initiatives appeared in the public domain between September and November 1998, when the White Paper was published.

Some of the changes with respect to training and the importance of NVQ were evident in the allocation of funds through the Training Support Programme. The Local Authority Circular, LAC(98)1 which was issued in January 1998 and more importantly, *Quality Protects*, (September 1998), and the government's response to the *Children's Safeguards Review*, (November 1998), provide clear and explicit commitments which are clarified in the White Paper. The official launch of the DoH sponsored research summarised in *Caring for Children away from Home; Messages from Research*, (DoH, 1998), demonstrated how far government policy was being influenced by the findings of research.

The changes are intended to confront the question of how social care should be delivered to different user groups as part of a reconstruction of the personal social services. In line with the *Messages from Research*, (DoH, 1998), this suggests that the government has affirmed a commitment to training as a mechanism, which underpins wider policy goals in the personal social services. It is worth reflecting on some of these changes to assess how far they represent substantial change with respect to residential child care.

Government recognises that an appropriately skilled, trained and qualified workforce needs to be available to provide quality services, which meet explicit standards. There is a commitment to continuing funding for training 'given the importance of ensuring that residential child care staff are qualified to do the work expected of them', (LAC(99)10 ANNEX 6 p22). For example, £2.5 million is committed to training to NVQ level 3 for 1999/2000 with an increase to £3 million for the following two years. There is a specific attempt to link the findings of research with further developments in residential child care. There is an explicit acknowledgement of the relevance of research by both Whittaker et al., (1998), and Brown et al., (1998), who examined the group care nature of residential child care. The Department of Health emphasises:

> *the value of in-service training involving the whole staff group, geared at ensuring that the team work to common objectives, common methods and in so doing forge a positive culture.*

by recommending that training is taken into children's homes where staff work as an alternative to sending staff on the more traditional offsite courses. In this way residential child care training is directed towards meeting the specified objectives of each and every children's home, (LAC (99) 10. ANNEX 6 p23).

And Now for Something Completely Different?

It is difficult to be certain that the changes indicated in the White Paper will all be achieved and how far any changes can be sustained over time. A more optimistic analysis suggests that there are good indications of serious intent in government policy but further and more consistent evidence is needed that some of these changes will be sustained over the long term and will produce a better future for all involved with residential child care. The Department of Health needs for example to publish information on progress being made in relation to numbers of residential workers achieving the NVQ award and how far best practice is becoming part of the national landscape. *The Quality Protects Newsletter*, of which there have been two editions at the time of writing, provides one example of attempts which are being made to keep people appraised of progress.

New policy suggests a future in which the aims and objectives of residential child care, along with other social care tasks, are likely to be clear and explicit within a national framework. It may be over optimistic to suggest that this will produce a New Jerusalem but it may be realistic to acknowledge the dawning of a new era. The 'Third Way' can provide services, which are not dependent on large institutions described by Hyland (1993), as 'yesterday's answers'. Tomorrow's services cannot be dominated by familial ideology, residues of the Poor Law and service providers who are constantly strapped for cash. The new era must be characterised by a commitment to meeting the needs of children and young people as citizens of the 21st century entitled to quality services when their families cannot or will not continue to look after them. The corporate parent of government rhetoric must provide good enough parenting which meets the standards specifically laid down in every official document from *Standards for Residential Child Care Services*, (DofH, 1994), to *Quality Protects*. The White Paper succinctly states the challenge for the new millennium:

> *the provision of social care which allows individuals to live their own lives and offers practical help based on research and other evidence of what works and free of unnecessary ideological influence.*

> (DoH, 1998b, para 5.15 p88)

A Strong Sense of Vision

The positive potential of NVQ 3 as a basic qualification has been examined above. The standards by which competence is evaluated are relevant to practice, having been systematically derived from the practice experience of what residential child care workers actually do. But NVQ is only a beginning and will never provide the sufficiently comprehensive approach implied in government policy. It is a sound foundation on which to build for the future. Recent research evidence, cited above, and earlier observations by Warner, (1992), suggest that the Dip.SW has not provided an appropriate structure or content for the professional level of qualification for the 30 per cent of all residential child care staff which Utting conservatively recommended should be professionally qualified. A radical shift away from the conventions of the past 25 years are required which secures the kind of future suggested by contemporary policy. What residential child care needs in this area is a separate and specific training, (Wagner, 1998, foreword to residential forum).

One way of developing this qualification is to examine the practices adopted by different European neighbours to provide services for children and young people living away from home. Warner recommended that the European model should be examined further 'in devising a professional qualification that fits residential child care', (para 7.30 p125). His inquiry commissioned research into the European tradition of the 'pedagogue' (Madge, 1994). Lane (1994) followed this recommendation though at the time he was not committed to a new and completely separate qualification. More recently this author has explored these arguments, (Crimmens 1998). Most importantly, recommendations for a new residential child care qualification for an occupational group to be known as 'social educators' was recommended by Roger Kent, (1997), as the future basis of residential child care in Scotland. Utting was strangely silent on the issue having already pledged his allegiance to the Dip.SW.

The response by CCETSW (1992) to the The Expert Group appears to have peremptorily rejected the Warner recommendation of moving away from Dip.SW as the recognised professional qualification or engaging with anything 'European'. This is hardly surprising given the political climate at the time, which was hostile and antagonistic to the possibility of further polluting national integrity with anything which culturally or politically resembled Europe. The climate of opinion has changed and the current government is expressly committed to further European-style developments. The time is therefore ripe for serious consideration of what is offered by social pedagogues or 'educateurs' which:

- Separates social care from social work and provide a professional integrity based on a common task and a common purpose.
- Fragments boundaries between traditional occupational groups to provide a new occupational grouping capable of meeting the challenges and expectations of modernised social care.
- Provides a vision, which starts to define common purpose in service provision to different user groups.
- Has a defined knowledge base, which could be incorporated into English academic disciplines.

Space does not allow for systematic evaluation of the potential value of social pedagogy. The further development of an occupational group, whose task is to focus on the problems of everyday living encountered by groups like young people living in children's homes, would appear to be consistent with the tasks defined in *Modernising Social Services*.

This could mark the 'golden opportunity' suggested by the residential forum for the development of a new residential child care profession in England. It is an opportune moment for the systematic investigation of curricula for the training of social pedagogues in the Netherlands and the orthopedagogues in Flanders. This would provide a start to defining a new tradition of social education based on the culture and experiences of providing residential childcare in the UK. According to the Residential Forum, a key issue is the creation of a common identity for residential child care workers, which is reflected in professional education and training.

The creation of a professional group of social educators working with a sense of common purpose towards agreed aims and objectives should create higher status and increased levels of morale and job satisfaction. This will be reflected in maintaining experienced, skilled and qualified staff working in residential child care. Stability does not in itself guarantee better quality of care and life experience for the young people who are looked after. Further research needs to be carried out to identify what part is played by better qualified staff in the process of producing quality residential child care to agreed national standards. This will only be possible if the cycle of the employment of untrained and unqualified staff in residential child care is conclusively broken. Only when the majority of residential child care staff are trained and qualified to a minimum standard will it become possible to identify the unique contribution provided by training.

CHAPTER 7

A Residential Staff Training Strategy in Liverpool

Sandy de Silva

Introduction

The well-publicised crisis in the residential care of children has highlighted huge problems in the organisation and delivery of such care. The difficulties of organising a residential care service have been given unprecedented prominence in professional debate. The most recent comprehensive survey of residential care for children was undertaken in the wake of abuse in Leicestershire homes, following the conviction of Frank Beck. The Warner Report, (1992), identified that 64 per cent of children living in local authority children's homes can be described as emotionally or physically abused and about one third are estimated to have been sexually abused. This pattern is apparent in the case of children looked after in Liverpool's homes.

The psychological damage to them and the imprints on their emotional and behavioural functioning may be such that many are unable to respond to high quality physical and emotional care. Some children looked after by Liverpool have lengthy care careers with moves and disruptions going back to their early childhood

Liverpool has 10 children's homes ranging in size from 6 to 12 places per unit. The functions of each unit varies, with some acting mainly to receive children admitted in crisis and others offering long-term care, secure accommodation or help to young people leaving care. There is one respite unit for children with a disability.

The Utting Report, (1991), identified training for residential workers as a crucial issue in the quality of care offered to children, but currently 60 per cent of Liverpool's residential staff do not hold a relevant qualification, including 30 per cent of all unit managers. Liverpool is not unique in this respect; the Warner Report confirmed such lack of qualifications as the norm. The current situation is highlighted in the previous chapter:

> *The overall picture we see is a children's homes' workforce trying to cope with difficult and complex tasks for which most have not been trained and for whom there are no plans to provide adequate training in the foreseeable future.*

> (Warner, 1992, para7.9, p116)

The Report also recommends work-based training for residential social workers as ensuring that learning is transferred back into the workplace. As Perlin and Schooler, (1978), state:

> *Work problems are intertwined with the social structure and organisation of the work place, and this requires collective rather than individual solutions.*

The Liverpool residential training strategy is grounded in the National Occupational Child Care standards and a systematic analysis of the role and function of residential social workers. This strategy is made up of a core curriculum of the underpinning knowledge skills and values for the NVQ level 3–4 .

Figure 1   *Core Curriculum linked to National Occupation Standards and the LAC Dimension*

LAC assessment and action documentation
Creating a protective environment
Communicating with children
Keyworking strategies
Health and selfcare
Child development
Identity
Trauma and attachment
Child protection procedures and its aftermath
The psychological impact of abuse
Self harm
Managing anger
Advocacy
Creating a stimulating educational environment
Family and social relationships
Building self esteem
Sexual health and HIV
First aid
Basic food hygiene
Integrating race, culture, language and religion into child care
Alcohol and drug abuse
Engaging with the youth service

One of the benefits of this strategy is that residential workers have to demonstrate a level of competence in the workplace evidenced by the completion of an NVQ portfolio. An increased competence in multi-disciplinary work is essential and therefore the strategy embraces inputs from education and health service professionals. As the 'trainer', my role within the strategy is to design, plan and evaluate the unit-based training and drive any policy initiatives relating to children in residential care. I am also responsible for advising and supporting both candidates undertaking the NVQ, and their assessors. The Directorate of Social Services has shown a strong commitment to the development of training for residential child care staff. In September 1998 Liverpool embarked upon a five-year strategy, which aims to ensure a fully qualified workforce in its residential establishments. Priority is being given to unqualified managers and deputy managers but all workers will be undertaking NVQ level 4 in either 'care' or 'community justice'.

Liverpool has a residential commissioning training group chaired by the residential divisional manager, which provides cover for staff, employs a full time NVQ residential co-ordinator, and holds a multi-agency forum where practice issues can be addressed.

Few of Liverpool's children's homes had statements of purpose but those that did tended to either be too general or out of date. Most homes had not developed any strategies to meet the needs of traumatised girls, ethnic minorities and care leavers. The behavioural control of adolescents was a major issue. In terms of the curriculum it is important that officers in charge of each home identify which of the modules would best meet the needs of the service provided by the home and the training requirements of the staff. Each children's home is entitled to six days training per year, plus additional training around restraint and control. The training is jointly evaluated with the officer in charge of each home in terms of an action plan that is discussed at the next training day and fed back to the commissioning group. However, at present, mechanisms for monitoring and evaluating unit-based training are not sufficiently connected to the organisational structure so that outcomes can be evaluated across the department.

Unit-based Training

The benefits of this type of training are that the whole staff group learns together and a culture of learning is created. The trainer can develop child care principles that are owned by the staff unit. It brings in issues of team building, opens up communication and creates opportunities for openness and sharing of feelings.

One of the aims of the training is to ensure that the home has a clear purpose and function and all the staff are made aware of this. Secondly, an atmosphere of mutual trust and co-operative working must be promoted. I do this by designing exercises where all members of the staff group are dependent on each other to complete the set tasks.

The training experience is presented as a process of learning together as a group in which the learning will be transferred back into practice in the workplace. The production of an action plan at the end of a training session is a key task, and it is expected that such a plan is further discussed at subsequent staff meetings. In this way, training can be a bridge between policy and practice, each informing the development of the other.

Residential workers are an integral part of the process of assessing the needs of the children in their care. The training equips them to complete the LAC Assessment and Action documents by providing residential workers with a range of techniques to work directly with children (e.g. an exercise that focuses on attachment and loss enables the worker to address these issues in the assessment process and feel more confident in participating in the review process). The training not only focuses on the disturbed behaviour of the child but underlying emotional and psychological trauma and how best to help these children recover from these experiences.

As a trainer, I am committed to a model in which practice and theory inform each other and this is what NVQ practice-based learning sets out to achieve in residential child care. In the training session, theoretical and conceptual knowledge is covered in the morning, while the afternoon is given over to more reflective practice, where staff can talk about case studies and explore the relationship between theory and practice. Case scenarios are discussed to identify risk factors in triggering past trauma experiences (for an example of the range of issues covered see Figure 2). As Ziegler, (1994), states, the effectiveness of treating traumatised children is directly related to the detail of interactions between adults and the children they look after. Every contact between a residential worker and a child, whilst a very small part of the puzzle, becomes critical to the healing process.

Childhood trauma, particularly if repeated and chronic, has a heavy developmental, physiological, emotional, social and behavioural impact. The case scenarios we use include examples of deliberate self-harm, inappropriate sexual behaviour, aggression, bullying, violence and intimacy avoidance. The Warner Report highlighted the two levels of need for improving residential care services as therapeutic help for children suffering from emotional and psychological problems and support for traumatised staff caring for them (see, for example, Chapter 8, p143). In my training I explain that traumatised children avoid closeness, which leads to feelings of vulnerability, and I seek to empower the carers to re-integrate the children's traumatic experiences in order that they can manage difficult behaviours and support the child in the placement. Staff also need the opportunity to reflect on their own emotions. I encouraged one of the staff to keep a reflective log as part of her NVQ portfolio which helped her to recognise the child's post-traumatic triggers and develop her own ability to deal with this. I have seen her become more confident in caring for this young person including advocating on the child's behalf. In the training I also use the Professional Accommodation Syndrome Theory (Morrison, 1996), to help staff to explore unhealthy processes in the unit. I have found that most of the staff feel undervalued and professionally abandoned. They sometimes comment that talking about the impact on them of their work can be seen as a sign of weakness and a lack of professionalism. The training explores ways of managing staff stress and the critical role of supervision, while recognising

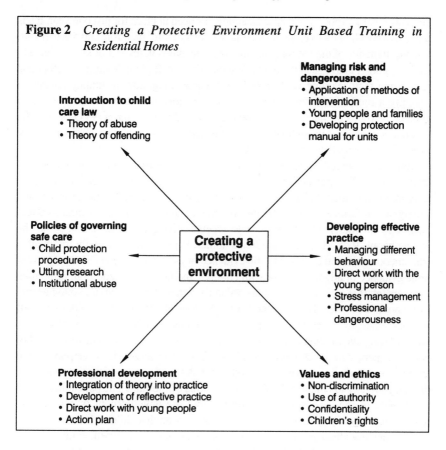

Figure 2 *Creating a Protective Environment Unit Based Training in Residential Homes*

Managing risk and dangerousness
- Application of methods of intervention
- Young people and families
- Developing protection manual for units

Introduction to child care law
- Theory of abuse
- Theory of offending

Policies of governing safe care
- Child protection procedures
- Utting research
- Institutional abuse

Creating a protective environment

Developing effective practice
- Managing different behaviour
- Direct work with the young person
- Stress management
- Professional dangerousness

Professional development
- Integration of theory into practice
- Development of reflective practice
- Direct work with young people
- Action plan

Values and ethics
- Non-discrimination
- Use of authority
- Confidentiality
- Children's rights

that supervision is not always available on a regular basis. We explore strategies for a unified approach to managing self-harm; the unresolvable nature of this issue is openly acknowledged and creative solutions arise. In consequence of this, staff are empowered to cope with an adolescent who is likely to deliberately self-harm.

Senior managers have a major role in addressing practice issues that come up in training. These issues are also fed to a multi-agency steering group, which includes representatives from health, education and social services and which looks at the joint commissioning of services for looked after children.

It has been difficult to train residential workers, who have undertaken training in an organisational environment that is characterised by rapid and continuous change, occupational insecurity, and a preoccupation with survival at both institutional and personal levels. Despite this there has been a thirst for knowledge and an openness to share and reflect on practice. Anxiety and stress are openly acknowledged and seen as normal in an environment where problems and mistakes are viewed as opportunities for learning. Liverpool's unit based training has been in place for just one year. It has acted as a bench mark to equip residential workers to fulfil their role and has met with the requirements of the national occupational standards in respect of knowledge and understanding. I have seen the benefits of the whole staff group learning together and translating their learning back into the work place, e.g. after a training course on creating a protective environment the staff developed an intimate care policy to protect the rights of the children in the home. The development of NVQs across the residential sector has meant that staff can gain a qualification and professional recognition for the work that they are doing.

What has emerged is the lack of clarity around the purpose and function of each home, and staff responsibilities with respect to the children they look after, where stresses on untrained staff are occasioned by increased numbers of inappropriate and emergency referrals. Despite the introduction of the *Looked After Children* documents, residential workers continue to receive inadequate information about the young people they admit into children's homes. Paperwork was usually fragmented and uncoordinated and showed little evidence of joint assessments. There was very little evidence of advocacy work with children and families. In addition, residential workers felt that their views were not valued and their concerns about young people were not taken seriously. The need for psychological support for children and staff has also emerged and as a result a jointly funded post from health and social services of a clinical psychologist has been created. This post is intended to provide psychological expertise to the children's residential child care service for Liverpool. It will provide a consultancy service and support for staff and an input into the residential training strategy to enhance the therapeutic skills of the staff. The psychologist will contribute to the assessment of children and the development of therapeutic programmes within residential care. This would mean that children's basic psychological needs, which underpin much of their emotional and behavioural disturbances, could be directly addressed in therapeutic and care management.

Conclusion

I have discovered a group of committed staff who, although many do not have the qualifications, have a wealth of experience in coping with children with complex needs. I am moved by the tenacity and skill of Liverpool's residential staff, and the wisdom and creativity of their interventions with traumatised children despite little support or professional recognition. In the future we need to raise the profile of residential workers nationally in order that their views are valued alongside other professionals involved in child care. In Liverpool we intend to involve care leavers in the planning and evaluation of residential child care training. We will develop more sophisticated evaluation mechanisms, which are linked to the organisational structures. For the future, we are planning to train residential workers and teachers together to look at the educational needs of looked after children.

SECTION 3

The Voice of the Child

CHAPTER 8

Speaking for Themselves: Two Care Leavers' Experiences of Residential Care

Interviewed by Ann Wheal

Answers and Comments by 'Ronnie'.

'Ronnie' is a teenager who prefers not to have his real name mentioned.

Were you given information that you could read and understand about your rights? Please give details
LAs tend to be selective about the information children receive, a bit like Serbian TV, LAs do not like children knowing certain information. For instance – Who Cares? Who knows? I never saw copies in the home I was in, this magazine was never to be seen. Information about advocacy groups such as Voice for the Child in Care (VCC). I never had a clue they existed for years.

However our children's home made sure that there were posters for Childline, only problem being there was limited access to the phone. There was also really nicely laid out and clear information on the numerous stages of the complaints procedure, no small print to let you know how long the stages take though.

What were the staff in the home like?
I always met three types of staff:

1. The ones who treated us like 'inmates'.
2. The ones who felt guilt, and could see what was wrong, but felt that to do something or say something would either risk their job or wouldn't make a difference anyway.

101

3. The ones who tried their utmost to look after us but were constantly fighting a system that stood against them.

The manager in my home went off sick for months but for the time I did know her she seemed to care and tried to change things. In her absence my local authority replaced her with someone from the department with orders to save money.

How were you treated when you arrived?
When I arrived I was treated like a textbook. I was assigned my allocated room, my allocated keyworker, my weekly 'care plan' and of course a copy of the rules. In addition to this I was treated as if I was a 'good boy' unlike all the rest, until I put a foot wrong and then I was an inmate just like the rest of them.

How were you treated whilst you were there?
Whilst I was there the 'textbook' became visible one minute and invisible the next, depending on the circumstances. The staff all made us feel as if we were held over a barrel and that if we did not follow their rules we would not get anything.

There was also an emotional abuse that happened whereby myself and other children were taught that we were not worth what we are given, for instance if you're in a review the staff and social services constantly remind you of the amount of money that is spent on your 'case'. If you asked for a grant for clothes you would be taunted about how much money you receive through the local authority, reminded of your parents obligation to provide for you and if you did not give up by then you're either refused or given a substantially reduced grant and made to feel guilty for ever asking, thus the chances of you asking again become remote.

My children's 'home' had a policy whereby criminal damage would not be tolerated. As you are probably aware most children who come in to 'care' are upset in one way or another. This is often expressed as anger. The corporate parent has not yet accepted this. In my 'home' if you were to get angry and break a plate, cup, saucer, wardrobe etc. you would not have help to discover why you felt that way, you would not be referred to counselling, you would not be supported to find other ways of expressing your anger. No, none of that, the corporate parent considers their furniture over their children. So in the 'home' I was in they would call the police and have you arrested for criminal damage, the supposed idea being that after six to eight hours in a police cell you would be cured of your 'disruptive behaviour'.

How were you treated when you left?
When I left the residential unit it was in difficult circumstances. The children's home was closed down, and us residents were rounded up, given a few hours notice of the closure and summoned to attend emergency reviews to discuss our placements. I was told by my LA that they had no residential or foster placements and that I would be going to bed and breakfast accommodation. I stated that I did not wish to go as I have never lived on my own before and that

Christmas was in two weeks time, I was told that you either go to B&B or return to live with your dad 100 miles away. I could not do this as we hated each other. For the duration of Christmas I was in a scummy B&B in East London with £40 a week to live on.

How did other people who visited the home treat you?
People who visited the home such as social workers walked past us and went into the office and chatted to the staff. If people needed information on our 'case' they did not ask us, they either asked staff or looked into our file to see how we were labelled.

Were your wishes, feelings and opinions taken seriously?
My wishes, feelings and opinions were requested, just as it requires in the Children Act 1989, however this was treated as a formality and I was not listened to. In my opinion the reason that this happens is that LA care is now a business with targets and expectations that need to be audited and so savings are made wherever they can.

Why is there no such thing anymore as social workers who champion the needs of the child. Social workers are merely messengers. With messages from managers with a duty to save money and the social workers end up with a role of taking stick from children and therefore treat children in turn with no respect.

What were the building and environment in which you lived like?
There were several residential placements in which I lived. I found them generally to be well looked after, however there was always a feeling of, not being my 'home', of being in a 'unit'. The state of the buildings reflected this, most of the rooms had bookcases and cabinets, however there were no books or ornaments. You could say this was because people felt we would break them. I am sure this played a part, however I felt it was always as if these 'homes' had no identity, no character or personality. It was always felt as if everything around you was shatterproof and inde-structible. A feeling that however much you banged and banged on the walls there would be no response. A feeling reflected in the system as a whole.

Did you know of and understand the complaints procedure?
The complaints system was a 'complicated joke'. The system allowed young people to feel as if there was a voice for them when things were not right. In my view the problems that occurred were that so many people had so many problems that even-tually LAs tried to take complaints seriously but through the sheer weight of complaints they could not acknowledge the vast amount of problems that existed.

This is echoed by the fact that when I placed a four page complaint into the hands of my LA they took a year to respond to what they call 'Stage 1'. I then placed a further complaint in under 'Stage 2' and to this day, three years later I still have no reply, and I'm still chasing it up but how long do you go on for?

How did other young people in the home behave and how were they treated?
When I first came to the 'home' the other young people were trying to make the most of what they had and had given up fighting a system that they felt they could not win against. I often think of posters of neglected children being portrayed as children huddled in a corner in fear. Most children I met were not quiet and they were not the little girl in the corner. These were children who had been silenced by a system and were shouting to be heard with nobody who cared or could do anything about their plight. These were children who were hurt inside and were asking for help, be it through throwing plates or breaking their wardrobe.

The young people I lived with were treated as inmates and were taught by staff that they were not valuable, and the viscious circle continued with us all being arrested and branded 'trouble'.

What help did you get with leaving care?
I was lucky, I was placed in a 16 plus project run really well by Barnardos, most children in our LA only get a 'six week independence training course' consisting of cooking lessons for two hours one evening a week for six weeks in total. Then its congratulations, you're independent now. The project I was in consisted of sharing flats with our own rooms and learning to cook, clean, budget, etc. The project taught me good skills and helped me as much as they could and the staff were generally excellent.

I was disappointed with my LA as the project was having problems with my social services department, as they were trying to reduce my funding. My LA, when I moved in, agreed with the Barnardos requirement of a package of assistance during my time at 16 plus. One of the requirements was a £1000 grant for setting up a flat when I left. When I left my LA went back on its 'word' and only granted me £300.

The Whole Thing! Experiences and Views on Residential Care by Maggie Lane

I have lived in both types of care, foster and residential, one foster placement and five residential units: a semi secure unit, a residential school, a large children's home, an average sized children's home and a pre-independence unit.

The foster placement and the first three units were short stay homes. So rather than confuse the issue I will concentrate on the average sized children's home in which I lived for three years, I would also like to concentrate a little on the pre-independence unit in which I lived for six months as I believe leaving care is a very important part of care.

How the staff in the home including the manager treated me
The staff were quite friendly and reasonably understanding, however with a home so big there was too many of them, and it was impossible to get close to one of them

even though we had key workers assigned to us. They could be very patronising at times and were rather strict. The manager or officer in charge as they were then called was a hands-on guy, and there was a lot worse than him in the other homes.

The complaints I would have on the staff side was that there wasn't any from ethnic minorities which I felt was particularly unfair to the black residents and they were very set in their ways on how to do things.

How I was treated when I arrived
I was treated very well. I was fed, informed of the basic rules and introduced to the other residents. This is a very scary experience for any child and at first I felt like an alien in someone else's home but after a week or so of caution, the other residents invited me into their group and I have to say made me feel more at home than the staff did by accepting me. After all it was their home and not the staff's.

How I was treated whilst I was there
I was treated very well most of the time when I was there, but there were a lot of rules and regulations to follow. After a couple of months I started seeing it as my home, and thankfully we got sofas instead of the chairs. I had some very good times there, and it was whilst in this home I had my first holiday. I began to get treated differently though when I became interested in young people's rights, especially by the manager. The staff approached me more so with caution than openness. I found it hard adjusting to losing people also, people who were like my brothers and sisters for years would move on and as they were never encouraged to come back, they never did.

I had been in the home two and a half years when the local authority decided to turn it into a short stay home. No consultation with the residents just a decision being made. It was decided that I could stay on until it was time for me to leave as I had lived there so long, but I found it very hard to adjust. I was in my last year at school and getting ready to take exams, whilst all the while there was disruption around me as new people came in (mostly much younger than me), and old people went out within six months. I was very unhappy as I felt that this wasn't my home anymore. So a week before my sixteenth birthday the staff asked me if I wanted to move into the pre-independence unit next door and I jumped at the chance.

How I was treated when I left
Just like those who had gone before me, the children's home where I had spent my teens, was now a no-man's land. They didn't invite me back nor did they come to visit me, even though I only lived next door to them. I must admit this was very hurtful. I saw a couple of the youngsters who I had lived with a couple of times but the people changed so quickly, there wasn't much point trying to keep in touch.

The pre-independence unit was worse on the inside than the children's home. The hallway was tiny, the lounge was very small and you couldn't swing a cat in the kitchen, the furniture was shabby and falling apart and the walls were nicotine stained. The only good thing about it was that you were allowed to have a black and white television in your room, a front door key and there were very few rules.

The first week I was there I got taken shopping and shown how to fill in benefit forms and that was my training complete. The officer in charge was trying it on (sexually) all the time with the young women, but we wasn't believed – until he jumped on a member of staff and got suspended. A couple of the young women were thought to be prostitutes and our one male resident basically sat outside all day eating magic mushrooms as he wasn't allowed in the unit as he had to look for work.

The information that I was given, and could read and understand about my rights
When I first went into the home, I was given a white piece of A4 paper which had the rules and regulations written on it in bold print. There wasn't one right written on it; when I asked about this I was told to ask my key worker about my rights.

How other people who visited the home treated me e.g. social workers
I had fourteen different social workers whilst I was in care and there was only one of these, who treated me both as an equal and an individual and I really respected her for that. She would take me out of the unit so I could speak my mind without fear of retribution from the staff or the other young people. Claire often took me back to my home town, and although I didn't understand it at the time, I now know that she was trying to keep me in touch with my roots. This proved very valuable in my later life and I am very grateful to her for that, as she is one of the few people in my life who has helped me to have a positive outcome.

The others patronised me or just didn't seem to have a clue how to treat me. They never took me out of the unit to talk over my concerns just into the home library, if not there into the dining room. They went behind my back, sided with staff and never even told me about what was happening in my home town, let alone take me back there for an afternoon. It's a real shame that social workers like Claire are in the minority.

How my wishes, feelings and opinions were taken notice of
They weren't until we set up an In-Care group, and then slowly but surely they began starting to listen to our wishes instead of just hearing us. Unfortunately there still wasn't much real consultation. A prime example of this was the home being changed into a short stay home, another example is that one of the smaller children's homes closed down, all the young people came to us, now they were consulted (talked at) and given fifty pounds each for their troubles, but we weren't even told until the day they arrived. Now I said they were consulted as opposed to listened to, as none of them wanted to leave their home and live in ours. Which resulted in one of the residents trying to set fire to our home. I believe the reason we were not listened to at first is because we didn't know about our rights, and it

was easier for the staff to do what they wanted, and not what we wanted in the short term. Just as for a parent it is easier in the short term to push a child around in a buggy instead of teaching her to walk, well with us it was easier for them to 'do their job' rather than allowing us to think.

The building and environment in which I lived

The children's home I lived in was in Lancashire. I had been moved from Bolton, it was night time when I arrived so I didn't take much notice of the outside of the building. On walking inside the building the first rooms that confronted me were the two offices; in the hallway the walls were white-washed breeze blocks with splatters of brown, the carpet in the hall and on the stairs was brown too. I remember this well as it was the colour I hated the most – the colour of my school uniform. I noticed a notice board on the wall with nothing on it except a couple of drawing pins. Then I walked through the double doors into the lounge, it was pretty much the same as the hall. There was an old TV in the corner. I was informed that the video was only allowed out at the weekend.

The kitchen and dining room were even worse; there were small white plastic tables and four grey plastic chairs around each one and a creaky old dresser in the corner where the crockery and cutlery where kept. The kitchen was almost totally covered in stainless steel and there was a lock on the kitchen door and a roller shutter on the breakfast counter. The room I liked best of all was the pool room: it seemed huge, the walls were the same but the floor was plastic. The only bad thing about the pool room was that all the windows in the room were fitted with security glass and it wasn't there to keep people out.

On the way up to my bedroom I was told I was the thirteenth resident and that I would be in a double room and possibly sharing with number 14 soon, as that was the amount of beds the home had and it wasn't at full capacity yet. I was more than happy to share the room in fact she could keep it, was what I decided on entering. I couldn't believe it, it was the same colour scheme as downstairs. There was one two door wardrobe, two desks and you guessed it two grey plastic chairs, two metal based beds with rubber mattresses and worse still there was a small sink in the corner with a prison mirror screwed to the wall above it.

When I went outside the next day I was horrified when I saw that we were separated from the rest of the estate by a large field, and the square buildings around it that looked like ours. There was a day centre for people with learning difficulties directly right of the home, a pre-independence unit directly left and an old people's home next door to that. You couldn't get more institutionalised than that.

The atmosphere of the home made up for this however as no matter how cold the building looked from the outside or the inside for that matter, the atmosphere was always warm and friendly due mainly to the other residents.

How I think other young people in the home behaved and were treated

When I first went into the children's home there was quite a mix of people; remands, abused young people, children with family problems but after a year or so, child abusers were allowed in which most of the residents were very unhappy about. Everybody, barring the child abusers, behaved reasonably average other than a little bullying going on. The child abusers sought out vulnerable people mainly survivors of abuse and preyed on them and the worst thing was that the staff protected the child abusers and not the victims, it was the victims who had to move out not the child abusers. It was different once the home became short stay, the remands got stopped because of their age, (normally seventeen) but the youngsters who did come in treated the place, young people and the staff like rubbish as they didn't see the place as their home. We were all treated the same – as second class citizens, and it was even worse if we happened to be black or female. Now I can't speak on behalf of the black people who were in the home as I wasn't one but I can tell you I witnessed a lot of ignorance and racism directed towards these young people from other young people sometimes but most of the time from the staff. As for us women, we were treated a little Victorian to say the least. We were not allowed to sit next to boys, our menstrual cycle was put on a chart in full view of every one. We were dished out as I fondly termed them sanitary bricks (maternity pads with thick rubber belts to hold them in place) by male members of staff. We were not allowed money for personal things such as razors, deodorant and shampoo instead we had to use our spending money to get anything decent. We were entitled to shampoo but we used to get a big five litre bottle of cheap stuff between us.

The help I got with leaving care

Very little, there wasn't an after care team in our area, so it was left to your key worker to help you. Mine helped me, by helping me to secure a flat out of town, showing me how to hang a pair of curtains and helping me spend my leaving care grant, nine hundred and fifty pounds, on a double bed, duvet and pillows, two pairs of curtains, an iron and ironing board and a washing up bowl. I later found out that they had kept some of my money but I never got any of it back.

Then there was nothing, no contact, again my former home was a no-man's land – just me aged sixteen in a two bedroom flat, with all my worldly possessions, the only things I did have too much of at that time was being alone and take-aways.

Eventually I got lucky though, if that is what you can call becoming homeless. When I did become homeless I decided to go back to my roots and plead with my family to put me up. I was ping-ponged between my sisters until they both got really fed up of me, and then I had to sleep in my old house where I had spent thirteen years of physical, emotional and sexual abuse at the hands of my mother. So in desperation I rung social services even though I was on a care order, I didn't have a clue who my social worker was by this time, so I spoke to the duty officer. She gave me the direct number for the after care team, even though you are supposed to be referred. I was then given a key worker who came out to meet me and she took me to lunch. To my dismay I noticed that she was heavily pregnant – which meant she'd be leaving too, she did a week later but this turned out to be very fortunate for me, because all the other key workers time was filled. I was very privileged (I was told) to get the manager, I thought he was going to be another patronising social worker but to my amazement he turned out to be sound and one of the most wonderful men I have ever met. 'My surrogate daddy' as I call him, a few other people and my own determination have really turned my life around. He got me a bedsit and then introduced me to a woman who worked for a young person's housing scheme. She got me into a short term house, I met a great bloke, we started a family and got a house together. Now me and Sie are married, we have two beautiful daughters and we both have great jobs. The only dream I haven't fulfilled yet is to become a fully fledged writer but I'm on my way – so watch out for my name though, as I am living proof that dreams can come true.

How we can improve residential care

The first thing that we must do is to demand that all young people are equals whether they live in a family home or are looked after. Educate the public so that they know that young people in residential care are not misfits, and make the tax payers care about the kind of care that children and young people are receiving with their tax money. We need to get rid of institutions altogether and only have satellite (family sized) units.

Above all we need to give young people hope, whether that be through education, employment, training or simply playing football with their friends and we must always remember that the most precious thing any one ever has is their identity and that this is no different for a child or young person. So we must always treat an individual as an individual.

We all may be equals but we are certainly not all the same.

Maggi and 'Ronnie' are founding members of *A National Voice*, a care organisation for young people, run by young people with support from an adult steering group. They aim to be a strong, valued organisation, which helps young people who are or have been looked after. They aim to create opportunities for the views of young people to be heard and to work for an improved care system.

CHAPTER 9

Empowering Children and Young People? The Possibilities and Limitations of the Complaints System

Nick Frost and Lorraine Wallis

Introduction

The search for empowering practice in residential child care has been a long and often painful one (see Frost, Mills and Stein, 1999, Chapter 2, for a detailed historical account). This chapter is a summary of our full report, *Cause for Complaint*, (1998), which outlines some recent research into one aspect of this search – the attempts since the Children Act, 1989, to implement a responsive and effective complaints system for children and young people in residential care.

Representations and Complaints Procedures

The procedure, introduced in the Children Act of 1989, enabled young people in care, as well as their parents, carers or anyone with 'sufficient interest in the child's welfare' to make a complaint or representation about any aspect of the care young people receive.

A young person or adult may make a complaint or representation, orally or in writing, to the Complaints Officer (CO) who is responsible for initiating the investigation. The aim should be to resolve the dissatisfaction as near as possible to the point at which it arose without recourse to a formal investigation. A formal investigation will begin either when the complaint cannot be resolved at this problem-solving stage, the complainant is not happy with attempts to resolve the complaint informally or if the complainant expresses a desire to go straight to the formal stage.

When a formal investigation begins the Complaints Officer will appoint an Investigating Officer to carry out the investigation. They should be a member of the social services department and should not line-manage the situation being investigated. The Complaints Officer will also appoint an Independent Person. Independent Persons are independent of the local authority and work alongside the Investigating Officer to ensure that the complainant receives a fair investigation. The Investigating Officer and Independent Person investigate the complaint and write a report outlining what action, if any, should be taken in response to the complaint. The authority should complete this stage of the process and report back to the complainant within 28 days of receiving the complaint. The complainant should receive formal notification of the local authority's response to the report.

If the complainant is dissatisfied with the result of the investigation, they have 28 days to inform the authority of this. The complaint then moves to the third stage, and the authority has 28 days to establish a panel, which should consist of at least one Independent Person. The panel will consider any further representations made by the complainant, local authority or the Independent Person who considered the original complaint; the panel then makes recommendations. If the complainant is dissatisfied with the outcome of the panel the matter may then be referred on to the Ombudsman.

The regulations also require that the local authority monitors the operation of this system at least every 12 months and that the local authority compiles a report on the findings.

The Theoretical Base: Children's Rights, Children's Welfare

A strong impetus for the development of the complaints procedure came from concerns about young people's need for protection from the state, highlighted by incidents of abuse in the residential care system, (Utting, 1991).

Protection is, however, only one of a range of rights the procedure may be defending. Drawing on Freeman, (1983), 'children's rights' can be in fact be understood as containing four dimensions:

- welfare rights
- protection rights
- social justice rights
- rights against parents

The first three of these are particularly relevant to this study of the complaints procedure and have been helpful in classifying the complaints young people may be making. Let us examine each in turn:

Welfare Rights
Freeman quotes The UN Declaration of Children's Rights as arguing that these are, 'fundamental rights' concerning 'the dignity and worth of the human person', (Freeman, 1983, p40). In our study we have framed these as 'provision rights' relating to young people's complaints about issues such as their material care, the conditions and the environment in which they live.

Protection Rights
Freeman states that this dimension is 'overtly concerned with protection', stressing the vulnerability of children, (Freeman, 1983, p43). In this context we focus on complaints about protection from other residents, staff or carers.

Social Justice Rights

Freeman states that these rights relate to, 'treating children like adults,' relating to, 'any rights currently enjoyed by adults', (Freeman, 1983, p47). We refer to this perspective as 'participation rights' – rights claimed by young people in terms of their right to take part in, or be consulted about issues which impact upon them.

We argue that the complaints procedure needs to be seen as protecting a continuum of rights, including participation, provision, and protection. The complaints procedure also needs to be located within a continuum of practice that is both empowering and participatory.

Methodology

Our research focused on the complaints procedure in five Northern local authorities working with the Children's Society, York, Independent Persons (IP) Project. The project provides IPs to act in both formal stages of the Representations and Complaints Procedure.

Data collected included a statistical analysis of 264 complaints referred to the York Independent Persons Project. Group, but also some individual interviews, were carried out with COs, IPs, carers and young people from a variety of local authority accommodation including foster care, respite care for young people with learning difficulties/disabilities, residential care and secure accommodation, (see Table 1).

More boys were interviewed than girls, 14 females and 30 males, and the interviewees tended to be in the older age bracket, 9.3 per cent under 13, 48.1 per cent, 13–15 years old, 42.6 per cent, 16–18 years old. The sample also included three black and four mixed parentage young people and five young people with learning difficulties.

On ethical grounds it was decided to use questionnaires rather than conduct face-to-face interviews with young people who had recently experienced a formal Complaints Investigation. Questionnaires were felt to be less challenging for these young people, who might have found recounting the events surrounding the investigation stressful. Seven out of 15 questionnaires were returned. However, 13 of the young people in the interview sample, outlined above, had made a formal complaint.

Table 1 Number of interviews with young people and staff/carers

Number interviewed	Residential care	Foster care	Secure accommodation	Respite care*	Total
Young people	34	10	5	5	54
Staff /carers+	21	17	3	1	42

*Five young people with learning difficulties/disabilities
+This includes interviews with five managers of residential units.

Practice Issues

Our research highlighted the extent to which practice surrounding the complaints procedure varied between authorities, within the residential setting and across care settings.

Practice in Different Local Authorities

The following account of the implementation of the complaints procedure in two of the local authorities gives a flavour of the procedure in practice.

In Local Authority A, young people in residential care had generally been informed about the process by staff although some learnt of it through posters. A leaflet had been designed especially for young people. In the children's home visited by the researcher, leaflets were only available on request from staff. There was no advocacy service for young people. Young people interviewed who lived in foster care did not know about the procedure.

An understanding had been agreed between the Complaints Officer and management that attempts would be made to resolve 'grumbles and gripes' informally after a spate of complaints about 'domestic' issues. The emphasis on informally resolving complaints meant staff sometimes filtered complaints by refusing complaints forms. However, none of the young people interviewed in the home felt that access to the procedure was a problem. Six out of nine of the young people were satisfied with the way their complaints were handled informally and felt that staff were always willing to help, the majority describing it as a 'good home'.

None of the staff had recent experience of a young person's complaint being investigated. The complaints procedure was covered in staff's formal induction. Staff felt they had information at hand on the procedure should they need it.

In Local Authority B, young people in residential care were told about the procedure when they first went to live in their unit when they were given a complaints form. In one unit in the authority leaflets on the procedure were usually to be found around the building. In another, they were usually only available from the staff and sometimes available in the unit. Information was also written about the procedure in booklets produced by the individual homes for new residents. The complaints procedure was also discussed at young people's meetings.

Staff felt quite separate from the procedure and did not feel that they were always given the opportunity to be involved in sorting out a complaint once it had been sent to the Complaints Officer. All staff had recent experience of a young person going through the complaints procedure. Some staff felt unable to offer the support they believed young people needed due to lack of knowledge of both the procedure and the progress of the individual complaints. The complaints procedure was included in an induction pack which new staff were taken through on their first days at work by a member of the staff group.

These examples highlight the ways in which practice may vary between authorities. These authorities contrast in terms of the training staff received, how prepared staff felt they were to deal with the procedure and the working relationship between staff and the Complaints Officer. There were also contrasts in how young people in residential care accessed complaints forms and how their awareness of the procedure developed and was reinforced.

Practice within Residential Care

Each home developed its own complaints culture, with particular understandings emerging of the way in which the complaints procedure worked in their unit, as outlined below.

In residential unit X, young people emphasised their positive relationships with staff. The procedure was seen as something only used by a small group of residents who were seen by other residents as difficult. Older residents reasoned they did not use the process because they were more mature and better able to negotiate over issues. Complaints forms had to be requested and were sometimes refused. There was no experience of a formal complaint being investigated by a resident whilst they were living in unit X. Only one resident knew who the Complaints Officer was.

In residential unit Y all residents were given a complaints form when they entered the unit and had to request further forms from staff. Three of the five young people interviewed described how the complaints procedure had become integrated in to the way in which complaints were addressed within their unit. If young people were unhappy with an issue they would write their 'complaint' on to a complaints form and give it to the manager of the home. A number of these complaints were dealt with by the manager without recourse to the formal procedure and to the satisfaction of the complainant. For some residents, using the complaints form in this manner was a way of ensuring that issues were taken seriously or were brought to the attention of the unit manager:

> *Because the manager wasn't there, it was like the weekend when I wrote it so I put it on his desk. He came in the morning, because normally I go to school before he gets here, so he had to look at that and when I come home from school he talked to me about it.*
>
> (young person in residential care)

This is an example of how complaints forms can become integrated into the way complaints are raised and dealt with within residential units and for this young person in a very positive way. A number of current residents had recent experience of the formal procedure and were familiar with the Complaints Officer and his role.

The promotion of the procedure within residential care had been more prominent than in other care settings. It is significant that 93 per cent of young people interviewed in residential care were aware of the procedure but only 20 per cent of young people in foster care were. None of the young people with disabilities we interviewed stated that they knew about the procedure. Young people in secure accommodation appeared more familiar with the internal procedure of dealing with complaints than the formal complaints procedure.

As we might expect, differences in awareness of the procedure are reflected in the use of the procedure. Data from York Project records indicates young people from residential care accounted for 86 per cent of the complaints made by young people in care. Only 9 per cent of these complaints were from young people in foster care, dropping to 3 per cent from young people who had left care, while 2 per cent of complaints were from young people in secure accommodation.

Activating the Complaints Procedure

Our research highlighted two key aspects of the process of activating the complaints procedure which were potential barriers to young people voicing their complaint:

- decisions around what is a valid complaint
- communicating the complaint

Decisions Around What is a Valid Complaint
Utting, (1991), was concerned that the effectiveness of the procedure would be determined by whether young people were able to formulate what has happened to them as a complaint. Our study gave some insight into how easy it is for young people to express their concerns as a complaint and what help they received.

The Children Act requires local authorities to provide publicity on the procedure. However, discretion is given to local authorities to publicise 'as they consider appropriate'. In 1996, Williams and Jordan found only 56.4 per cent of County Councils in England had such publicity and only 12.5 per cent of authorities in Wales.

Four of the five local authorities in the study had a leaflet specifically for complaints about children's services. There was little information about the types of issues they could complain about. Most forms referred to how the young people might be feeling, for example:

> *If you are having difficulties and feel you are being treated unfairly or ill treated, or no one will listen to your point of view, you have a right to complain.*

Only two leaflets actually gave concrete examples of the types of complaints the process could be used for, for example, 'if you have been refused help unfairly'. The emphasis was on complaints relating to issues of protection or provision rather than participation in decision-making.

When young people raised concerns with adults this provided an opportunity for adults to influence young people's perceptions of what was a legitimate complaint. In one residential unit staff tried to ensure that young people were aware of a range of issues they might complain about through discussion at young people's meetings.

> *When we do have young people's meetings one of the tasks is to look at the things around the building that are going wrong. The shower in that toilet might not work, and frequently if it's not done, say 'put in a complaint' – so they understand that it could be about anything, they are aware.*

(residential worker)

The following discussion compares young people's and adults' views of what are appropriate complaints, they are grouped under concerns about participation, provision and protection. These are the three aspects of children's rights which are relevant to our study.

The Children Act guidance is clear that the procedure covers issues of decision-making, 'a complaint may arise as a result of an unwelcome or disputed decision' (para. 10.5). Whilst the young people interviewed sometimes had complaints about the rules and routines of their unit, generally young people and carers felt that it was not appropriate to use the complaints procedure to address these. At one unit a group of young people felt there was no point in using the complaints procedure to try to alter bedtimes which they felt were unrealistic in terms of both the timing and routine they had to adhere to. When asked if they had tried to complain about bedtimes they commented:

> *They have kids meetings on a Monday and every time they say to us, 'what do you want to say in the meeting' and we say, 'we don't want to go to bed at that time, it's not fair' – people aren't tired, people are kicking off.*

(young person in residential care)

Rules are one aspect of living in residential care which young people felt it was not worth complaining about, often reflecting feelings of lack of influence within the home or with social services. Young people could be complaining about their right to participate in making those rules but for young people not used to partici-pation or being heard this did not seem an option.

Complaints about participation could range from decisions about placement moves to issues around the rules and routines of bed times. There is a possibility of the latter being defined as a management issue and returned to the unit to be resolved rather than entering the formal procedure. We are left to ponder whether this response would help to challenge the way rules and routines are decided, or if the formal procedure would be any more effective?

Issues of Provision
Whilst one in five of young people interviewed in residential and foster care had current or past concerns about their social worker, only one had made a formal complaint. One manager noted that young people did not tend to see even lack of continuity of contact with a social worker as a valid reason to complain. He explains:

They (young people) have some serious complaints at meetings, sometimes, but they never register it or even see it as a complaint. Young people don't want a change of social worker, 'I've got a new social worker, why can't I have the old one?' Now that to me is a complaint but no one registers that complaint, you're lucky if it gets into the minutes.

(manager of residential unit)

Adults may have a vital role in identifying issues that can be complained about. Three young people interviewed had considered making a complaint about their social worker and adults had influenced their final decisions. One young woman was in the process of making a formal complaint about lack of contact with her social worker, and staff had encouraged her to make the complaint. In contrast, another young woman in residential care described how her social worker was 'doing nothing' for her. She saw little of her social worker, who had not even attended her recent review. She had talked to staff about her social worker's behaviour and about wanting to change her social worker but they had replied, 'You need a good reason, not just because you don't like them.' This young woman did not make a complaint. It seems that young people do need guidance about what is a legitimate complaint but sometimes they are not receiving this guidance.

The crucial role adults can play in defining an issue as worthy of complaint is again illustrated when we look at the issue of provision for cultural needs. Our interviews included three examples of young people who were unhappy about the extent to which their cultural needs were being met in care. It is interesting to follow this young black woman's story to trace how she perceived whether she had cause for complaint.

The young black woman lived with a black foster carer:

I always say in my reviews that I would like to have more black friends. One of the questions they asked was, 'how do you feel in your culture' and I felt that the only culture I get to learn from is Val [foster carer] and my family. I don't really have any black friends and also if they were in care it's better because then they understand as well don't they? But I've never met any so you wonder if there are any don't you?

(young person in foster care)

Her foster carer also felt it was important for her to develop friendships with other black young people. The young person felt nothing had happened as a result of raising her concern, rather, the responsibility for meeting this need had been turned back on her. She felt she had made efforts to meet other black young people but these had been unsuccessful for a number of reasons. Whilst feeling the responsibility lay with social services to arrange for young black people in care to meet she had resigned herself to what she felt was a lack of response.

When a young person feels she is receiving a consistent message at her review that she has no cause for complaint, she is unlikely to pursue this complaint by other routes.

Again, this demonstrates the key role adults can play in giving young people signals about what is a legitimate complaint and the role reviews may play in identifying them.

In contrast to the other issues, bullying was seen by young people in this sample as a very clear reason to use the complaints procedure. In our sample, thirteen of the young people talked about intimidation or assault by another resident and eight had turned to the complaints procedure to deal with the issue. However, some young people felt that others were put off using the complaints procedure because of fears that the bullying would increase.

The appropriateness of the formal complaints procedure for this type of complaint was sometimes questioned by staff who had experience of the procedure being used in this way. Staff felt that bullying needed to be seen in a wider context, i.e. as a result of an inappropriate placement of a certain resident. This raised questions for staff about how complaints were defined, what was seen to be the focus of the investigation, and the extent to which those investigating the complaint took context into account. They also questioned the impact the procedure had on the issue.

Another way of exploring understandings of legitimate complaints is through those complaints which have gone through the formal procedure. We can never know how representative these complaints are of all the complaints made, since some complaints are dealt with informally, through problem solving, and there is little information on complaints that are dealt with in this way. We can group these complaints made by young people into the rights which young people are seeking to uphold (see Table 2). Young people are more likely to be making complaints that relate to protection, such as assaults by staff and residents and bullying or provision, for example, being denied food or lack of after care support. They were less likely to complain about issues relating to participation, in practice these are predominantly complaints about consultation in relation to moving placement.

The project records cover a four year period but the emphasis on complaints about protection issues has not varied over that time. The focus of the complaint does not vary with the gender of the young person making the complaint. However the age of the young person making the complaint does appear to have a significant impact on which rights young people are seeking to uphold. These findings need to be treated tentatively because of a number of cases where the age of the child was not clear.

Table 2 The rights which young people's complaints seek to uphold

Rights	Number	Percentage
Protection	35	46.0
Provision	24	31.6
Participation	7	9.2
Other	10	13.2
Total	76	100.0

The mean age of young people complaining about issues relating to protection such as bullying was 14.1. By comparison, the average age for young people making complaints about provision was 15.5 and for complaints about participation rose to 15.7. This evidence may indicate that it is only as young people in care grow older that they recognise their right to be more involved in decisions being made about their care. Or perhaps it is only when they are older that young people feel confident enough to begin to challenge those decisions.

Communicating the Complaint

In most of residential and foster care settings, being able to make a complaint had become dependent upon having access to a complaints form. Complaints forms contain information about the procedure, the address of the CO and a form that the complainant can fill in with brief details of their complaint. This practice proved to be a barrier to the procedure for some young people.

Whilst in some homes forms were left on tables or pinned to walls, in others complaints forms were only available on request, from staff. Only a small number of young people said they had been denied a complaints form when they requested one. Nevertheless, some young people perceived this type of access to forms as problematic and they developed strategies to overcome it, as this young person describes:

> *It [the booklet] said just ask for a complaints form but when your living-room's only like two doors away and the office is right outside, you knock on the door and say, 'can I have a complaints form' they [other young people] might hear you. So you ask for somebody else to get it for you and you stay up in your room and they come and give it you, you write it.*

(young person in residential care)

The experiences of young people lead us to question whether the best way for young people to communicate their complaints is in writing. Young people felt there were no real alternatives. The written form was seen as preferable to telephone calls because young people were often unable to make a private phone call. The SSI review of the procedure pointed to the importance of young people having access to private telephones (SSI, 1994). Sinclair and Gibbs' research found only 34 per cent of young people said they could make a private phone call with *no* permission, (Sinclair and Gibbs, 1996). It is important to bear in mind young people's notions of privacy. Making a phone call in the office not only involves asking permission, but may not always appear to young people as private space, as this young person explains:

> *I'm all right about writing it [the complaint] down and handing it in. Because if you are using the phone in the glass office, the kids and that can hear you talking through it.*

(young person in residential care)

Faced with no viable alternative, young people continue to write their complaints. However, young people had alternatives to suggest. Some young people said they would prefer to complain directly to a person who visited their unit on a regular basis. This would make the process of complaining more tangible. As one young person suggested:

> *Put the complaints department in here. I think we should have someone from complaints visiting every week, every couple of weeks, just visiting to see what's going on. If they're sending complaints in, it's like it's not getting seen too quickly.*

(young person in residential care)

Young people wanted access to someone on a regular basis; this would also enable them to inquire directly about the progress of any complaint they had made. Young people seem to make a connection between length of the procedure and the fact their complaint is communicated in writing:

> *I prefer to talk to somebody. Because complaints, they take too long to go through don't they? I reckon that they should just get something else done with it.*

(young person in residential care)

An important finding of this research is how fixed ideas have become about the medium for making a formal complaint in the authorities studied. More examination needs to take place of the different mediums that could be used for making complaints and how to offer young people real choices about how they complain. The accepted practice of writing complaints and using complaints forms may account in part for the uneven use of the procedure by young people living in different types of accommodation. Reliance on this form of communication inevitably raises questions about excluding from the process vulnerable groups such as young people from ethnic minorities or those with disabilities.

How Young People and Others Experience the Investigation

Although it was planned to look at young people's experience of using the complaints procedure through questionnaires, inevitably the interviews included young people who had, or were in the process of, making a complaint. The focus of the complaints made by the young people we interviewed is not representative of the range of complaints investigated by the project. Nevertheless, it is important to explore issues these young people raised about how the process and outcome of the procedure is experienced.

Seven young people had experience of a formal investigation. Beyond an expectation that once they had sent off the leaflet someone would get in touch with them, young people had little idea what making a complaint involved. Indeed only two of the seven young people who returned the questionnaire said they knew what would happen after they sent their complaints form off.

Four of the seven young people interviewed who had gone through an investigation felt unclear about what was happening to their complaint during the investigation, and this had often been translated into an assumption that nothing was being done. Some young people felt they had not been informed of their complaint's progress.

> *I wasn't being informed of when they [the investigators] were meeting with whoever or when there was going to be a meeting. They just told me when they came to [interview] me, that's how I knew about it.*
>
> (young person in residential care)

Another young person understood that her Independant Person (IP) would be 'sorting things out' but was unclear about the details.

> *I don't know what's going to happen. I didn't really see much response because she (the IP) was supposed to come to us again. She never did.*
>
> (young person in residential care)

In part this can be explained by young people's understanding of what they are told and their expectations about how things will be dealt with. Young people and IPs may have very different understandings of the length of time required to collect information, particularly if the young person has no idea how much work this would involve. If this sort of information is not communicated to young people, maybe even written down, they might conclude, inaccurately, that 'nothing seems to have happened'.

Dalrymple and Payne (1994) explain that five of the nine young people they interviewed felt nothing appeared to happen until they were appointed an advocate. Their research indicates the vital role which advocates can have in the process by tackling some of the problems which this research has highlighted, e.g. helping young people clarify their complaint and passing information on to young people. This perspective is supported by Sir William Utting in *People Like Us*, (1997).

Our analysis of records of complaints processed by the York Project indicates that young people are more likely to withdraw their complaints than adults (16 per cent of all complaints made by young people). 42 per cent of the complaints withdrawn were made about staff conduct. A clear message arising from this research is that some young people need the opportunity of having independent support, both before and during the process, if they are going to use the procedure effectively. We would argue that this would have the effect of improving young people's participation in the procedure more than any other single reform.

Support

What support did young people receive? From the questionnaires filled in by Investigating Officers and young people who had made a complaint, we can develop a picture of the types of support available to young people during an investigation. The single most important source of support was staff who accounted for support to 41 per cent of the young people making complaints. A quarter of young people had support from staff only.

Whilst there was a heavy reliance upon staff support, staff themselves did not always feel able to offer young people the support they needed to make a complaint. For some this was due to lack of information about the procedure. For others it was not always an appropriate role for them to play. Some staff felt they were placed in the role of advocating for the young people making complaints and that this was a difficult position for them to sustain, for example, if the complaint was against another member of staff. Staff in three out of five residential settings said they had sometimes felt compromised when supporting young people with a complaint about other staff members. One way of dealing with this 'conflict of interest' was by being clear with young people that they wanted to remain neutral:

> *You've got a complaint, write it down, I'm neither supporting you nor arguing against you, I'm just helping you fill in a piece of paper.*

(residential worker)

Eight of the 22 staff interviewed from residential care felt compromised by their role and unable to offer the support they felt young people needed:

> *Pressure from the authority has been put on staff not to assist or encourage a young person to make a compliant.*

(residential worker)

Again, the experiences of these staff point to the importance of young people in residential care having more independent support. Yet existing research indicates a limited availability of such support for young people in residential care. Research carried out in 1996 found only 33 per cent of authorities in England and Wales had developed an independent visitors scheme, (Knight, 1998). In 1996 there were only 28 Children's Rights Officers in England and Wales, (Utting, 1998).

Timescale

Timescale for the procedure was an issue for all those involved in the process. Analysis of the project records shows young people were twice as likely as adults to have their investigation completed with the 28 day timescale. Nevertheless, there was an overwhelming consensus amongst young people that the investigations took too long to complete.

For young people who are complaining about bullying and still having to live with the bully, time is of the essence. Here a young person recounts a Complaints Officer's response to his complaint about another resident.

They said they were going to come down for a visit in 3–4 weeks, 3–4 weeks!
That's a bit long, I can still get bullied in that time.

(young person in residential care)

Indeed, young people who had perhaps been living with a situation for some time were often expecting a quick response when they finally put in a formal complaint to someone seen to be more powerful. Sometimes young people had expected action within a week if bullying was the focus of their complaint. If young people continue to live in the situation they are complaining about and it appears as if 'nothing's happened' – the process will appear to take an eternity. The investigation can also become irrelevant if it starts too long after the event young people complained about. One IP, commenting on an investigation that had taken five months, said:

When I saw him [the complainant] during the process, he considered the initial meeting so distant from the initial incident that he genuinely had diffi-culty in recalling the sequence of events about which he had complained. When I saw him some three months later to report the findings he was quite disinterested in these.

(Independent Person)

Timing and communication, then, are vitally important. Certainly, delay seems to be a factor in reducing the credibility of the complaints procedure amongst young people.

Outcomes

The communication of outcomes, particularly to young people and Independent Persons, was noted as a problem area in our research. Young people are generally less focused on the details of the process and more concerned about the impact the procedure will have on their problem. Existing research highlights that young people wish to see change effected as a result of the procedure, (Dalrymple and Payne, 1994). A Social Services Inspectorate report, (1994), noted the area needed more attention. Indeed, others have questioned whether COs were able to acquire information from the operational side to find out if recommendations were being implemented, (Voice for the Child in Care, 1993).

Whilst the records from the York Project indicate that young people's complaints were as likely to be upheld as adults, young people raised issues about the extent to which they felt the procedure was able to have an impact on the problem they had complained about. The impact of the procedure had two dimensions. Young people making a complaint were looking for an immediate effect whilst the investigation took place, such as members of staff being removed, a bully made to feel intimidated by the process. Young people also wanted to see action taken as a result of the investigations.

Of the young people replying to the questionnaire, six had completed an investigation. Three felt the issue they had complained about was resolved as a result of the investigation. However, only two of the seven young people interviewed who had been through, or were currently going through, an investigation into a complaint felt that the investigation had an impact on the behaviour of staff and residents they had complained about. The other five young people had mixed views about the impact that making a complaint had. One issue they raised was not seeing action result from the recommendations made in their report. A young person who made a complaint about a member of staff commented:

> *Nothing happened so it was a waste of time but I wasn't going to stop it because I wanted people to listen to us. But you think, when you get it all, 'why did I bother?' When you get this report with everything upheld on it, you think, 'what was the point?' Everything upheld, nothing done about it.*
>
> (young person in residential care)

Three other young people who were complaining about bullying had expected that the young person would be removed as a result of the complaint. This had not happened and they had continued to feel vulnerable.

Confidence in the Procedure

Lack of impact, as the young people perceived it, led four of the 12 young people who had experience of an investigation to conclude that it was not worth complaining. With this avenue for complaining effectively closed, one young person felt there was 'nothing you could do'.

However, five young people interviewed, even if they were dissatisfied with some aspects of the process said they would continue to use the procedure which must be the acid test for it. Indeed, only two of the seven young people returning the questionnaire said they would not use the procedure again.

Nevertheless there is a danger that young people who have not been through the complaints process may absorb some negativity about the procedure. This is certainly the case for young people in residential care, as one young person explained:

> *I've heard that many stories about it, I'm not going to even bother. It takes too long, they throw it away. They're useless. I've heard it off a lot of people, sounds as if it might be right!*
>
> (young person in residential care)

There is clearly a need to encourage young people to have confidence in the procedure. This might, however, be hard to secure when their peers have negative experiences of the system when they generally have ambivalent feelings towards social services, (Utting, 1997). In short, young people in residential care are dependent on the efforts of staff to renew their faith in the procedure, staff who might very well be disillusioned themselves about the process.

Empowerment

There is evidence of some young people using the procedure to feel powerful in their negotiations with staff. The opposite side of the coin is that young people are often not using the procedure because they feel powerless, a common phenomenon amongst the young people we interviewed for this study. Despite the ideology of complaints procedures, that customers and their wishes are sovereign, it is as a result of powerlessness or vulnerability that most complainants became 'customers' of welfare agencies. This observation is particularly pertinent for young people who have entered care and who turn to the complaints and representations procedure for redress to a concern.

Young people in care could experience powerlessness at a number of levels. On an individual level some young people felt they had no power and so there was no point in complaining:

> *They don't listen; we're just kids. We have no power.*
>
> (young person in residential care)

At an institutional level, young people had varying experiences of participation in the running of their residential home. Some young people felt they were informed of rules without consultation or discussion:

> *They've done a whole load of new rules that we don't know anything about. We didn't get a say in that...They don't even tell us.*
>
> (young person in residential care)

Others felt powerless in the face of social services:

> *It's not right 'cos it's the government making rules and social services, it's not the staff here. I think it should be the staff here and the children that are actually living in that place to make the rules as well. We should all get a say in the rules.*
>
> (young person in residential care)

Not all young people saw social services as all powerful. Some saw Social Services as remote and having little impact on their daily lives. The complaints procedure, which they equated with the Social Services, was seen to be ineffective:

> *It's part of the same thing; it's just social services. Don't do jack for us now. Social services do not have any impact on the home, how good it was run anyway. All they could do was move them, not change things.*
>
> (young person in residential care)

Feelings of powerlessness at a number of levels are an important context for understanding why some young people in residential care felt the complaints procedure was not an effective tool for responding to their needs. This issue needs to be addressed, as Utting, (1997), has endorsed, through collective young people's organisations.

Conclusion

Before drawing any conclusions from our study we wish to make two points which place our work in a broader context.

First, whilst children's rights can be helpful in promoting high quality substitute care there are other dimensions of quality which need to be taken into account. An emphasis on rights can become an end in itself – switching the focus away from process (how things are done) and outcome (what happens as a result) issues. Additionally the focus on children's rights is difficult where the rights claims of particular individuals are in conflict. There is also a possibility of conflict between an individual's rights and those of a group – where an individual claims a right to play loud music late at night, for example. It follows therefore that in providing quality care we need to implement children's rights within a wider empowering framework, which can respond to the complex realities of looking after children.

Second, complaints systems themselves also need to be placed in a wider context. Complaints procedures alone cannot provide a safe, quality environment for children. Rather they should form part of such an environment for children. Utting, (1997), makes a similar point when he argues that children and young people can only be truly safeguarded by high quality management practice. This seems to be the intention of the Labour Government's *Quality Protects* programme. It is important to note that complaints procedures are not a 'magic wand' in relation to issues in residential settings, but can form part of an effective package of safeguards.

How effective is the current system? Our findings suggest that:

- Awareness of the procedure varies across local authorities and from unit to unit.
- Access to complaints procedures varies from unit to unit.
- Different homes seem to develop different 'complaints cultures'.

Whilst some variability between units is to be welcomed, in so far as it responds to the different needs of different groups of young people, it is important that local authorities ensure that minimum standards are guaranteed.

Essentially, young people require adequate information about the complaints procedure, that is appropriate to their age group, ethnic background and their ability. Once they have this they need to be able to access the system through written and verbal points of access. They also need guidance about whether the issues which concern them constitute a complaint. When they have activated the process they need support in ensuring that the complaint progresses, towards a timely and fair resolution.

Our evidence suggests that young people in residential care use the complaints system more that young people in foster care, but that nevertheless, the current procedure does not command much credibility from these young people. Credibility would be increased if complaints were dealt with within reasonable timescales, if young people received feedback on the progress of their complaint and if they saw change as a result of their complaint. It is important to point out, however, that representations and complaints procedure can only form part of an effective system for protecting and enhancing the welfare of children and young people. We conclude with a reform that would add a crucial element to the effective safeguarding of children and young people in care:

> *...those in care or have been in local authority care should be represented by bodies which not only act as advocates but also contribute to the development of policy and practice nationally.*

(Utting, 1997, para 10.17).

We should welcome government funding for just such an initiative which will be led by the voluntary organisation, First Key.

It is important that the contribution to positive practice made by an effective complaints procedure should be seen in the wider context of high quality provision, protection and participation which effectively empowers children and young people.

CHAPTER 10

Safety in Numbers? Promoting Children's Rights in Public Care

Carolyne Willow

> *Children in the care of local authorities have been abused and neglected by the care system that was supposed to look after them.*
>
> (Modernising Social Services White Paper, 1998)

The more we learn about the history of children's residential care the clearer it becomes that those who have needed the greatest care and attention have been let down the most. Individual lives have been damaged and destroyed and residential care itself has been discredited. Those who work in children's homes must now suffer the same social stigma as tax collectors and traffic wardens. Over the past two decades alone, large numbers of children in residential care have been raped, beaten, bullied, threatened and routinely humiliated. A few have even died. The catalogue of abuse is so huge that we should perhaps ponder whether the idea of residential care for children should be buried in a millennium casket together with other failed social experiments such as child prisons, or 'secure training units'.

The End of an Era of Residential Care?

Tempting though it may be to draw a line under residential care, four positive aspects remain. First, several thousands of children benefit from care and support which so far has proven impossible to provide in any other setting but residential care. Second, many young people continue to have good experiences of residential care and – given the choice – would opt to live in groups rather than in their own or a substitute family. Third, residential care offers young people the chance to live with peers who have had similar experiences, it gives them access to a large number of adult carers with whom they can form positive relationships, and they are not pressurised to 'fit in' to a family. Finally, there remains a large body of staff working in the residential sector who have a great deal to offer children.

Working in residential care can be the most rewarding of all forms of social work with children but it can also prove the most demanding. That is why today's advocates of children's residential care frequently argue that this sector should set out to recruit the best social work practitioners and managers rather than those who are just entering the profession, or who simply see residential care as a step on the ladder to 'real social work'. For many years, looking after children within residential care was perceived (and treated) as second-rate social work, as Barbara Kahan, (1994 p255), explains:

> *The task of looking after children and young people living away from home in groups...has traditionally been underestimated and undervalued. People assume it is a 'natural' role like parenting in a child's home.*

The challenges and complexities of looking after children are now widely recognised. The importance of recruiting the right people and ensuring staff have access to relevant training and support have been central recommendations of all major reports and inquiries into residential care across the past decade. The other principal message from many of these investigations is that the voices of children and young people individually and collectively, as the main consumers of these services, have been widely and frequently ignored.

The *Quality Protects* programme, launched by the Department of Health in 1998, to radically overhaul services for children in need, and especially for those in care, places great emphasis on hearing the views of children and young people who use these services. There is now a growing consensus that, for residential care to come off the critical list and recover from its injured past, children must be heard and their views and ideas acted upon – in individual care planning, in the day-to-day running of their homes, and in broader policy development and organisational decision-making.

Review Meetings

> *They never ask me anything about how I'm doing in care – they just pretend I'm not there.*

> *As soon as I talk someone interrupts then they change the subject, so when I do get to talk they then tell me that the subject has been discussed and we are on to something else.*

(young people talking about participation in review meetings in Fletcher, 1993, p56)

Key decisions are made about individual children's lives at review meetings. Article 12 of the United Nations Convention on the Rights of the Child (see below) states that whenever decisions are made which affect a child, she or he should be able to express and have her or his views taken into account. There is no age limit on participation – the test is whether or not a child is able to form a view.

In the early 1980s the young people's organisation NAYPIC (National Association of Young People in Care) published *Gizza Say* which argued the case for young people to be actively involved in review meetings, (Stein and Ellis, 1983). The title of the publication was taken from the then popular Boys from the Blackstuff television series, whose central character Yosser Hughes was desperate to find work and habitually asked anyone who would listen to 'gizza job'. Yosser didn't get very far; advances in young people's participation in review meetings have also been painfully slow.

The Children Act 1989 strengthened young people's right to participate in review meetings (Regulation 7 Review of Children's Cases 1991), and the Looking After Children Assessment and Action records provide an excellent basis for improving dialogue and communication between children and social workers. Yet young people continue to experience the same kind of isolation and frustration in these meetings as their contemporaries from previous decades. While it is clear that many more local authorities are encouraging young people to physically attend their review meetings, real participation continues to be hindered by the way meetings are planned and conducted, (Grimshaw and Sinclair, 1997).

Some years back when I was a children's rights officer I accompanied a girl who lived in a children's home to her review meeting. At the beginning, the chair-person invited those taking part to introduce themselves. Each of the professionals in the room gave their full name and title. When it came to the girl's turn she said her name and added 'subject' as her title. That was the word next to her name on the social worker's report for the review meeting. This was a poignant reminder of how the established behaviour of professionals can have a dehumanising effect on children. The National Children's Bureau has produced a young people's guide to help them prepare for their review meetings, (Wheal and Sinclair, 1995). And many local authorities are now appointing specialist 'reviewing officers' to chair meetings. However, there is a great deal residential social workers can do to help young people prepare for their review meetings, (Willow, 1996 pp97–102), and participate fully in them. Here, managers of homes have a pivotal role in ensuring that basic preparations have taken place, such as asking young people their views on who should attend, when and where the meeting should be held and what needs to be on the agenda. They can also check that staff have spent time with young people in advance, planning their contribution, and working out what questions they want to put to the professionals attending.

Too often review meetings are used as an opportunity for professionals to discuss the perceived shortcomings of young people rather than as a chance for young people to scrutinise what professionals have (or have not) done for and with them in the preceding months. If review meetings are to be effective in planning children's care their focus should not only be on the needs and behaviour of young people. These meetings also need to examine the actions of professionals, and question how the way services are delivered impacts on the development and welfare of young people. If this were to happen as a matter of course we might see more enlightened practice when young people request a change in social workers or keyworkers for example. Currently such requests are routinely refused even when it is evident that the relationships are serving little benefit to young people or professionals alike.

When I was a children's rights officer I supported a young woman who asked to change her social worker because she didn't get along with him. She explained that she found it hard to relate to men. The social worker agreed that their relationship was very poor and that they had exchanged very few words in the years he had been 'working with her'. Yet he and his manager refused to make alternative arrangements; the only reason they gave for reaching this decision was that it was impractical to offer a choice of social worker. The young woman then made a complaint under Section 26 of the Children Act 1989 which was jointly investigated by an independent person not employed or associated with the local authority; her complaint was upheld and she was finally allocated a female social worker. If children are to have any real influence when decisions are made which affect them, they need to enjoy positive relationships with the professionals who are responsible for 'looking after' them. Blanket policies, which deny children a choice of social workers or keyworkers can, in this respect, result in removing children's right to play an active part in decision-making.

Choosing the Right Staff

The Warner recommendation (1992) that young people should be involved in the recruitment of staff is another obvious starting point for improving the quality of care in the residential sector. Young people's involvement in the recruitment of staff is crucial for two main reasons. First, it conveys to young people that they matter; it validates them as people. Second, it gives a powerful signal to candidates that young people are valued, and that their judgement is respected. It is not that young people have a special insight by dint of their experiences or a sixth sense, that they can spot a paedophile or paedophobe where adults are unable to. There is no reason to believe that young people are any better or worse at weeding out at interview abusive adults who have cleverly avoided prior detection. But it is likely that they will make other discoveries that adult interviewers miss. A friend of mine – a young care leaver – was on an interview panel a couple of years ago. One of the candidates failed to make any eye contact with her, or other interviewers who had been in care. Instead, he concentrated on trying to impress the manager on the panel, and heavily peppered each of his interview answers with social work jargon. He didn't get the job.

Young people have to spend hundreds of hours with staff who work in residential care. They know what kinds of people they get along with, and they are more likely to invest in relationships with staff they have recruited. If young people lack experience or knowledge in certain areas – such as the organisation's equal opportunities policy or key legislation such as the Children Act 1989 – training should be provided, rather than this used as an excuse to exclude them.

It should not be assumed that only teenagers or care leavers can take on this important responsibility. The youngest person I have been on an interview panel with was nine years old. We were recruiting an adult advisor for a NAYPIC local group.

House Meetings

It is usual practice for most community homes to hold 'residents meetings' where young people come together – often with staff – to discuss issues arising from group living. While there are good examples of these meetings working for the benefit of young people, they are frequently seen as a waste of time by young people because, all too often, they serve as an opportunity for staff to impose their agendas. This is alarming as house meetings are an essential mechanism for children and young people to positively contribute to the running of their home. In 1997 the Who Cares? Trust carried out a survey into the experiences and views of over 2000 children in public care. The survey asked children to list what they would change about living in residential care if they had the chance. Their top five answers were (1998 p63):

	would change
More pocket money/allowance	(42%)
Bedtimes	(29%)
More freedom to be out	(18%)
More activities/outings	(9%)
Better accommodation	(7%)

Apart from pocket money/allowances, all of the above issues can be largely dealt with by young people and staff together; they do not necessarily require policy changes or the active involvement of senior managers or elected members. House meetings can also present valuable opportunities for young people and staff to work out strategies on how to address matters which cannot be resolved at a local level, such as gaining an increase in clothing or leisure allowances. Yet their potential for enabling young people to make decisions about their home, and impact on wider policy matters, is hardly ever fully exploited. Such meetings can help relationships between young people and staff, and ensure that young people know they will be taken seriously if they have concerns or complaints:

> *For me care has been a positive experience...the unit where I was living encouraged a culture of participation and involvement in the day-to-day running of the home. I believe that developing such a culture depends on the value the people in charge place on listening to what young people say and taking them seriously. The head of the home encouraged us to have house meetings...I knew that if I was unhappy about something I would have the space to talk to someone individually with the knowledge they would take me seriously.*

(Patel in Dalrymple and Hough, 1995)

It is remarkable that so many local authorities have not seen a need, or facilitated training and support, for young people in running productive house meetings. Training departments frequently arrange training for staff teams across social services departments on 'working together' and 'team-building' yet little investment has been made in meeting young people's needs in this area. Staff only have to work with each other; young people have to live with each other. Clearly this is another opportunity to improve the quality of life in residential care, while also offering children with low self-esteem or confidence the opportunity to develop their communication skills and assertiveness.

Independent Advocacy

While local authorities are endeavouring to improve the care they offer to looked after children, there is an immediate need to ensure that these children have access to independent advocates for information, support and advice. Local authorities, while acting as 'corporate parents', have even more of a responsibility than ordinary parents to ensure the children they look after can turn to people outside their immediate situation when they are unhappy, confused or just in need of a listening ear. It is a historical irony that the first local authority to establish a children's rights service subsequently achieved notoriety for the abuse of children in its care. In 1987 Leicestershire county council recruited Mike Lindsay as the UK's first children's rights officer. Twelve years later about one-quarter of local authorities fund or support local children's rights and advocacy services, and many more are setting them up. Most children's rights or advocacy officers are employed by voluntary organisations contracted by local authorities to provided an independent service to local looked after children. Some services remain within local authorities, based within their arms-length inspection or quality assurance units, although this is increasingly rare.

To local authorities it can often seem that children's rights and advocacy services are causing more problems than they are solving. When new services are established it is usual for issues that have been simmering away for months or years to suddenly boil over, as young people gain the strength and confidence to challenge poor practice. Often the first few years of these services are concentrated on addressing basic care issues, which then clears the way for more general (and positive) developmental work. Shane Ellis, a former NAYPIC development worker and children's rights officer explains:

> *Good care services require good management; effective selection, recruitment and induction processes; regular staff supervision and continued staff development; and all this within a common value framework and a clear shaped purpose. When this is in place the children's rights officer may be really effective in enabling children's and young people's perceptions to be voiced and to be heard. Until then they resemble the sorcerer's apprentice: bailing out an unrelenting and formidable tidal wave*
> (Ellis and Franklin in Franklin, 1995 p98)

Sir William Utting commended children's rights services in *People Like Us* (1997 p111):

> *One of the most beneficial developments of the last decade has been the arrival and gradual development of children's rights services for young people looked after by local authorities.*

Local authorities are now being encouraged to set up children's rights services (*Quality Protects*, 1998; *Modernising Social Services*, 1998), and a new national development manager has been appointed by Children's Rights Officers and Advocates (CROA) to support them in doing so. Young people are central to the development of local children's rights and advocacy services – in recruiting staff, setting out targets and priorities, running projects and evaluating the impact of such services (CROA, 1998).

A Rights Culture

Until a few years ago it was the norm within local authorities for children's rights to be seen as the exclusive interest of children's rights and advocacy officers. But the existence of local children's rights and advocacy services is not an excuse for local authorities to abdicate their responsibility to comprehensively promote children's rights. The United Nations Convention on the Rights of the Child, which the UK Government ratified in December 1991, places a duty on local authorities to promote children's rights (Association of Metropolitan Authorities and Children's Rights Office, 1995). Its 54 Articles grants a set of 40 rights to people under 18 years, covering a range of matters such as the right to express and have their views considered, protection from all forms of violence, and the right of young disabled people to 'fullest possible social integration'. Article 42, like the Children Act, requires public authorities to inform young people of their rights.

Table 1   The United Nations Convention on the Rights of the Child – a Selection of Key Articles Relevant to Residential Care

Article	Summary of right
2	Children have the right not to be discriminated against
3	In all actions concerning children their best interests should be a primary consideration
12	Children have the right to express and have their view taken into account in all matters affecting them
13	Children have the right to freedom of expression
14	Children have the right to freedom of thought, conscience and religion
15	Children have the right to freedom of association and right to peaceful assembly
16	Children have the right to privacy
19	Children have the right to be free from all forms of violence

20	Children who are separated from their parents have the right to 'special protection and assistance'
21	In the process of adoption, children's best interests shall be the primary consideration
22	Children who are refugees have a right to 'receive appropriate protection and humanitarian assistance'
23	Disabled children have a right to 'a full and decent life, in conditions which ensure dignity, promote self-reliance, and facilitate the child's active participation in society'
25	Children who live away from home have a right to 'periodic review' of their treatment and circumstances
37	The arrest, detention or imprisonment of children should only be used as a last resort, and for the shortest appropriate period of time
	Children who are deprived of their liberty should be treated with 'humanity and respect'; they should be separated from adults unless it is not in their best interests; and they have the right to maintain contact with their families
39	Children who have been neglected, abused or exploited have the right to rehabilitative care
40	Children who are alleged to have committed a crime have a right to be treated with dignity and worth
	Governments who ratify the convention should seek to promote wherever appropriate measures for dealing with children who offend which avoid the use of judicial proceedings

The Children's Rights Office estimates that over 100 local authorities in England and Wales have signed up to the convention. This is an impressive number but it is not a realistic indicator of how much activity is taking place at a local level to implement the Convention. There is still a great deal to be done; passing a report through a council committee is very different from setting in place co-ordinated measures to implement the Convention across the organisation.

Although progress on implementation overall has been poor – especially in comparison with other activities to promote 'equal opportunities' in relation to sex, race and to some extent disability – there are some excellent examples of local innovation. Durham County Council's Investing in Children project brings together a wide range of local organisations to promote active partnerships between adults and children:

> *At the very heart of Investing in Children are two very simple ideas. Firstly, all of the different organisations have got to learn to work together for children and young people. Secondly, adults don't always know best, and unless we find ways of including children and young people in deciding what should be done, we will sometimes get it wrong.*

Young people in Durham have carried out several pieces of research to find out what services children and young people want from their local council. One of the four priority areas identified by young people was transport; field work is currently being carried out by young people to obtain information about transport policy and systems across the country and in other European countries. Their findings will be fed into the relevant council committees, with the aim of making *practical* change.

On 20 November, 1998 (the ninth anniversary of the Convention being adopted by the United Nations), North Tyneside Council launched its Children's Charter to a large conference of young people. As part of its efforts to promote children's rights in a variety of accessible ways the council has produced a CD-ROM for young people celebrating their Charter, which is based on the Convention. Milton Keynes Council has established an authority-wide project to promote and implement the Convention, while in Bolton work on the Convention was spearheaded by a high profile training seminar for senior councillors and managers from all council departments.

The time has yet to come where job adverts and recruitment packs from local authorities positively promote their organisation's commitment to the Convention, and there is still a reprehensible lack of any form of training on the Convention for council employees and elected members. Yet in those local authorities where projects based on the Convention have been set up, a great deal of activity and goodwill has been generated. Importantly, a range of new alliances between young people and adults have been forged, and children have been made aware of their rights, often for the first time.

Working within the framework of the Convention on the Rights of the Child gives an unequivocal message to children and adults alike that children matter. Adopting a children's rights approach to service development, especially in the residential sector, can help create a culture which is forward-looking and celebratory rather than pessimistic and regretful.

Many of the rights which children in public care now enjoy, at least in theory, were fought for by their predecessors, in the 1970s and 1980s. NAYPIC campaigned for complaints procedures for children in care; argued against the 'order book' where young people in care had to exchange vouchers in designated shops for clothes; they showed the harmful effects of bulk-buying food and toiletries; and they lobbied for young people's participation in review meetings. Black and In Care conversely showed that black young people's fundamental needs – such as positive black role-models, information about their heritage, food and hair and skin care – were not being met by a care system run by predominantly white people.

While the idea of rights for children in care has arguably come of age in the 1990s, its roots – as the activities of NAYPIC and Black and In Care members show – are to be found in previous decades. It was the 1975 Children Act which first gave children in care a legal right to be consulted on matters which affected them. And the first local in-care group was set up in Leeds in 1973, called Ad-Lib (short for 'adolescent liberation').

In-care Groups

There are now over 35 in-care and after-care groups across the UK, (Patel, 1997), and the Department of Health has funded the establishment of a new

English in-care organisation, A National Voice, which had its official launch at the House of Commons, in June, 1999. This national organisation will work with young people at a local authority level to help them establish local and regional groups that offer children in and leaving care peer support and information on their rights. Local authorities wishing to promote children's rights in residential care can support young people's groups through the provision of grants and support in kind such as computer equipment, meeting places and facilitating access to senior managers and elected members.

While it is now generally accepted that children and young people who are looked after have a right to be part of an in-care group, to have an independent advocate, or to attend review meetings for example, we must not overlook the one most basic right they have as children: to lasting relationships with adult carers.

When the Who Cares? Trust survey (see above) asked young people to list the best things about being in care, the most frequent answer was 'having someone who cares' (1998 p58).

It is a sad indictment on the care system that care leavers, when reflecting on their childhoods, frequently proffer that things would have been much different if only they had had one person to whom they could have turned. A recent publication written for young people in care, (*Voice for the Child in Care*, 1998), describes the often harrowing experiences of more than 20 young people in care, and powerfully argues the case for independent advocates. Maurice, now an adult in his thirties, gives advice to young people about finding someone special:

> *You need to come across a person in the world in whom you can find some solace, someone who actually listens to you, whoever it may be, a teacher at school, a friend, whatever . . . The hardest thing in the world is to hope and to trust; to overcome the feeling that everyone and everything is just an utter pointless waste. If you can link in with someone and begin to talk about your experiences, then you can gain the strength to move on from them.*
>
> (Voice of the Child in Care, 1998).

It is perhaps naive to expect large bureaucracies to always deliver these 'special relationships'. A few years ago I was working with a group of young people who were to perform a play at a large social care conference. I raised the possibility of the press being present at the event, and asked whether they should discuss this with their parents and carers. A 13 year-old boy replied that he didn't need to talk to anyone: 'I've got no-one; I'm on my own'. He had lived in residential care and foster care for several years, yet somehow the system had failed to give him even one special and lasting relationship. The government's response to the Children's Safeguards Review explained:

> *Parents bring love to their children. Public agencies cannot equal that but they can and must work to provide placements which offer the opportunity of*

*developing appropriate attachments as a foundation of healthy growth and
development.*

(1998 p10)

The *Quality Protects* programme aims to address this shortcoming by setting a
target that no child in care should have more than three placements a year, still too
many. Meanwhile, there are other ways of ensuring children have access to
positive and lasting relationships with adults. The concept of the 'independent
visitor' was born from the need to provide children who had little or no contact
with their birth families, access to fulfilling relationships with adults outside of the
care system. Although 'looked-after' children have had a legal right to independent visitors since 1991, when the Children Act was implemented, few local
authorities have given these services a high priority.

Local authorities are now being encouraged, through the *Quality Protects*
programme, to prioritise the establishment of independent visitor services, and
befriending and mentoring schemes. Hopefully, those who have not yet developed
these services will learn from the successes of existing initiatives, especially those
which specifically recruit adults with care experience themselves.

If residential care for children is to rebuild its reputation, and gain public confidence, especially among children, a sea-change in attitude is needed, both within
and outside of the system.

Making Connections

Residential care does not exist in a vacuum, the type of society it operates in
inevitably affects the way people who live in groups are perceived and treated. The
origins of residential care in Britain lie in the 17th century workhouse, where poor
children were separated from their parents and made to work in return for a roof
over their head and meagre food rations. Two over-arching sentiments prevailed;
that the 'able-bodied' poor should be punished; and that destitute children needed
to be rescued from their feckless parents and inculcated with decent values. This
obviously affected the way those who administered poor relief treated children,
and encouraged disparaging public attitudes towards them.

As we approach the new millennium, poor children are still far more likely to
enter public care than their more affluent contemporaries, (Bebbington and
Miles, 1989), and their care status continues to carry enormous stigma. The
public remain muddled about why children are in public care, most believing
they have committed offences and are just bad. The punitive nature of New
Labour's approach to children who get into trouble undoubtedly feeds the
public's lack of compassion for this small group of people. Similarly, the fact that
months before we enter the 21st century we are still debating whether UK law
should allow adults to hit children inevitably affects adults' relationships with
children in residential care.

Parents in the UK are able to hit children and use the legal defence of 'reasonable chastisement', which has its origins in a case dating back to 1860. It is not uncommon to hear staff in residential care bemoan the fact that at home they can 'smack' their children for wrong-doings while at work they have to 'put up' with all kinds of misbehaviour and misdemeanours. The same is true for teachers, who lost their right to hit children in state schools in 1987.

Joined-up Rights

That the law condones parental physical punishment but prohibits violence by teachers or social workers is a clear example of the need for joined-up rights. Adults and children alike need to hear and understand that any form of violence in any type of relationship is wrong. It does not make sense that residential social workers are legally permitted to hit their own daughters and sons in between shifts, yet at work they are somehow meant to rely on non-violent forms of discipline in their relationships with children whom they probably regard as more 'difficult'.

Importantly, changing the law in relation to parental physical punishment would also help increase expectations among children that they will not be hurt. If children enter residential care with little experience of non-violent relationships with adults, they are less likely to question and raise their voices if staff push them around or frighten them.

If children in the UK lived in a society which loudly celebrated its non-violent approach to parenting, alarm bells would ring when adults tried to hurt them. At the moment, we have a situation where inquiry after inquiry tells us that children who were physically abused believed what was happening to them was normal, and that nobody would take much notice if they raised their voices in opposition. While everyone remembers the sexual abuse of Frank Beck in Leicestershire children's homes, less attention is given to the gross physical abuse which characterised his regime of terror. In fact, several years before Frank Beck stood in the dock for his reign of abuse as manager of the Beeches, he appeared in court for beating a ten-year-old child, (Kirkwood, 1993; D'arcy and Gosling, 1998). Among those advocating for Beck was a fellow councillor who wrote a glowing testimonial. Beck was acquitted; a less complacent attitude towards physical violence against children would probably have prevented him from damaging numerous young lives.

As a society we cannot come close to guaranteeing children safe and positive experiences in residential care until their overall status markedly improves. If children are to count in residential care, they must also matter on a macro-scale. While we have a 'law and order' agenda which runs counter to children's most basic needs, (Goldson, 1999), and politicians openly condoning, even encouraging, violence against children, (Willow and Hyder, 1999), it is difficult to foresee any significant change. The proliferation of recent initiatives to safeguard children in residential care are long overdue yet they must not eclipse bigger questions about children's position in society, their powerlessness vis a vis adults, and the need for our society to become pro-children. The summary report of the Review into Children's Safeguards cautioned:

> *Bear in mind that the abuse of children in institutions is part of the wider issue of the abuse of children generally. The bottom line is drawn by the values and attitudes to children which characterise the society in which we live.*

(1997, p1)

We must not fall into the trap of believing that children's homes are uniquely unsafe; children have also been harmed by people paid to care for them in penal settings, residential schools, foster care, nurseries and in their own homes. Attempting to fix residential care without also addressing children's wider position in society is like trying to put together a jigsaw of blank pieces of wood – the pieces may fit but the big picture will always be missing.

SECTION 4

Locking up Children

CHAPTER 11

The Politics and Process of Child and Youth Imprisonment

John Pitts

Introduction

From its inception, the failure of the prison to rehabilitate its inmates or to control the lawlessness within its walls, has been answered by new forms of imprisonment. Yet, these new prisons have rapidly taken on the pernicious characteristics of the institutions they have superseded, prompting further calls for newer and better prisons. Often, prison administrators have responded to these calls by creating special units, prisons within prisons, wherein those unmanageable prisoners who are believed to have subverted the rehabilitative goals of the prison and instigated the violence and chaos, can be isolated and their corrosive influence contained. From the 1970s, this tendency towards the diversification and proliferation of custodial penalties elicited demands from reformers for 'alternatives to custody'. However, aggressive criminal justice policies and judicial scepticism often meant that, far from diverting serious offenders from imprisonment, 'alternatives to custody' have been the means whereby less serious offenders have been propelled further up the sentencing tariff. In this chapter I shall argue that these tendencies are nowhere more evident than in the youth justice systems of the UK. In doing so, I shall draw upon the lessons of the 1960s, 1970s and 1980s, as well as the lessons of the 1990s.

A Troubling Institution

In the early 1960s, a series of 'disturbances' in Home Office administered approved schools prompted the development of units in which the 'hard core' of 'troublemakers', believed to have been at the root of these disturbances, were to be contained. In 1966, following disturbances at Carlton House Approved School, the Durand Committee recommended that a mechanism be devised for the transfer of 'Senior boys who are unruly or subversive and have shown themselves quite unsuitable for Approved School Training' to prison department Borstals, and the construction of 'one or two closed units'. The size and number of these closed units grew steadily through the late 1960s and 1970s, (Millham 1977).

With the advent of the Children and Young Persons Act (1969), control of the riot-prone approved school system was transferred to local authority social services departments. The 'schools' were re-designated Community Homes (with Education) (CHEs) and, nominally at least, adopted a therapeutic, rather than a disciplinary, orientation. Moreover, unlike the approved schools, the heads of the CHEs were able to select their inmates on the basis of their 'treatability'.

The 'Widening of the Net of Control' and the Politics of Minimalism

Stanley Cohen, (1985), has observed that since the 1960s, the net of official control over socially deviant populations has widened steadily, bringing new and less problematic groups under the surveillance and control of official agencies, and blurring the boundaries between 'institutional' and 'community corrections'. This thesis, which described observable processes occurring in the real world, also contributed to the emergence of a new politics within the field of crime and justice, described by Thomas Matiesen (1974) as 'abolitionism' and by Elliott Currie (1985) as 'progressive minimalism'. Progressive minimalism, as it expressed itself in the youth justice arena, was founded upon four central propositions:

1. That the crime perpetrated by working class children and young people was more or less innocuous and that intervention in their lives was motivated by elitist, middle class concerns about the morality of the poor, rather than the crime perpetrated by their children.
2. That victimisation was not therefore a serious problem, and was best dealt with by indigenous mechanisms of social control rather than state intervention.
3. That rehabilitation, treatment or social and economic intervention to prevent or eradicate crime were demonstrably ineffective and that young people in trouble should, if necessary, simply be granted their right to due process of law.
4. That, left to their own devices, children and young people would 'grow out of crime'.

As the 1970s progressed it was apparent that the progressive minimalists had a point. The early 1970s saw a rapid expansion of formal intervention by police officers from the newly created police 'youth and community bureaux', in the lives of children and young people involved in petty crime. Between 1965 and 1977 the numbers of 10–17 year olds cautioned by the police rose from 3,062 to 111,922.

This contrasts with juvenile prosecutions, which underwent a far more modest rise from 123,166 in 1965 to 133,638 in 1977. This growth in cautioning doubled the numbers of children and young people entering the youth justice system and, for some of these youngsters, early official intervention accelerated their progress through the system, (Wilkins, 1964, Young, 1971, Thorpe et al., 1980, Pitts, 1988).

In the 1970s, local authority social services departments, brought into being by the Social Services (Reorganisation) Act (1970), were also committed to earlier intervention with troubled or troublesome families, as a means of preventing the reception of their children into care. However, early intervention meant that social workers sometimes came upon previously undiscovered problems, some of which were very serious. However, as the 1970s progressed, spending cuts meant that under-staffed social services departments lacked the resources to respond adequately to these problems. Moreover, they often lacked sufficient evidence to initiate care proceedings. As a result, in cases where the child 'at risk' was also an offender, they would sometimes use juvenile justice legislation to remove children and young people from problematic families, (Thorpe et al., 1980).

As the 1970s progressed, the numbers of children and young people being presented for assessment for placement in CHEs increased steadily. But, of course they could not all be accommodated in CHEs which tended, as a result, to 'cream off' the most treatable candidates who were usually younger, less disturbed and often, but by no means always, guilty of less serious offences (Millham, 1978). Nonetheless, as Cornish and Clarke, (1975), have observed, for most of the boys placed in CHEs, institutionalisation represented, at best, a temporary interruption of their criminal careers. 75 per cent of the boys discharged during their study were re-convicted within two years. Moreover, there was no difference in re-conviction rates between boys discharged from 'therapeutic community' regimes and traditional regimes.

These findings are important, indicating that even when CHEs were able to control the 'quality' of their intake, this had little impact upon their re-conviction rates. Moreover, there is no evidence that these institutions were rendered more manageable by selectivity, since the rate at which they shipped troublesome inmates out to closed units did not diminish either. This suggests that the troubles afflicting these institutions may well have been rooted in the institutions themselves rather than the 'quality' of their intake. (Cornish and Clarke, 1975, Thorpe et al., 1980, Morris et al., 1980).

For children under 14 who were deemed to be 'unmanageable' in both the CHE system and the closed units, the DHSS created four Youth Treatment Centres. These centres catered for children who had committed grave crimes and the 'worst of the worst' from the CHEs. The first YTC, in Brentwood, Essex, like the Medway Secure Training Centre (STC) opened in 1999, attempted to bring some of the most difficult and disturbed children in the country together under one roof. Like Medway STC, Brentwood YTC was first vandalised and then burned by its inmates. Commenting upon the likelihood of such institutions reducing the criminality of their inmates, Masud Hoghughi, (1983), then principal of Aycliffe, a residential unit for seriously disturbed young people in the North East of England, and professor of psychology at Newcastle University observed:

> *Quite extensive evidence suggests that no amount of tinkering with institutional structures, programmes and procedures has any important or long-term impact on the propensity to re-offend. I would simply say that because the political and professional fashion of an era leads us to expect that a particular provision, such as a Borstal or community home is the 'right' place for processing delinquents into law-abiding citizens does not make them so. We have too many social white elephants, from the re-organisation of the National Health Service to Youth Treatment Centres and the proliferation of 'observation and assessment centres' to have much faith in fashionable wisdom. Nor have any but a small confused band of those who run institutions for delinquents ever claimed any expertise in curbing further delinquency.*

(p206)

The growing residue of children and young people who could not be accommodated within the CHE system and its secure off-shoots were consigned to prison department institutions. Between 1969 and 1977 the number of juveniles sent to detention centres rose by 158 per cent from 2,228 to 5,757. Between 1971 and 1977 the proportion of 14–17 year olds in the Borstal population rose from 484 (1 in 8) to 1,935 (1 in 3). In effect, during this period, the detention centres and Borstals, (subsequently re-designated Young Offender Centres and Young Offender Institutions) became a resource and an expansion tank, for local authorities attempting to discharge their child care and juvenile justice functions under the 1933 and 1969 Children and Young Persons Acts. The extent to which social services and prison department residential/custodial institutions were fulfilling overlapping functions is illustrated by the fact that, in 90 per cent of cases, social workers had recommended borstal training in their social enquiry reports, (Cawson, 1975) . As to the effects of incarcerating 14 and 16 year-olds in prison department establishments; in 1994 the Penal Affairs Consortium observed that:

> *The Home Office Prison Statistics for 1992 contain the latest reconviction figures for 14–16 year olds released from Prison Service custody: these are for those released in 1987 and followed for four years. 81% of boys in this age group leaving Detention Centres and 85% of those leaving Youth Custody Centres were reconvicted within two years. The figures after four years were 90% and 92% respectively. The figures for girls aged 15 and 16 leaving Youth Custody Centres were 49% after two years and 55% after four years.*

A System in Crisis

By the late 1970s, more adult professionals were doing more things to more young offenders, at an earlier stage in their 'criminal careers', than at any time since the establishment of a separate youth justice system in 1908. Early official interventions which identify young people as 'criminal', may reinforce their 'deviant identity', so projecting them deeper into the youth justice system. This tendency will be accentuated if justice system professionals fail to 'manage' the sentencing process by developing a network of genuine 'alternatives to custody', access to which can only be triggered if the youngster's offences are sufficiently serious.

The evidence is fairly clear. When, in the 1960s and 1970s, larger numbers of youngsters were inducted into the system at an earlier stage, the proportion entering custody increased markedly. Whereas in 1965, 21 per cent of convicted young offenders were dealt with in attendance centres, detention centres and Borstals, by 1977 this proportion had risen to 38 per cent. As a result, the justice system inherited by the Conservative government of Margaret Thatcher in 1979 was locking up more and more less problematic children and young people. As happened again in 1999, this was forcing older juveniles up into the adult system where they were placing enormous strains on prisons which were at bursting point already, and costing the government a great deal of money.

Reform by Stealth

The Thatcher government's sabre-rattling 'law and order' rhetoric notwithstanding, the 1982 Criminal Justice Act was the law which initiated the rationalisation of the youth justice system of England and Wales. By the mid-1980s, government youth justice policies were primarily concerned with the cost-effective management of the youth justice system. This led to a unique situation in which the most vociferous 'law and order' government of the post-war period found itself presiding over unprecedented reductions in the numbers of young people consigned to custody. This occurred, moreover, in a period in which the crime rate rose to record heights, (Pitts, 1996).

However, the Conservative Government's first foray into penal reform was something of a fiasco. The 1982 Criminal Justice Act handed juvenile court magistrates the power to commit juveniles to what were now called Youth Custody Centres for six months or for two consecutive periods of six months if they deemed it necessary, rather than remitting the case to the Crown Court for sentencing. This was obviously a gesture of solidarity with the magistrates, a key political constituency for the Conservative Party. However, it was accompanied by a plea from Home Office minister Leon Brittain that they use this power only when absolutely necessary, utilising the new three-week 'short, sharp shock' regimes in detention centres to the full, and youth custody sparingly. In the year following the introduction of the 1982 Act, the borstal/youth custody centre population rose by 65 per cent while the short sharp shock was effectively rejected by the juvenile bench. As a result of this experience, it is now an established political precept that if politicians hand more power to the bench, or even hint that they wish magistrates to make greater use of their existing powers, they will. This is why, subsequently, Home Secretaries Hurd, Waddington and Baker, and the Lord Chancellor's department, took to sending the bench unequivocal messages about reducing sentence lengths and using alternatives to custody whenever possible, in an attempt to manage, and in so doing inject some rationality and proportionality into, sentencing within the youth justice system. This remarkable strategy, coming as it did from an administration elected a few years before on a draconian 'law and order' ticket, required an unusual, and on the face of it unlikely, political alliance, with the 'progressive minimalists' of the left, comprising youth justice professionals, penal reform groups, progressive Home Office civil servants and academic criminologists.

Decarceration

The first major outing for the government's 'delinquency management' strategy came in 1983, when the Department of Health and Social Security launched its Intermediate Treatment (IT) Initiative, in which £15,000,000 was granted to non-governmental agencies to develop 4,500 alternatives to custody, over three years, in collaboration with the police and juvenile court magistrates. Between 1981 and 1989 the numbers of juveniles imprisoned in Young Offenders Institutions fell from 7,700 to 1,900 per annum.

However, the radical reductions in custodial sentencing during this period are not solely attributable to changes in 'sentencing culture' and the provision of alternatives to custody, although this may have played a minor role. The levels of custodial sentencing in areas where 'Initiative' projects were established tended to be 2–3 per cent below the national average (9 per cent versus 11.4 per cent of all sentences, NACRO, 1989). Supporters of the Initiative maintain that this lower rate testifies to the effectiveness of the government and youth justice professionals in persuading magistrates and judges to change their sentencing practices. However, it could also be the case that Initiatives were established in areas which already had low custody rates, since a pre-condition for funding was that the police and the juvenile bench should be in favour of, and willing to use, alternatives to custody. Moreover there were, at the same time, reductions in custodial sentencing in many non-Initiative areas where no additional 'alternatives to custody' were established or popularised by project workers. If these reductions in custodial sentencing were a product of changed sentencing patterns, we might reasonably expect the proportion of custodial sentences imposed by juvenile courts to drop markedly vis a vis non-custodial sentences. In fact, as Anthony Bottoms, (1990), discovered in his evaluation of the IT Initiative, sentencing patterns within the juvenile courts remained remarkably constant during the Initiative period.

It is more likely that the major contributory factor to the reduction in custodial sentencing during this period was the marked reduction in the numbers of children and young people entering juvenile courts. Whereas in 1980 71,000 boys and girls aged 14 to 16 were sentenced by the juvenile courts in England and Wales, by 1987 this figure had dropped by 37,300, a reduction of over 52 per cent. Far more tightly regulated forms of police cautioning and other, less formal, modes of pre-court diversion were 'starving' the courts of juvenile offenders, causing some youth justice workers to proclaim, prematurely in the event, the advent of 'custody-free zones', (Rutherford, 1986). Between 1980 and 1987 the cautioning rate for girls aged 14 to 16 rose from 58 per cent to 82 per cent. For boys the figures were 34 per cent and 58 per cent respectively. The implications for would-be reformers appears to be that diverting youngsters away from the justice system at an early stage may be more effective than attempts to change the attitudes and behaviour of sentencers.

So pleased was the Home Office with these results that it planned to enshrine its achievements in the Criminal Justice Act (1991) and to pursue a similar strategy for young adult offenders, whose custody rate was climbing. As the junior Home Office minister John Patten, (1991), rather quaintly observed:

> *I want to promote a cultural change not just in the probation service but among the sentencing classes. The punishing classes and the helping classes are now talking to each other in a way they never did before.*
>
> (The Guardian, 12/4/91)

The Renaissance of Youth Imprisonment

However, record hikes in the crime rate, and youth riots in out-of-town housing estates in 1991 and 1992 were to force John Major's government to defend its minimalist policies on youth crime. But it was the murder in 1992 of two-year-old James Bulger by two truanting ten-year-olds, which put youth crime unequivocally back on the 'front page'. As a result, the key reforms of the 1991 Criminal Justice Act were abandoned. In March 1993, only five months after the newly implemented Act had abolished custody for children under 15, Kenneth Clarke, the Home Secretary promised to create 200 places in new 'Secure Training Centres' for 12 to 15 year olds. This *volte face* signalled a new era in which crime in general, and youth crime in particular, were to be moved back to the centre of the political stage.

The Tough Get Going

Seeing the Tories in disarray, Labour mounted a full-scale attack on their 'law and order' record, orchestrated and led by their new shadow Home Secretary, Tony Blair. Under the Tories, Blair claimed, crime in general and youth crime in particular was running out of control. Not only had they created a moral vacuum in which crime flourished, the Tories had, he said, also shown themselves to be incapable of forging the radical measures needed to contain it. Labour, Blair maintained, would be 'tough on crime' and 'tough on the causes of crime' and, in the ensuing debate, the Labour Party deployed the entire lexicon of 'get tough' soundbites in an attempt to wrest the political initiative on 'law and order' from the Conservative's grasp.

If Labour's message was unfamiliar, its delivery held even more surprises. Ken Livingstone who, as leader of the GLC, had entertained Sinn Fein's Gerry Adams and Martin McGuiness at County Hall, called for longer prison sentences. David Blunkett, shadow Health Secretary and erstwhile leader of Sheffield City Council, the eponymous 'Socialist Republic of South Yorkshire', demanded the reintroduction of national service. And, with that touch of ambiguity which was to become his political hallmark, Tony Blair called for a regime of 'tough love', a phrase he had borrowed from US president Bill Clinton, in which secure confinement would be tempered with a responsiveness to the offender's needs.

Prison Works?

In October 1993, Michael Howard, the new Conservative Home Secretary told the Conservative Party's annual conference that:

> *Prison works, it ensures that we are protected from murderers, muggers and rapists – and it makes many who are tempted to commit crime think twice... This may mean that many more people will go to prison. I do not flinch from that. We shall no longer judge the success of our system of justice by a fall in our prison population.*

In July 1994 Tony Blair became leader of the Labour Party and Jack Straw became shadow Home Secretary. While not subscribing directly to Howard's proposition that 'prison works', Straw subsequently emphasised his commitment to:

> *consistent and progressive sentencing so that criminals know far more readily what they can expect. At present so many of them think they are living a charmed life and are too often surprised when they end up in jail.*
>
> (The Observer, 1/2/98)

The youth court bench, realising which way the wind was blowing, began to impose custodial sentences in earnest. The population of young offenders under sentence in penal establishments, which had fallen steadily between 1983 and 1993, rose by nearly 60 per cent from 5081 to 8500 in 1998.

Jack Straw's Stratagem

As Shadow Home Secretary, Jack Straw's job was at once simple and daunting. He had to retain the political initiative, which Tony Blair had seized in the furore surrounding the Bulger case. This task was central to what had now become the 'New Labour' project, not least because Blair's claim to the leadership of the Labour Party was predicated, in large part, upon his virtuoso parliamentary performances at the time of the Bulger case. These performances simultaneously enabled the party to speak with one, albeit meticulously rehearsed, voice and give expression to 'the mood of the country' on the issue of 'law and order'; an issue previously viewed as the sole preserve of the Tories. Straw's task was to plant firmly in popular consciousness the idea that New Labour was now the 'natural party of law and order'. New Labour, he claimed, would offer not a radical departure from, or a reversal of, the Conservative's stated objectives on youth crime, but rather a policy which integrated popular Conservative 'law and order' concerns with vastly improved economy, efficiency and effectiveness.

However, as the 1997 general election approached, Jack Straw had to contend with the fallout from Michael Howard's decision to become the 'hard-right candidate' in the impending, post-defeat, Conservative Party leadership contest. Knowing that he would probably never have to 'deliver', Howard's 'law and order' promises became ever more extravagant. But now Jack Straw was committed, and his only option was to match Howard's increasingly eccentric bids. Howard had toughened the Probation Service, Straw said it should be tougher still. Youth on the streets, Howard told the police to act decisively, Straw promised to pass a law against it. Secure Training Centres – New Labour now liked them, but wanted 10 and eleven-year-olds sent there too.

Hard Labour

Some commentators imagined that, despite their 'tough' pre-election law and order rhetoric, New Labour's front bench, once elected, would reveal policies, which aimed to solve the complex problems of crime and victimisation in an increasingly polarised society. There was also a belief, in some quarters, that in the new era of 'post-ideological' politics announced by Tony Blair (a politics based on 'what works' rather than the 'tired old slogans'), the issues of crime and justice would no longer be exploited for political and electoral advantage. And there was also a modicum of hope, amongst justice system professionals, for practical policies which reflected what had been learnt about the internal dynamics of youth justice systems in the preceding thirty years. By and large, this optimism has proved to be unfounded.

Kicking Arse in Worcester

The *Crime and Disorder Act* (1998) was New Labour's flagship and epitomised the New Labour project. Aimed at 'Worcester Woman' rather than 'Clapham Claimant' or 'Jarrow Job Seeker', the Act promised the Conservative voters who had defected to Labour in 1997 that it would contain the threat posed to their property, person and peace of mind by the 'neighbours from hell', and their perfidious progeny.

Although the Act was presented as self-evidently sensible, bi-partisan, popular, 'evidence-based', inspirationally led and, therefore, beyond all criticism, its apparent political neutrality could be subverted at a stroke if political necessity demanded. Thus, in 1999 the Home Secretary, Jack Straw, suddenly exhumed Michael Howard's 'three strikes and out' sentencing policy for juvenile burglars in response to a call from party HQ to 'showcase' a tough measure in order to boost flagging opinion poll ratings.

New Labour's youth justice strategy drew heavily upon The Audit Commission's report *Misspent Youth*, (Perfect and Renshaw 1996). *Misspent Youth* was, first and foremost, concerned with whether, or not, the youth justice system of England and Wales offered 'value for money'. Its authors brought extensive experience and considerable expertise in economics and social policy to their task but, in the wake of a whirlwind consultation exercise with a selected group of psychologically-oriented criminologists, they also chose to deliberate upon the origins of youth crime and the likely impact of a range of interventions upon young offenders.

The central message of *Misspent Youth* was that, of the £1 billion spent annually on youth justice services in England and Wales, 70 per cent was spent on administration. The remaining 30 per cent was spent on largely ineffective interventions with young offenders when they eventually completed their journey to the serious end of the system. Nothing, they noted, was spent on preventing young people getting into trouble in the first place:

> *The current system for dealing with youth crime is inefficient and expensive, while little is being done to deal effectively with juvenile nuisance. The present arrangements are failing the young people – who are not being guided away from offending towards constructive activities. They are also failing victims – those who suffer from young people's inconsiderate behaviour, and from vandalism and loss of property from thefts and burglaries.*

(p96)

Prevention

Thus, New Labour's youth justice strategy was, in large part, a reaction to the apparent moral nihilism of the progressive minimalism of the mid-1980s and the evident inability of delinquency management strategies to contain or reduce youth crime. However, economic stringency and the dominance of individualistic explanations of youth crime offered by *Misspent Youth* dictated that unlike the 'preventive' initiatives of the 1960s, 1970s and early 1980s, which stressed the importance of responsiveness to the needs of the young offender, the provision of a wide range of supportive and 'preventive' services in the community, preventive intervention in the late 1990s was re-positioned within the youth justice system. The key conceptual reference points in the construction of this strategy were derived from *Young People and Crime*, a study undertaken by John Graham and Ben Bowling for the Home Office, and the aforementioned Audit Commission report *Misspent Youth*. Having identified a broad range of social, economic and cultural 'variables' which correlate positively with youth crime, but venturing no view about how these 'variables' interacted, both documents commended a preventive strategy at the core of which were tightly focused, time-limited, cogni-tively-oriented courses in behavioural control for the parents, teachers, trou-blesome children and delinquents. These interventions, it was argued, 'are those which research points to as the most thorough and best designed programmes showing the most promising results.' (Farrington, 1996). These programmes were to be 'delivered' by the Youth Offending Teams YOTs, recommended to the government in *Misspent Youth*, which comprised representatives from all of the agencies involved in the youth justice system.

However, what was ostensibly a quest for economy efficiency, effectiveness and consistency marked the convergence of two contradictory approaches to the problem of youth crime; 'progressive minimalism' and 'low tariff' preventive intervention. *Misspent Youth* simultaneously extolled the virtues of multi-agency youth diversion panels, originally established spontaneously in many areas in the 1980s, to keep youngsters out of the system (Pratt, 1989), while endorsing the new thrust in centre left social policy, towards robust early inter-vention with troublesome populations, in order to nip their socially deviant proclivities in the bud. Thus the YOT emerged with a structure which had origi-nally been designed as a mechanism for keeping youngsters out of the youth justice system, and a remit to draw younger, less problematic children, young people and their parents into the system.

The Logic of Systems

Like all 'systems', New Labour's youth justice system had a logic of its own. This is hardly news, changed system 'inputs' trigger changed system outputs, that is why they are called 'systems'. The problem was that Jack Straw's Home Office appeared not to have thought through the logic of the new system they had brought into being. New Labour's new youth justice system allows formal pre-emptive intervention with populations previously beyond the reach of the youth justice and child protection systems via *Child Safety, Anti-Social Behaviour, Child Curfew* and *Parenting* orders. This is likely to draw in a new, much larger, population of youngsters. These measures, which blur the distinction between offending and offensiveness, and effectively reduce the age of criminal responsibility to zero, are likely to set in train many new 'system careers', not to mention a significantly enhanced workload for the European Court of Human Rights.

The ending of police discretion in repeat cautioning and its replacement by one 'reprimand' and one 'final warning', will mean that a larger number of children and young people in trouble will enter the system, and will exhaust this option, at a younger age and an earlier stage in their offending careers. While the final warning will probably deter around 70 per cent of them, the remaining 30 per cent of this larger and younger population will now enter the youth court.

The effective repeal of the 'absolute' and 'conditional discharge' in the youth court, a disposal previously imposed in 28 per cent of cases, will mean that a larger number of young people entering court for the first time will be made the subjects of an 'Action Plan Order', a 'Reparation Order' or a 'Supervision Order'. The belief that young offenders will simply be 'turned around' at this stage by the 'evidence-based' measures which underpin these orders is rooted in a demonstrable misreading of that evidence. (Pawson and Tilley, 1997. Matthews and Pitts, 1998). Consequently, the 55 per cent, or so, of these youngsters who re-offend, (Audit Commission, 1996), are likely to receive the new, partially indeterminate, 'Detention and Training Order' (DTO) or have a 'residence requirement' inserted in their supervision order.

The extension of the power of the youth courts to remand children and young people directly into secure and penal establishments, the unequivocal signals sent to magistrates by the expansion of secure and custodial provision, and the Home Secretary's observation, in spring 1998, that 'prisons are a demand-led service, if the courts want to impose custodial sentences, it is my job to provide the cells,' have all fuelled the use of custodial disposals by sentencers. This process will be moved up a gear in 2001 with the introduction of a 'three strikes' sentencing strategy for young burglars announced in 1999. With the advent of the 'Secure Training Centres', the numbers of 12–15 year olds sentenced to DTOs will increase substantially and quickly fill the 200 available places. This is likely to mean that existing young offender institutions will have to be re-designated, and growing numbers of 15 year olds will be pushed up into young offender institutions proper. Norman Warner, chair of the Youth Justice Board of England and Wales, has confirmed that this is likely to be the case in the 'short-term'. There is, as yet, no official word on why or when this situation is likely to change.

The fact that it has brought into being a system which will pull in a greater number of younger, less problematic, children and young people; to subject them to modes of intervention which have not been shown to be particularly effective, belies the alleged radicalism of the Crime and Disorder Act, (1998). As a consequence, many more of them will be dispatched to young offender institutions from which, Sir David Ramsbotham the Chief Inspector of Prisons has said, anybody under 18 should be removed. Ramsbottom has been attacked by Junior Home Office Ministers for his failure to appreciate the ways in which New Labour plans to modernise what they now describe as 'the juvenile secure estate'.

The Secure Estate We're in

Following their election in 1997 the Labour government established a Youth Justice Taskforce to report upon the state of the 'juvenile secure estate'. The taskforce considered the arrangements for detaining young offenders in Young Offender Institutions (YOIs) run by the prison service, secure accommodation run by local authorities; and the Glenthorne Youth Treatment Centre run by the Department of Health. Its final report (1998) concluded:

> *The different types of facilities for young people that constitute the secure estate are in need of major reform. Current arrangements are both inconsistent and unsatisfactory. Young offender institutions are too large. Bullying and abuse of one young offender by another occurs too often while the education offered is often poor. Some young offender institutions, notably Lancaster Farms, have made major efforts to provide good services but even in these cases there is scope for improving links between the supervision a young person receives inside the institution and the supervision provided when the young person returns to the community.*

Responsibility for the 'secure estate' was handed to the newly constituted Youth Justice Board of England and Wales. Their remit is to mould the existing ragbag of institutions into a coherent system with 'a structured and caring environment', which 'addresses the individual needs and welfare of the young people and the risk of harm they pose to themselves', and 'reduces offending behaviour'. Significantly, in stating its official 'vision', the Board notes that the achievement of these goals will be contingent upon the capacity of community-based programmes of preventive intervention at earlier stages in the process, to halt the progress of children and young people up the sentencing tariff. However, as I have argued above, there is considerable evidence that the 'community penalties' introduced by the Crime and Disorder Act will not achieve this goal and may, instead, draw more youngsters into a system career. This is not just because, as I have suggested, the proposed cognitive-behavioural and restrictive interventions are likely to have only a limited impact upon youth offending. It is also the case that the Youth Justice Board's implicit plea for a strategy of 'delinquency management', is likely to fall upon deaf ears amongst the politicians, judges and magistrates who, for the foreseeable future, are unlikely to countenance 'alternatives to custody' for more serious offenders.

It is therefore likely that the growing demand from sentencers for secure provision, which has been evident for most of the 1990s, will dilute still further the educational and rehabilitative resources available to young prisoners. It will also make the task of developing penal regimes which do not worsen the problems which brought the children and young people into custody in the first place, even harder (for a fuller account see the following chapter by Stephen Shaw and Clare Sparks).

Yet, like governments throughout the preceding 100 years, New Labour enthusiastically adopted plans for a new kind of children's prison; a Secure Training Centre (STC), rather than responding to the dismal news about secure provision and youth imprisonment by placing an embargo upon the further development of penal institutions. The new STCs, the Home Office maintained, were to be robustly managed in accordance with clear goals. They were to be 'transparent' in their operation, utilising only proven rehabilitative programmes within a professional regime which accorded with 'best practice' in the residential care sector. Yet the first STC, run by Rebound ECD (education, care and discipline) a subsidiary of Group 4 and Tarmac was very quickly in trouble.

By the autumn of 1998, the staff of Medway STC were getting very jumpy indeed, as they were 'bitten, hit and head-butted' by children, some of whom were teetering on the edge of mental illness. More than 100 assaults on staff were recorded in the centre's first seven months of operation, along with £100,000 worth of damage. Over the period, 35 of the original 100 staff resigned and an increasingly perplexed and frustrated Home Office finally decided it was time to call in reinforcements. Nick Cohen writes:

> *The despised public-sector prison service has now been ordered to draw up riot control plans better suited to Strangeways or Fort Apache or the Bronx. According to the latest leaked documents from the Home Office – and I don't know what morale's like in Whitehall but I'm getting more Home Office leaks than Christmas cards this season – 'prompt and effective' measures must be planned for when 'there is a major threat to overall control'. Containing the 12 year-olds is so arduous a task that the most senior and hard-bitten security officers in the prison service, known as 'Gold' commanders, are on alert. 'Strategic command of an incident will rest with a Prison Service Gold,' the memo continues, 'who will operate from the Headquarters Control Suite.' Gold's swat team will be authorised to use 'basic and advanced control and restraint techniques'.*

(Hey, Tony, leave those kids alone, The Observer, 20/12/98)

So much for the 'restraint' guidelines of the Children Act 1989.

In January 1999, the Social Services Inspectorate submitted a damning report on Medway STC, recommending that it be shut down and that the other five STCs under construction, at an estimated cost of £30,000,000, should be put on hold. Paul Boateng, recently transferred from the Department of Health, where he launched the *Quality Protects* initiative to safeguard children in residential care, refused to be drawn on the issue of closure, referring to the Medway trainees as 'little monsters'.

Undaunted, the Youth Justice Board invited the major children's charities to bid for contracts to run the remaining three Secure Training Centres. They declined on the grounds that they regarded STCs as ill-considered, ill-conceived, politically inspired and inimical to the interests, and a threat to the well-being, of the troubled younger offenders for which they were designed. On hearing this, a senior figure associated with the Board, and a confidante of Home Secretary Jack Straw, opined loudly that these people should 'grow up' and get to grips with the political realities of what New Labour had taken to calling 'the real world'.

Spencer Millham, (1977), has shown that in the UK, the failure of, or crises within, each new form of secure provision for juveniles has always spawned another type of institution which promptly finds that it is heir to all the difficulties which confounded the institution it has superseded. So why do we persist? Millham answers:

> *In the old approved school system demonstrations that the failure rates were enormous or that the institutions had a host of other difficulties were irrelevant for policy, simply because residential institutions have one enormous advantage over community care. Behind their walls the children are invisible.*
>
> (Millham, 1977, p23)

CHAPTER 12

The Rights and Wrongs of Youth Custody

Stephen Shaw and Clare Sparks

In April 1990, during the wave of prison riots, which followed the insurrection at Manchester's Strangeways prison, there was a major disturbance involving young people at Pucklechurch remand centre outside Bristol. What happened subsequently remains a matter of controversy. The official report suggests that prisoners were left naked under blankets for two days. It adds:

> *The treatment of inmates after surrender has to be criticised. It should not have been only the Board of Visitors who noted the unfortunate remarks referring to the breaking of limbs. There is no doubt that at the time the inmates were very frightened. The treatment of the clothing and personal possessions of the inmates is wholly unjustifiable. No explanation or justification has been given why personal possessions such as watches and earrings should be removed.*

(Lord Justice Woolf, 1991)

Every institution looks back to a golden age. In the case of the Prison Service, and its responsibility for young offenders, there is tendency to idealise the pre- and post-war Borstals when caring, motivated 'housemasters' instilled the values of the English public school into the delinquents in their charge. There is ample evidence of these benevolent intentions. But the reality – perhaps best captured in books such as Brendan Behan's *Borstal Boy* and Alan Sillitoe's *The Loneliness of the Long Distance Runner* – was a good deal rougher. Indeed, the use of physical violence by staff was almost certainly much more prevalent in the 1950s and 1960s than it is today. That said, the systematic brutalising of young people at Pucklechurch after the riot in Easter 1990 is an illustration of the ever-present potential for abuse by staff.

In this contribution, we look at the characteristics of the young offenders and of the 'secure estate'. We highlight the differences between the various young offender institutions and consider criticisms made by HM Chief Inspector of Prisons, Sir David Ramsbotham, and by Sir William Utting. We detail New Labour's critique of youth justice, and explore the consequences of measures in the 1998 Crime and Disorder Act – in particular, the establishment of the Youth Justice Board and the new Detention and Training Order. We conclude with some recommendations for better practice.

Categories of Abuse

We begin with the issue of physical abuse, the potential for which we regard as intrinsic to the prison experience. The maintenance of order in all custodial institutions ultimately depends on the use of coercive power. There has been some level of staff-on-prisoner violence throughout the Prison Service's history, and this has come to public notice recently in a series of allegations against staff at HMP Wormwood Scrubs. However, taken overall, we judge the Prison Service in England and Wales to be relatively free of the staff violence which characterises so many other prison systems.

The much greater potential for abuse (whether physical, psychological or sexual) exists *between* young people in custody and may be said to derive more from a lack of care on the part of the prison authorities rather than from their oppressive practice. Bullying, battering, 'taxing' (theft and robbery) and violent initiation ceremonies (sometimes with a sexual element) have been features of almost all penal institutions housing children and young offenders.

Many of these attacks are never recorded as such by the authorities – either because of direct intimidation or because of the inmate code of silence ('I fell over in the showers'). Likewise, there is little official evidence of the sexual abuse of children and young people in custody (whether it involves adults or other youngsters). Sir William Utting (1997) expressed his surprise at this lack of information in his landmark report *People Like Us*. In the Prison Reform Trust's evidence to Utting, we said that the authorities had investigated some cases of abuse by adults in the past, but we knew of no published accounts.

As with violent and sexual assaults, little is known about the incidence of racial harassment – again whether from staff or from other prisoners. Report after report from Boards of Visitors, the local watchdogs, and from HM Chief Inspector of Prisons, contain bland assessments that 'race relations' are not a 'problem'. The Prison Inspectorate has been weak on race issues throughout its existence and there is a strong case for a separate thematic review on the issue.

The ultimate abuse and lack of care is of course suicide and self-injury. Here at least there is some firm evidence, albeit inquest verdicts tend to understate the number of suicides. Self-injury statistics are unreliable both in terms of reporting and recording. But we do know that in 1997, of the 70 self-inflicted deaths in Prison Service custody (i.e. one death every five days), 16 involved prisoners under the age of 21. We also know that in 1990, Philip Knight, a 15 year old prisoner held on remand at Swansea prison, took his own life. At least two other 15 year olds have killed themselves in young offender institutions during the 1990s.

There are, of course, many causes of suicide and parasuicide. But fear of other prisoners undoubtedly plays a significant part. For this reason, the Prison Service has spent much time developing policies and practices to combat bullying. (Although widely recognised and understood by both staff and prisoners, 'bullying' is an unfortunate term, suggesting a degree of childishness. Intimidation, assault, robbery, should be called what they are.) Since 1995/96, all establishments – whether for adults or young people – have been expected to develop anti-bullying strategies (See also *Bullying in Prison: A Strategy to beat it*, (1998) Prison Service). In early 1999, the Prison Service issued comprehensive new anti-bullying guidance which charges governors to ensure six key elements in their local response:

1. That bullying will not be tolerated.
2. That monitoring and evaluation processes should be put in place.
3. That a 'whole prison approach' should be taken to changing the climate and culture.
4. That supervision and detection should be improved.
5. That victims should be supported.
6. That bullies should be challenged with the aim of replacing anti-social with pro-social behaviour.

No-one could do other than welcome this strategic approach, but it is not possible to tackle bullying effectively if a jail is in poor physical shape and if its regime is boring. Penal institutions for children and young people differ widely, but report after report from the indefatigable David Ramsbotham, Chief Inspector of Prisons, has drawn attention to serious deficiencies in the quality of care. Something of the flavour may be gained from these extracts:

Of 'disgraceful' Werrington YOI (inspected June 1998):

> *To find children no longer eating together, but forced to take their food back to their cells, which are little more than lavatories, to eat, being limited to two evenings of association in a week, on landings where there are no chairs, so the time amounts to little more than an hour and a half standing outside rather than inside a cell, would be bad enough if found in any juvenile establishment...I have not come across such totally deliberate and unnecessary impoverishment of children anywhere and suspect that, were Werrington to be a Secure Custody Unit in the hands of the Social Services, it would be closed for lack of provision of appropriate facilities.*

> Report of a Short Unannounced Report on HMYOI Werrington.
> HM Inspector of Prisons (1998)

Of Dover YOI (inspected May 1996):

> *...The six bed dormitories in which the majority of young prisoners were housed, apart from being ramshackle in appearance, were the setting for untold bullying and criminal corruption. They were a veritable 'jungle' in which the strong preyed on the weak and where most who entered the*

establishment had to physically fight to survive or exist as a vulnerable prisoner, subjected to continual intimidation and insult.

> Report of a Full Inspection on HMYOI Dover.
> HM Inspector of Prisons (1997)

Of Feltham YOI (inspected October/November 1996):

Feltham is bursting at the seams. It is not an institution able to tackle re-offending but a gigantic transit camp, in which day to day activities are dominated by the process of finding beds for ever increasing numbers, particularly of young remand prisoners, and ensuring that they get to court on time.

> Report of a Full Inspection on HMYOI Feltham.
> HM Inspector of Prisons (1997)

As prison reformers, we can but deprecate conditions and treatment of this kind. But we also sympathise with the managers of young offender institutions. First, they have little or no control over intake: no prison or YOI can put up a 'full up' sign. Moreover, at a time when the numbers in custody overall have risen at an unprecedented rate (as a broad rule-of-thumb, the prison population in England and Wales grew by 10 per cent in each of the five years between 1993 and 1997), the system responds by sending prisoners far across the country to wherever there is an available space.

Second, just as there is no control over intake, most managers have only limited sway over resources. Although the Prison Service is much less centralised than was once the case, and responsibility for many budgets has been devolved to establishment level, many spending heads and priorities are still determined at the centre. In some cases, these priorities are politically determined. The twin escapes of top-security adult prisoners from Whitemoor and Parkhurst in September 1994 and January 1995 set off a wave of spending on extra security throughout the prison system. It also had a direct impact on regimes – either because certain activities were barred or because prison officers had been diverted to other tasks.

A third problem concerns staffing. Nobody joins the Prison Service expressly to work in a young offender institution. Indeed, many may end up doing so against their wishes or expectations. No less fundamentally, the numbers and grades of staff tend to reflect the demands and traditions of the much larger adult estate. Similarly, the YOI rules made under the Prison Act 1952 read essentially like the adult prison rules. There are one or two changes in terminology but no fundamental shift of emphasis.

A fourth problem, linked to that of staffing, is the lack of specialist training for staff who work with young offenders. It is inconceivable in any other aspect of residential care that none of the staff looking after a group of children or young people would not have had specific training in working with this age group. While some training has been developed, most notably by the Trust for the Study of Adolescence, there is no obligation on governors of young offender institutions to ensure training for their staff in the specific issues they will face working with this age group.

The Trust for the Study of Adolescence (TSA) carries out research into issues relevant to adolescence such as teenage parenthood, family break-up, communication, drugs and poverty. Working in partnership with Lancaster Farms YOI, the TSA has produced a training manual for staff, *The Nature of Adolescence – Working with Young People in Custody*. This challenges staff to reconsider young offenders' behaviour in the light of their own feelings and activities when they were young. The training package, which has been lauded by Sir David Ramsbotham, has been offered to staff at many prisons holding young offenders, but it is not obligatory.

The Ramsbotham and Utting Reports

Sir David crystallised his criticisms of young offender institutions into a landmark report, *Young Prisoners* (1997). Arguing that there was, 'a clear obligation on custodial authorities to locate young prisoners in establishments where regimes help them to mature, examine their behaviour, and change,' Sir David said that, 'of all the parts of the Prison Service that we inspect, the one that gives all of us in the Inspectorate the greatest cause for concern is the Young Prisoner estate.' He added:

> It is the plight of children that alarms us most, not least because of the conditions in which they are held in Prison Service establishments in many cases they are far below the minimum conditions in Social Services Department secure units required by the Children Act 1989 and the UN Convention on the Rights of the Child. Indeed I can find no evidence that the Prison Service has acknowledged the Children Act 1989 as having any relevance to children held in Prison Service establishments. More damage is done to immature adolescents than to any other type of prisoner, by current conditions. There is no such thing as a neutral environment in custodial institutions. Young prisoners are either helped or damaged by the experience.
>
> > Young Prisoners: A Thematic Review, pp 6, 13.
> > HM Chief Inspector of Prisons (1997c)

Ramsbotham called upon the Prison Service to relinquish responsibility for all children under the age of 18. In the interim, children should receive individual attention, assessment, close supervision and education/training according to their individual needs. There should be a focus on working closely with families, a much under-used resource throughout the penal system. Training should be expanded. He records the current position as follows: 'Specific training for dealing with adolescents was sporadic and confined to wing or unit staff. Staff in other areas of the establishment such as Reception, Induction, PE and Healthcare were generally excluded from such courses'. And the aims and values of both the Children Act and the UN Convention should be incorporated into a new set of rules and practices.

Ramsbotham also proposed that local authorities should pay the costs of children in custody, thus removing the current financial disincentive against using their own secure estate. (Sad to say, the Chief Inspector's continued emphasis on the word 'children' to refer to those under 18 has been regarded as 'emotive' by some Prison Service officials.)

Perhaps because they form such a small proportion (1–2 per cent) of all children living away from home, *People Like Us* (1997) has relatively little to say about the problems faced by children living in penal institutions. Sir William Utting drew heavily on inspection reports from HM Chief Inspector of Prisons, and *People Like Us* was in fact published on the same day as the Chief Inspector's thematic review *Young Prisoners*.

However, in a subsequent article, *Children in Prison* (1998). Utting has drawn attention to possible breaches of the UN Convention on the Rights of the Child in the treatment of children on remand:

> *Children were said to be allocated to wherever a vacancy could be found, sometimes at great distance from home and family, overcrowded, in local prisons, sharing accommodation (even cells) with adults, moving around the system without access to educational or leisure facilities. Such conditions do not need to be widespread to constitute a public scandal and an obvious falling away from the basic requirements of the Convention.*

Regrettably, it is not clear from this passage whether Utting considers a 'falling away from the basic requirements' to constitute a breach of the Convention.

But Utting is forthright in arguing that 'children on remand should not be in the penal system at all, and *People Like Us* criticises the failure of government to implement Section 60 of the Criminal Justice Act 1991 which was intended to end the use of Prison Service custody for the remanding of juveniles. Somewhat optimistically, he suggests that the Crime and Disorder Act 1998 may provide 'a belated approach to removing the problem.' In contrast, the Penal Affairs Consortium, which is made up of all the principal representative bodies like the Prison Governors Association and NAPO plus interest groups like NACRO and the Prison Reform Trust while welcoming some of the Act's provisions has expressed its concern about the provisions in Section 98 of the Act which provide for vulnerable 15 and 16 year old boys to be remanded to local authority secure accommodation if a place is available and for other 15 and 16 year old boys to be remanded to Prison Service custody. The Consortium comments that:

anyone of this age held in an overcrowded and overstretched penal estab-
lishment is potentially vulnerable to criminal contamination, depression
and self harm'.

The Crime and Disorder Act. Penal Affairs Consortium (1998)

The basic problem is insufficient local authority accommodation, given the rise
in the number of young people in custody during the 1990s. The Penal Affairs
Consortium has suggested that one way forward may be to abandon the pledge to
end the remanding of all juveniles, and to begin with 15 year olds before moving
on to those a year older.

Utting appears to be at one with Sir David Ramsbotham in locating inconsis-
tencies in the treatment of children and young people within 'the current managerial structures and policy priorities'. Sir David has repeatedly called for
functional management within the Prison Service (that is, grouping young
offender institutions, women's prisons, other specialist jails, altogether) as
opposed to the service's present system of management by geographical areas.
A compromise has been reached whereby an enhanced directorate of regimes
within Prison Service Headquarters now contains specialist women's policy and
young offenders policy units, each headed by an assistant director. However,
although these units offer support and advice and have responsibilities for
policy development, they do not have line management responsibilities, nor do
they have any allocated budget. Utting says: 'From the perspective of the safeguards review, the post of assistant director needs the line management clout to
achieve local delivery of the distinctive policies for the welfare of children in
penal settings ... '

Utting accepted that the Children Act did not apply to young offender institutions, but argued that the principles therein should be incorporated into revised
YOI rules, the statutory instrument which interprets the Prison Act 1952. A
revision of the YOI rules is now planned by Prison Service Headquarters, although
it seems unlikely they will be promulgated until the second half of 1999 at the
earliest. (A revision of the prison rules for adult prisoners should come into effect
in early 1999.)

The Children in Custody

The population of young offenders under sentence, which fell by a half between
1980 and 1993, rose by nearly 60 per cent in the four years to 1997 (see Table 1).
It reached 7,949 in mid-1997 and has risen to over 8,500 since then. At the end of
September 1998, 1,625 convicted young offenders were aged 17 or under (1,549
boys, 76 girls), and 6,893 were aged 18–20 (6,630 young men, 263 young
women). In addition, around 3,000 young offenders (736 aged 15–17) were held
on remand. Home Office 1998) *Prison Statistics England and Wales 1997*; (Home
Office 1998).

Table 1. Average population of young offenders in custody under sentence by sex

	1987	1988	1989	1990	1991	1992	1993	1994	1995	1996	1997
Male	9329	8263	6997	6247	5683	5443	4925	5137	5659	6363	7698
Fem	227	183	173	154	100	139	156	139	183	252	251
All	9556	8446	7170	6401	5793	5572	5081	5276	5842	6615	7949

Source: Home Office (1998) *Prison Statistics England and Wales 1997*, Table 3.7

While most young offenders serve a relatively short sentence there is a significant and growing minority who will serve over three years. The average sentence length of those discharged in 1997 was 11.3 months for male young offenders and 8.6 months for females. In mid-1997 just over 40 per cent of young offenders were serving sentences up to 18 months, 32 per cent were serving over 18 months and under three years, the remaining 28 per cent were serving over three years. (Home Office 1998).

These bare statistics tell only part of the story. What sort of youngsters are they who end up in custody? Not surprisingly, we find considerable overlap in the characteristics of children and young people in penal establishments and those in other forms of institutional care.

Indeed, no-one entering a young offender institution, and talking to the children and young people themselves, can fail to be struck by the levels of damage and disadvantage which they exhibit. However a proper socio-economic breakdown of those in YOIs is not available. For a representative sample we are reliant upon the 1991 *National Prison Survey*, but this expressly excluded juveniles under 18. (It would be beneficial were the survey conducted routinely – say every five years.) At that time, it was found that 38 per cent of young prisoners had been in local authority care at some point in their childhood. A similar proportion had suffered psychiatric problems. Levels of literacy and numeracy and social skills were also painfully low.

Since then, Sir David Ramsbotham has carried out a smaller sample survey of young men and young women in custody for his thematic review. This identified various factors in the criminal and social histories of the young people held in the prison system.

Amongst the boys and young men, a very high proportion had a history of care or social services contact. Half of those aged under 18 came into this category. Despite this, many remained in contact with members of their family. Indeed, many had been living at home prior to their custody – usually with one parent, usually their mother.

Over half had been excluded, or had excluded themselves, from school with almost two-thirds stating that they had no educational qualifications. Two-thirds had also been unemployed before they entered custody, and a like proportion admitted to misusing drugs at some time in their lives. Around a quarter had been under the influence of alcohol at the time of their offence. A significant minority (17 per cent) admitted to having suffered either physical, sexual or emotional abuse, although it is likely that this figure is an underestimate. Ten per cent of the young men admitted to self harming (HM Chief Inspector of Prisons, 1997).

For young women in custody the figures are similarly telling. Just over a quarter of young women had been in care during their childhood, a lower rate than the 40 per cent of young men interviewed. But nearly half of the young women said they had experienced sexual abuse, 37 per cent said they had attempted suicide and 15 per cent said that they had self harmed.

Over three-quarters of the young women reported having used drugs or alcohol: 56 per cent said they had a problem with drugs, 29 per cent with heroin. Nearly 40 per cent of the young women had children themselves (HM Chief Inspector of Prisons, 1997).

It is a feature of all young offender institutions that those kept in custody rarely use formal channels of complaint to air their grievances. No doubt a general distrust of authority is one reason, along with a lack of written skills. But having suffered so much already in their lives, we wonder if the petty cruelties and inconveniences of prison life are seen as simply not worth the bother.

A Range of Institutions

At the time of Sir David Ramsbotham's thematic review, children and young adults were held in no fewer than 41 different Prison Service establishments. The main institutions holding male juveniles and young offenders are listed below (population and certified normal accommodation as at 31 August 1998).

However, in addition to these more or less specialist institutions, remanded boys and other young offenders can routinely be held in separate wings/units in adult prisons.

All girls and female young offenders are held in jails shared with adult women. Indeed, until recently, it was an article of faith that the presence of older women exercised a 'calming' effect on the young people, the adults in effect acting as older sisters or as substitute mothers. The Prison Service acknowledged that this mixing conflicted with the precepts of the domestic prison rules and the (advisory-only) European prison rules promulgated by the Council of Europe.

All of this has changed as a consequence of a legal challenge (the Flood Judgement – handed down on 22 August 1998) which made it unlawful for convicted female young offenders to be held in mixed accommodation with adult prisoners. (R v Accrington Youth Court, Governor of HMP Risley and Secretary of State for the Home Department ex parte Clare Louise Flood.) This has resulted in the Prison Service building or converting accommodation to provide discrete, dedicated units. The first two units at HMPs Holloway and New Hall opened in late 1998.

Establishment	Location	CNA	Occupancy
Aylesbury	Bucks	318	304
Brinsford	Staffs	477	491
Castington	Northumberland	330	320
Deerbolt	Co. Durham	432	419
Dover	Kent	316	290
Feltham	Middlesex	849	893
Glen Parva	Leics	720	814
Hatfield	Essex	180	151
Hollesley Bay	Suffolk	45	45
Huntercombe	Oxon	368	352
Lancaster Farms	Lancashire	496	483
Onley	Warwickshire	640	603
Portland	Dorset	516	562
Reading	Berks	263	232
Stoke Heath	Shropshire	646	579
Swinfen Hall	Staffs	319	311
Thorn Cross	Cheshire	316	234
Werrington	W. Yorks	188	150
Wetherby	W. Yorks	360	304

C.N.A. stands for Certified Normal Accommodation, which is the number of prisoners that the establishment is designed to hold.

This array of institutions – some with small numbers of young people, others vast penal colonies – differ markedly in the quality of care they offer. For example, a couple of miles from the centre of the pleasant county town of Lancaster can be found what is widely regarded as the best young offender institution in Britain and one of the most successful new jails ever opened. Although in fact designed as an *adult* prison, Lancaster Farms YOI has, under its banner, 'Preventing the Next Victim', proved a pioneer in the safe, humane and purposeful custody of young people. There is a distinct vision and clarity of purpose. Staff are well-trained and enthusiastic (and all staff who come into contact with young offenders have received the Trust for the Study of Adolescence training, including cleaners and caterers. The prison regime is innovative, providing a high level of activity and regular contact with community groups. The education department has achieved success with a potentially volatile, fast-moving population. And special initiatives such as an anti-bullying course and another on 'Coping in Custody' have tackled key issues. (Sparks, 1997)

Three hundred miles to the south, on the western outskirts of London, near Heathrow, is a much more troubled establishment. Feltham, with nearly 900 prisoners, is the largest concentration of young lawbreakers anywhere in Europe.

Perhaps this very size is part of the problem. It may not be coincidental that the only other YOI of similar size, Glen Parva in Leicestershire, has also had an unhappy history. Sir David Ramsbotham stormed out of his inspection of Glen Parva, so dismayed was he with what he found, and the establishment is currently one of a small number designated by the Prison Service as in need of 'special managerial attention'.

Between these two extremes may be found all manner of other establishments, differing hugely from one another in terms of size, history, tradition, architecture, performance and reputation. One sometimes reads glibly of the prison 'system' or the young offender 'system'. What strikes the observer most forcefully is the absence of the very characteristics, such as planning, unity of purpose, interconnectedness, which might be felt to constitute a systematic approach to the problems of youthful incarceration.

New Labour's Critique

It was this absence of systems which was at the heart of New Labour's critique of youth justice arrangements. Through a series of documents issued while still in Opposition, and culminating in the 1997 White Paper with the decidedly populist title *No More Excuses: A New Approach to Tackling Youth Crime in England and Wales*, (Cm 3809) Jack Straw outlined far reaching reforms to all aspects of youth justice. A raft of consultation papers were issued more or less coindicental with the White Paper, albeit they allowed scant time for a considered response before the deadline.

The measures were subsequently given statutory form in the Crime and Disorder Act 1998. In this contribution, our concern is solely with the *custodial* and *sentencing* implications of the Act. In passing, however, we note there is a great deal to be welcomed in the Act's emphasis upon local crime prevention strategies and partnerships, and a great deal to regret in its abolition of *doli incapax*, its plans for child curfews, and its use of severe criminal penalties to back up two new civil procedures designed to prevent anti-social behaviour and to control the movements of convicted sex offenders.

The Act also empowers courts to remand young people from the age of 12 upwards to secure accommodation where this is deemed necessary to protect the public. Section 98 of the Act provides that boys of 15 and 16 may be remanded to local authority secure accommodation if they are judged to be 'vulnerable' and a place is available. Those who do not meet the criteria will continue to be remanded to a remand centre or prison until such time as sufficient alternative accommodation is on stream.

Of even greater significance, sections 73–79 of the Act introduce a new, comprehensive custodial sentence for 10–17 year olds called the Detention and Training Order (DTO).

The circumstances in which a Detention and Training Order may be imposed are as follows:

- For 15–17 year olds, for any imprisonable offence sufficiently serious to justify custody under Section 1 of the Criminal Justice Act 199.
- For 12–14 year olds, who are, in the opinion of the court, persistent offenders, for offences serious enough to justify custody under the 1991 Act.
- For 10 and 11 year olds, for persistent offending and only then when the court considers that only custody is sufficient to protect the public from further offending.

Courts may impose Detention and Training Orders of 4, 6, 8, 10, 12, 18 and 24 months provided they do not exceed the adult maximum.

It is intended that the provisions will be implemented in Summer 1999. The sentence will be extended to 10 and 11 year olds at the discretion of the Home Secretary, 'only if it should prove necessary or desirable, to include them.' (Home Office, 1998).

One half of the order will be served in custody. It will be for the Home Secretary (or, rather, his agents) to decide, 'whether this is served in a secure training centre, a young offender institution, local authority secure accommodation, a youth treatment centre or any other secure accommodation'. Offenders may be released early or late from detention, to reflect good or bad progress against the sentence plan set at the beginning of the order. The Home Secretary has the power to release offenders from the detention and training element of the order one month early, for orders of eight months or more, but less than 18 months, or either one or two months early for orders of 18 months or longer. He also has the power to apply to the youth court for late release for periods of the same lengths. The Detention and Training Order thus has a degree of indeterminacy not seen in youth justice since the abolition of Borstal training and its replacement by youth custody over 15 years ago. Indeed, the indeterminate element in a Borstal sentence had in practice all but disappeared by the time the sentence as a whole was abandoned in 1982. In a very real sense, the DTO represents a return to the 1950s.

The Youth Justice Board

The key player in the future of youth custody will be the Youth Justice Board. Chaired by Lord Warner of Brockley (author of the Warner Report on children's homes (HMSO, 1992) and, more controversially, formerly policy adviser to Jack Straw), the Board will have a remit covering four main areas:

1. To monitor the operation of the youth justice system, including the youth courts and the local Youth Offending Teams.

2. To advise the Home Secretary on standards for the Youth Offending Team and the juvenile secure estate.
3. To disseminate good practice.
4. To advise the Home Secretary on the operation of the youth justice system in delivering its aim of preventing offending.

The fourth objective may seem somewhat ambitious!

The Board will also have a role as a purchaser of services. In other words, it will agree contracts for custodial services whether from the Prison Service, from local authorities, or from the privatised secure training centres. (Secure training centres are new establishments designed to house offenders formerly sentenced to Secure Training Orders and now sentenced to Detention and Training Orders under the Crime and Disorder Act. To date, just one secure training centre has opened. The Medway secure training centre in Kent opened on 17 April 1998 and holds 40 persistent young offenders aged between 12 and 14. Its first months of operation have been dogged by stories of disturbance and it has been the focus of much press attention. The second secure training centre at Onley opened in May 1999 and the preferred bidder (Securicor) for the third centre at Medomsley in County Durham has recently been announced. Two further centres are planned at Sharpness in Gloucestershire and in Nottinghamshire.) The closest model for these arrangements is the internal market within the National Health Service.

No provider is likely to be allowed a monopoly, and a mixed market will develop. As a sole purchaser, the Youth Justice Board will have a great opportunity to drive down costs and drive up performance.

The Way Forward

What more can be done to improve standards of care and prevent a recurrence of the scandals which have befallen so many YOIs – Feltham, Glen Parva and Werrington, notable among them? We believe action is required on the following agenda:

Enhanced Inspection
HM Chief Inspector of Prisons currently has two teams of inspectors which means the average YOI can expect a full inspection only once every six or seven years. At a minimum, he should be given a third team – perhaps dedicated to inspecting YOIs, certainly with an enhanced complement of those with specialist expertise in child care and child development issues.

Greater Openness
It should be a characteristic of all institutions holding young people that they should be open to a range of outside influences and maximise their community ties. This is a huge agenda, involving everything from sharing the institution's sporting and other

facilities with community organisations through to full integration of regimes and activities with those which the young people would enjoy on the outside.

Effective and Appropriate Training

The Warner Report emphasised the need to weed out those not suitable for working with children. Yet governors of YOIs have only limited control as to which staff work in their institutions. All staff coming in contact with young offenders should benefit from appropriate training – both at the start of their service and regularly during it. The training package designed by the Trust for the Study of Adolescence should be mandatory. However, we agree with Sir David Ramsbotham that it should be supplemented by other local and national training.

Clarification of Legal Status

In recent years, the Prison Service has placed much greater emphasis upon standard-setting and the auditing of performance against specific targets. We applaud these developments. But audit against standards is the final element in a process which must be traced back much earlier. The intermediary stage is to design YOI rules reflecting the distinct and special needs of children and young people (as we report, work on revising the YOI rules should be printed by the end of 1999). The primary stage is a modernised Prison Act, placing clear responsibilities upon the penal authorities and recognising the UK's commitments under the UN Convention on the Rights of the Child and clarifying where, if at all, the Children Act has implications for Prison Service policy and practice.

At first sight, this agenda may seem bureaucratic, over-concerned with process rather than the quality of service, detached from the reality of the lives of the people who live in or work in young offender institutions. It is of course true that the penal experience is very imperfectly captured by notions of rules, audit, training and inspection. What matters most to people in places of detention (of whatever age) is the relationship – if any – which they enjoy with their jailers, and the contact – if any – which they are able to maintain with their family and friends.

Some people do have a natural aptitude and sympathy for working with young people. The very best practice is almost always driven by a peculiarly talented and energetic individual. But getting these things right is not a matter of chance. The structure needs to be one in which those with talent can flourish and those who would be better employed in other directions can be identified and helped aside. This has most definitely not been the case in youth custody for many years. It is all the more important now given that the necessary 'care', affection and encouragement which all young people need may seem out of step with a media, public and political climate in which youthful lawbreakers are demonised and in which the social benefits of custody are trumpeted at every opportunity.

But even if all of our agenda were achieved, the dangers and dilemmas of penal incarceration for children would remain. In his *Prison Service Journal* article, Sir William Utting (1998) concludes:

> *Prison is no place for children, particularly for un-convicted children. It is difficult, if not impossible, to meet their needs there. I believe that children are at greater risk of abuse and general harm in penal settings than they now are in any other.*

Institutional reform can only go so far. By their very nature, institutions for young offenders have a tendency to corrupt. No YOI is so good that delinquent young people should be sent there in the belief that it will make them behave better. Many YOIs are so bad that even the least recidivistic offender leaves more equipped and determined on a career of crime.

References

Abrahams, C. and Mungall, R. (1992) *Exploding the Myths*, London, NCH Action for Children

Aldridge, M. (1994) *Making Social Work News,* London, Routledge

Aries, P. (1962) *Centuries of Childhood*, Harmondsworth, Penguin

Association of Metropolitan Authorities and Children's Rights Office (1995*) Checklist for Children: Implementing the UN Convention in Local Authorities*, London AMA

Barter, C. (1996) *Nowhere to Hide: Giving Young Runaways a Voice*, London, Centrepoint and NSPCC

Bates, J. and Pugh, R.(Eds.) (1997) *Emotionally Competent Child Protection Organisation*, Aldershot, Ashgate

Bebbington, A. and Miles, J. (1989) The Background of Children who Enter Local Authority Care, *British Journal of Social Work*, 19, 5, 349–68

Beitchman, J., Zucker, K., Hood J., Da Costa, G. and Akman, D. (1991) A Review of the Short-term Effects of Child Sexual Abuse, *Child Abuse and Neglect* 15. 537–56

Beitchman, J., Zucker, K., Hood, J., Da Costa, G., Akman, D. and Cassavia, E. (1992) A Review of the Long-term Effects of Child Sexual Abuse, *Child Abuse and Neglect* 16. 101–18

Boswell, G. (1995) *Violent Victims: The Prevalence of Abuse and Loss in the Lives of Section 53 Offenders*, London, The Prince's Trust

Bottoms, A. E., Brown, P., McWilliams, B. Mc.Williams, W. and Nellis, M. (1990) *Intermediate Treatment and Juvenile Justice*, London, Home Office

Brannan, C., Jones, R. and Murch, J. (1993) *Castle Hill Report Practice Guide,* Shropshire County Council

British Association of Social Workers (19xx) *Code of Ethics*, BASW

Brown, E., Bullock, R., Hobson, C., and Little, M. (1998*) Making Residential Care Work: Structure and Culture in Children's Homes,* Aldershot, Ashgate

Bullock, R. (1991) Residential Care for Children – What We Know and What We Don't Know in DoH, *Residential Care for Children, Report of a Seminar 30 October – 1 November 1991*

Calam, R. and Franchi, C. (1987) *Child Abuse and its Consequences,* Cambridge, Cambridge Univ. Press

Cawson, P. (1975) *Changes in Intakes of Special Units*, Unpublished, London, DHSS

CCETSW (1992) *Residential Child Care in the Diploma in Social Work,* London

Child Care Register. London. ICSE

Children's Rights Officers and Advocates (1998) *On the Rights Track. Guidance for Local Authorities on Establishing Children's Rights and Advocacy Services*, Local Government Association

Cliffe, D. (with Berridge, D.) (1991) *Closing Children's Homes: An End to Residential Childcare?* London, National Children's Bureau

Cobley, C. (1995) *Child Abuse and the Law,* London, Cavendish

Cohen, S. (1985) *Visions of Social Control,* Cambridge, Polity Press

Colton, M. J. and Hellinckx, W. (1993) *Child Care in the EC*, Aldershot, Arena

Corby, B., Doig, A. and Roberts, V. (1998) Inquiries into Child Abuse. *Journal of Social Welfare and Family Law* 20, 377–95

Cornish, D. and Clarke, R. (1975) *Residential Treatment and its Effects on Delinquency*, (Home Office Research Study No.32), London, HMSO

Crimmens, D. (1997) Staff Development Strategies in Residential Child Care. In *Interface or Interference; the First Line Management of Residential Care for Children and Young People,* Report of a developmental workshop run jointly by the Support Force for Residential Child Care, the Social Services Inspectorate and the National Children's Bureau, Residential Care Unit, 24–25 April 1995

Crimmens, D. and Vaughan, G. (1992) *Residential Child Care in Humberside. A Training and Development Strategy,* Hull, University of Humberside

Crimmens, D. (1998) Training for Residential Child Care Workers in Europe: Comparing Approaches in The Netherlands, Ireland and the United Kingdom, *Social Work Education,* 17, 3

D'arcy, M. and Gosling, P. (1998) *Abuse of Trust,* Bowerdean

Dalrymple, J. and Payne, M. (1994) *They Listened to Him: A Report on the Evaluation Project of the Advice, Advocacy and Representations Service for Children (ASC),* ASC/ Manchester Metropolitan University

Dalrymple, J. and Hough, J. (1995) *Having a Voice, An Exploration of Children's Rights and Advocacy,* Birmingham, Venture Press

Dartington Social Research Unit (1995) *Child Protection: Messages from Research,* London, HMSO

Department of Education (1991) *Competence for a Changing World,* Guidance Note No.8. cited in Howarth and Morrison op.cit.

Department of Health (1991) *Statutory Instruments no. 894, the Representations Procedure (Children) Regulations,* HMSO

Department of Health (1991) *The Outcome of an Investigation Concerning St. Charles' Youth Treatment Centre,* London, DoH

Department of Health (1993) *Report of the Follow Up Inspection of the Community Homes for Children in Leicester,* HMSO

Department of Health (1994) S*tandards for Residential Child Care Services: A Handbook for Social Services Managers and Inspectors, Users of the Services and their Families.* Social Services Inspectorate, London, HMSO

Department of Health (1996) *Focus Teenagers: Research into Practice,* HMSO

Department of Health (1997) *A Matter for Investigation,* HMSO

Department of Health (1998) *Caring for Children Away from Home: Messages from Research,* Chichester, Wiley

Department of Health (1998) *Health Secretary Outlines Reform of Social Services System.* Press release (98/0557), 30th November 1998

Department of Health (1998) *Health Secretary Pledges to Transform Children's Services.* Press release (98/388), 21st September 1998

Department of Health (1998b) *Modernising Social Services: Promoting Independence, Improving Protection, Raising Standards,* The Stationery Office

Department of Health (1998*) Quality Protects. Objectives for Social Services for Children,* The Stationery Office

Department of Health (1998) *Social Services Failing Children in Care, Says Inspectorate.* Press release (98/387), 21st September 1998

Department of Health (1998) *Social Services Training to Get Extra £20 Million.* Press Release (98/0532), 18th November 1998

Department of Health (1998*) The Quality Protects Programme: Transforming Children's Services,* DoH

Department of Health (1998c) *The Government's Response to the Children's Safeguards Review,* Cm 4105, London, The Stationery Office

Department of Health and Social Security (N. Ireland) (1985) *Report of the Committee of Inquiry into Children's Homes and Hostels,* Belfast, HMSO

Department of Health *Employment of Residential Child Care Workers,* London, DoH

Department of Health (1992) *Choosing with Care: The Report of the Committee of Inquiry into the Selection, Development and Management of Staff in Children's Homes,* DoH

Department of Health (1998) *Caring for Children Away from Home: Messages from Research,* DoH

Employers organisations (1999) Independent Sector, Children's Residential Homes Survey 1998. June. London

Farmer, E. and Pollock, S. (1998) *Sexually Abused and Abusing Children in Substitute Care*, Chichester, Wiley

Farrington, D. (1996) *Understanding and Preventing Youth Crime*, York, Joseph Rowntree Foundation

Fédération Internationale des Communates Éducatives (1998) A Code of Ethics for People Working with Children and Young People, *FICE Bulletin* No.14, Summer

Fletcher, B. (1993) *Not Just a Name, the Views of Young People in Foster and Residential Care,* National Consumer Council

Franklin, B. (1995) The Case for Children's Rights: A Progress Report, in Franklin, B. (Ed.) *The Handbook of Children's Rights,* Routledge

Franklin, B. (1995) *The Handbook of Children's Rights : Essays in Comparative Policy and Practice,* London, Routledge

Freeman, M.D.A. (1983) *The Rights and Wrongs of Children,* Frances Pinter Publishers

Frost, N., Mills, S. and Stein, M. (1999) *Understanding Residential Child Care,* Ashgate

Gabbidon, P. and Goldson B. (1999) *Preparing to Care: Induction and Practice Development for Residential Social Workers,* London, National Children's Bureau

Goffman, E. (1968) *Asylums : Essays on the Social Situation of Mental Patients and Other Inmates*, Harmondsworth, Penguin

Goldson, B. (1999) The Contemporary Politics of Child Punishment: From Bulger to Medway, in *Childright* 155, April

Graham, J. and Bowling, B. (1995) Young People and Crime. London, Home Office

Grimshaw, R. and Sinclair, R. (1997) *Planning and Reviewing under the Children Act 1989: Research Messages for Local Authorities,* National Children's Bureau

Gwent County Council (1992) *Ty Mawr Community Home Inquiry*, Gwent CC

Hetherington, R., Cooper, A., Smith, P. and Wilford, G. (1991) *Protecting Children: Messages From Europe*, Lyme Regis, Russell House Publishing

Hill, M. (1990) The Manifest and Latent Lessons of Child Abuse Inquiries, *British Journal of Social Work*, 20, 197–213

Hills, D., Child, C., Hills, J. and Blackburn, V. (1997) *The Evaluation of the Residential Child Care Initiative. Final Report,* London, The Tavistock Institute

HM Chief Inspector of Prisons (1997), *Young Prisoners: A Thematic Review*, Home Office

HM Chief Inspector of Prisons (1997), *Reports on Feltham, Dover and Werrington*, Home Office

HM Inspector of Prisons (1998) *Report of a Short Unannounced Report on HMYOI Werrington*

Hoghue, M. (1983) *The Delinquent*, London, Burnett Books

Home Office (1967) *Administration of Punishment at Court Lees Approved School,* London, HMSO Cm. 3367

Home Office (1991) *The National Prison Survey,* Research Study 128

Home Office (1997) *No More Excuses: A New Approach to Tackling Youth Crime in England and Wales,* Cm. 3809, HMSO

Home Office (1997) *Prison Statistics England and Wales*

Home Office (1998) *Crime and Disorder Act 1998: Introductory Guide*

Home Office (1998) *Prison Population Brief*

Home Office (in conjunction with the Department of Health) (1992) *Memorandum of Good Practice on Video Recorded Interviews with Child Witnesses for Criminal Proceedings,* London, HMSO

Horwath, J. and Morrison, T. (1999) *Effective Staff Training in Social Care,* London, Routledge

House of Commons (1998) *Children Looked After by Local Authorities. Health Committee, Second Report,* Vol. 1. Report and Proceedings of the Committee. Vol. 2. Minutes of Evidence and Appendices

Howe, D. (1992) Child Abuse and the Bureaucratisation of Social Work, *Sociological Review* 40, 491–508

Howe, Lady E. (1992) *The Quality of Care.* Report of the Residential Staffs Inquiry chaired by Lady Howe, LGMB

Howitt, D. (1995) *Paedophiles and Sexual Offences Against Children,* Chichester, Wiley

Hunt, G. (1998) *Whistle-blowing in the Social Services,* Arnold

Hunt, P. (1994) *Report of the Independent Inquiry into Multiple Abuse in Nursery Classes in Newcastle upon Tyne,* City Council of Newcastle upon Tyne

Hyland, J.(1993) *Yesterday's Answers: Development and Decline of Schools for Young Offenders,* London, Whiting and Birch

James, B. (1994) *Handbook for the Treatment of Attachment Trauma Problems in Children,* USA, Lexington Books

Jenkins, P. (1992) *Intimate Enemies: Moral Panics in Contemporary Great Britain,* New York, Aldine de Gruyter

Jones, A. (1996) *Report of the Examination Team on Child Care Procedures and Practice in North Wales,* London, HMSO

Joss, R. (1991) Professional Competence and Higher Education. in Yelloly, M. and Henkel M. (1995) *Learning and Teaching in Social Work: Towards Reflective Practice,* London, Jessica Kingsley p58

Kahan, B. (1994) *Growing Up in Groups,* London, HMSO

Karban, K. and Frost, N. (1998) Training for Residential Child Care: Assessing the Impact of the Residential Child Care Initiative. *Social Work Education,* 17, 3

Kempe, C., Silverman, F., Steele, B., Droegemueller, W. and Silver, H. (1962) The Battered Child Syndrome, *Journal of the American Medical Association,* 181, 17–24

Kent, R. (1997) *Children's Safeguards Review,* Edinburgh, The Stationery Office

Kilgallon, W. (1995) *Report of the Independent Review into Allegations of Abuse at Meadowdale Children's Home and Related Matters,* Northumbria CC

King, M. and Piper, C. (1990) *How the Law Thinks About Children,* Aldershot, Gower

Kirkwood, A. (1993) *The Leicestershire Inquiry 1992,* Leicester, Leicestershire CC

Knight, A. (1998) *Valued or Forgotten? Disabled Children and Independent Visitors,* National Children's Bureau

LaFontaine, J. (1998) *Speak of the Devil: Tales of Satanic Abuse in Contemporary England,* Cambridge, Cambridge Univ. Press

Lancashire County Council (1992) *The Scotforth House Inquiry,* Lancs CC

Lane, D. (1994) *An Independent Review of the Residential Child Care Initiative,* London, CCETSW

Levy, A. and Kahan, B. (1991) *The Pindown Experience and the Protection of Children: The Report of the Staffordshire Child Care Inquiry 1990,* Staffs CC

Lewisham Council (1995) *The Leeways Enquiry Report,* Lewisham Council

Little, M. (1999) New Research in Residential Care, *Children and Society* 13.1, 61–66

Lynes, D. and Goddard, J. (1995) *View from the Front, the Users View of Child Care in Norfolk,* Norfolk County Council Social Service Department

Lyon, C. (1997) Children Abused within the Care System: Do Current Representations Procedures Offer the Child Protection and Family Support? In Parton, N. (Ed.) *Child Protection and Family Support: Tensions, Contradictions and Possibilities,* London, Routledge

Lyon, C. and Parton, N. (1985) Children's rights and the Children Act 1989, in Franklin, B. (Ed.) *The Handbook of Children's Rights,* Routledge

Macfarlane, A. (1970) *The Family Life of Ralph Josselin,* Cambridge, Cambridge Univ. Press

Madge, N. (1994) *Children and Residential Care in Europe,* London, NCB

Masson, J. (1990) *The Children Act 1989: Text and Commentary,* Sweet and Marshall

Matthews, R. and Pitts, J. (1998) Rehabilitation, Recidivism, and Realism: Evaluation Violence Reduction Programs in Prison, *The Prison Journal,* 78, 4

Millham, S. (1977) Intermediate Treatment: Symbol or Solution? *Youth in Society,* 26: 22–24

Ministerial Task Force on Children's Safeguards (1998) *The Government's Response to the Children's Safeguards Review,* The Stationery Office

Morris, A., Giller, H., Szwed, E. and Geach, H. (1980) *Justice for Children,* London, Macmillan

Morris, J. (1995) *Gone Missing? A Research and Policy Review of Disabled Children Living Away from their Families,* Who Cares? Trust

Morris, J. (1998) *Still Missing? The Experiences of Disabled Children and Young People Living Away from their Families,* Who Cares? Trust

Morrison, T. (1996) *Protecting Children, Challenges and Change*

NACRO (1989) *The Custodial Sentencing of Juveniles,* NACRO Briefing, London

Nava, M. (1988) Cleveland and the Press: Outrage and Anxiety in the Reporting of Child Sexual Abuse, *Feminist Review* 28, 103–121

Parton, N. (1996) Social Work, Risk and the 'Blaming System'. In Parton N. (Ed.) *Social Theory, Social Change and Social Work,* London, Routledge

Parton, N., Thorpe, D. and Wattam, C. (1997*) Child Protection, Risk and the Moral Order,* Basingstoke, Macmillan

Patel, S. (1997) *The Directory of In-care and After-care Groups Run by Young People in the United Kingdom,* Save the Children

Pawson, R. and Tilley, N. (1997) *Realistic Evaluation,* London, Sage Publications

Payne, C. (1999) If You Can't Beat Them…Join Them. *Social Caring.* The Official Newspaper of the Social Care Association, Issue 2, June

Penal Affairs Consortium (1994) *The Case Against the Secure Training Order,* London, The Penal Affairs Consortium

Penal Affairs Consortium (1998) The Crime and Disorder Act

Perfect, M. and Renshaw, J. (1996) *Misspent Youth,* London, The Audit Commission

Perlin, L. and Schooler, C. (1978) The Structure of Coping, *Journal of Health and Social Behaviour,* 19th March, 1–23

Pitts, M (1992) *Somewhere to Run,* unpublished University of Exeter BA dissertation

Pitts, J. (1988) *The Politics of Juvenile Crime,* London, Sage

Pitts, J. (1996) *The Politics and Practice of Youth Justice,* Mclaughlin E. and Muncie J. (eds.), Controlling Crime, Sage Publications/Open University Press

Pitts, J. (2000) *Discipline or Solidarity: The New Politics of Youth Crime,* Basingstoke, Macmillan

Pollock, L. (1983) *Forgotten Children: Parent-Child Relations from 1500–1900,* Cambridge, Cambridge Univ. Press

Pratt, J. (1989) Corporatism, the Third Model of Juvenile Justice, *British Journal of Criminology,* 29, 236–54

Precy, G. (1999) Nothing's Sacred. *Community Care,* 7th October, p27

Prison Service (1998) *Bullying in Prison: A Strategy to Beat it,* London, Home Office

Rees, G. (1993) *Hidden Truths: Young People's Experience of Running Away,* London, The Children's Society

Residential Care Association (1974) *The Dalmeny Papers,* RCA

Residential Forum (1998) *A Golden Opportunity: A Report on Training and Staff Development for People Working in Residential Services for Children and Young People,* London, NISW

Rutherford, A. (1986) *Growing Out of Crime,* Harmondsworth, Penguin

Shaw, C. (1998) *Remember My Messages,* Who Cares? Trust

Simons, K. (1995) *I'm Not Complaining But, Complaints Procedures in Social Service Departments,* Joseph Rowntree Foundation

Sinclair, I. and Gibbs, I. (1996) *The Quality of Care in Children's Homes,* Working Papers Series B, No. 3, University of York. Social Work Research and Development Unit

Sinclair, I. and Gibbs, I. (1996a) *Quality of Care in Children's Homes. Report to the Department of Health,* University of York Social Work Research and Development Unit

Sinclair, I. and Gibbs, I. (1998) *Children's Homes: A Study in Diversity,* Chichester, Wiley

Social Care Association (1999) *Lay Visitors,* London, SCA (Education)

Social Care Association (1999b) *Line Management of Residential Services,* London, SCA (Education)

Social Service Inspectorate (1994) *Second Overview Report of the Inspection of the Complaints Procedure in the Local Authority Social Services Department,* HMSO

Social Service Inspectorate (1996) *The Inspection of Complaints Procedures in Local Authorities Social Services Departments: A Third Overview,* HMSO

Social Services Inspectorate (1988) *Report of an Inspection of Melanie Klein House CHE by the Social Services Inspectorate,* London, Department of Health

Sparks, C (1997) *Lancaster Farms: Preventing the Next Victim,* Prison Reform Trust

Stein, M. and Ellis, S. (1983) *Gizza Say. Reviews and Young People in Care,* NAYPIC

Stein, M., Frost, N. and Rees, G.(1994) *Running the Risk,* London, The Children's Society

Support Force for Children's Residential Care (1995) *Code of Practice for the*

The Children Act 1989, The Stationery Office

The Children's Society (1994) *The Independent Person Project Evaluation,* The Children's Society

Thorpe, D., Smith, D., Green, C. and Paley, J. (1980) *Out of Care,* London, Allen and Unwin

UNICEF (1998) *Implementation Handbook on the UN Convention on the Rights of the Child*, UNICEF

Utting, Sir W. (1991) *Children in the Public Care : A Review of Residential Care*, London, HMSO

Utting, Sir W. (1997) *People Like Us. The Report of the Review of the Safeguards For Children Living Away From Home*, London, The Stationery Office

Utting, Sir W. (1998), Children in Prison, *Prison Service Journal*, November

Voice for the Child in Care (1994) *An Evaluation of the Independent Person Service in London*, VCC

Voice for the Child in Care (1998) *Shout to be Heard, Stories from Young People in Care*, London, VCC

Wagner, G. (Ed.) (1988) *A Positive Choice. Report of the Independent Review of Residential Care*, London, HMSO

Wallis, L. and Frost, N. (1998) *Cause for Complaint – The Complaints Procedure for Young People in Care*, The Children's Society

Ward, L. (1997) *Seen and Heard, Involving Disabled Children and Young People in Research and Development Projects*, Joseph Rowntree Foundation

Wardhaugh, J. and Wilding, P. (1995) Towards an Explanation of the Corruption of Care, *Critical Social Policy*, 44, 4–31

Warner, N. (1992) *Choosing with Care — The Report of the Committee of Inquiry into the Selection, Development and Management of Staff in Children's Homes*, HMSO

Webster, R. (1998) *The Great Children's Home Panic*, Oxford, the Orwell Press

Wheal, A. and Sinclair, R. (1995) *It's Your Meeting: A Guide to Help Young People Get the Most from their Review*, London, National Children's Bureau

Whitaker, D., Archer, L. and Hicks, L. (1998) *Working in Children's Homes. Challenges and Complexities*, Chichester, Wiley

White, I. and Hart, K. (1995) *Report of the Management of Child Care in the London Borough of Islington*, Islington LB

Wilkins, L. (1964) *Social Deviance, Social Policy, Action and Research*, London, Tavistock

Williams, C. and Jordan, H. (1996) *The Children Act 1989 Complaints Procedure: A Study of Six Local Authority Areas*, University of Sheffield

Willow, C. (1996) *Children's Rights and Participation in Residential Care*, London, National Children's Bureau

Willow, C. and Hyder, T. (1999) The Myth of the Loving Smack, in *Childright*, 154

Woolf, Lord Justice (1991) *Prison Disturbances April 1990*, Cm 1456, HMSO

Wraith, R. and Lamb, G. (1971) *Public Inquiries as an Instrument of Government*, London, Allen and Unwin

York Independent Person Project (1997) *Good Practice Guidelines for Investigating Officers and Independent Persons*, The Children Society

Young, J. (1971) *The Drugtakers: the Social Meaning of Drug Use*, London, MacGibbon & Kee/Paladin

Ziegler, D. (1994) A Residential Care Attachment Model, In James, B. (1994) *Handbook for the Treatment of Attachment Trauma Problems in Children*. USA Lexington Books

Index